KT-446-152

URY

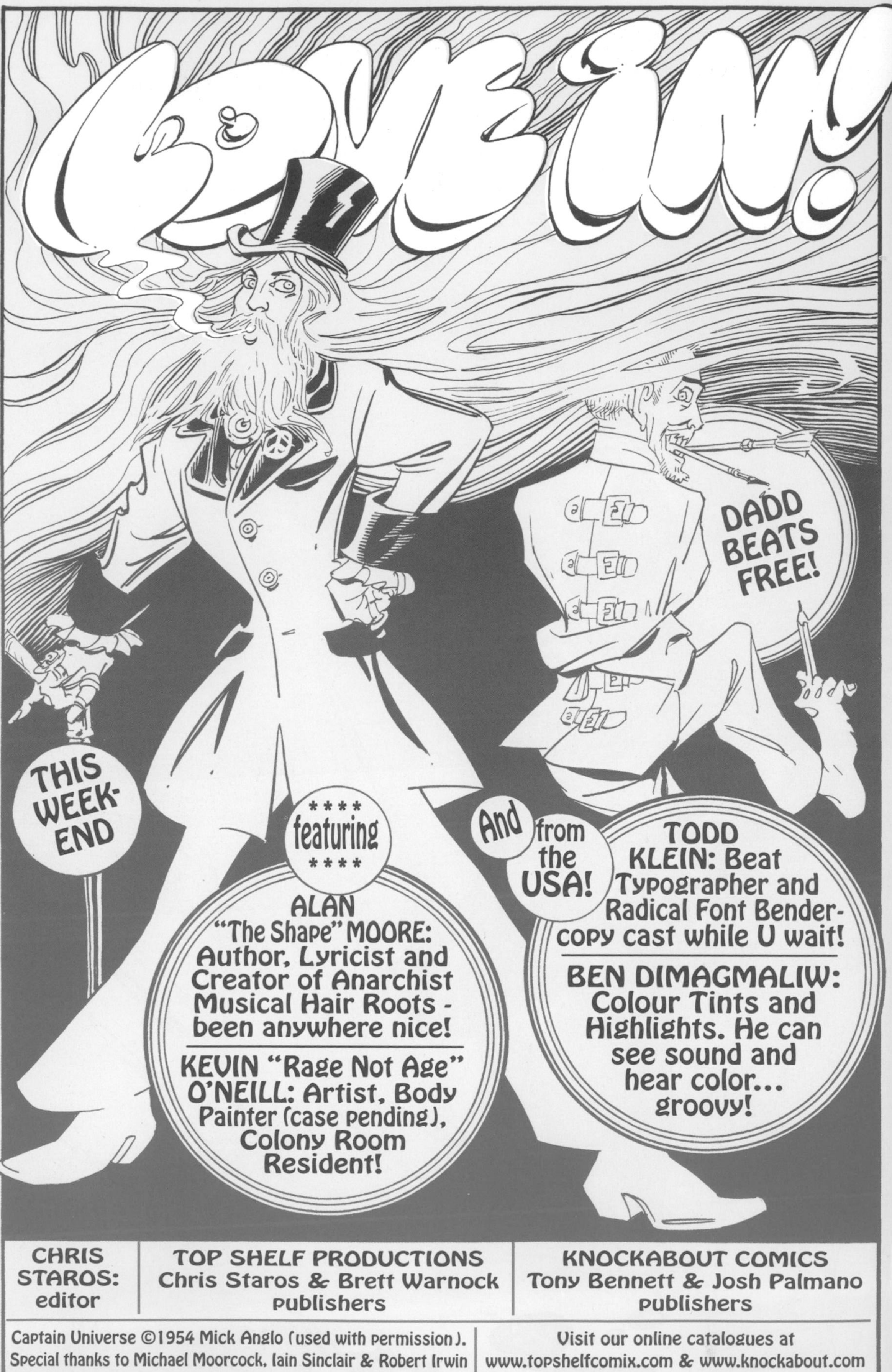
COME IN!
DADD BEATS FREE!
THIS WEEK-END
**** featuring ****
ALAN "The Shape" MOORE: Author, Lyricist and Creator of Anarchist Musical Hair Roots - been anywhere nice!
KEVIN "Rage Not Age" O'NEILL: Artist, Body Painter (case pending), Colony Room Resident!
And from the USA!
TODD KLEIN: Beat Typographer and Radical Font Bender- copy cast while U wait!
BEN DIMAGMALIW: Colour Tints and Highlights. He can see sound and hear color... groovy!

CHRIS STAROS: editor

TOP SHELF PRODUCTIONS
Chris Staros & Brett Warnock
publishers

KNOCKABOUT COMICS
Tony Bennett & Josh Palmano
publishers

Special thanks to Michael Moorcock, Iain Sinclair & Robert Irwin

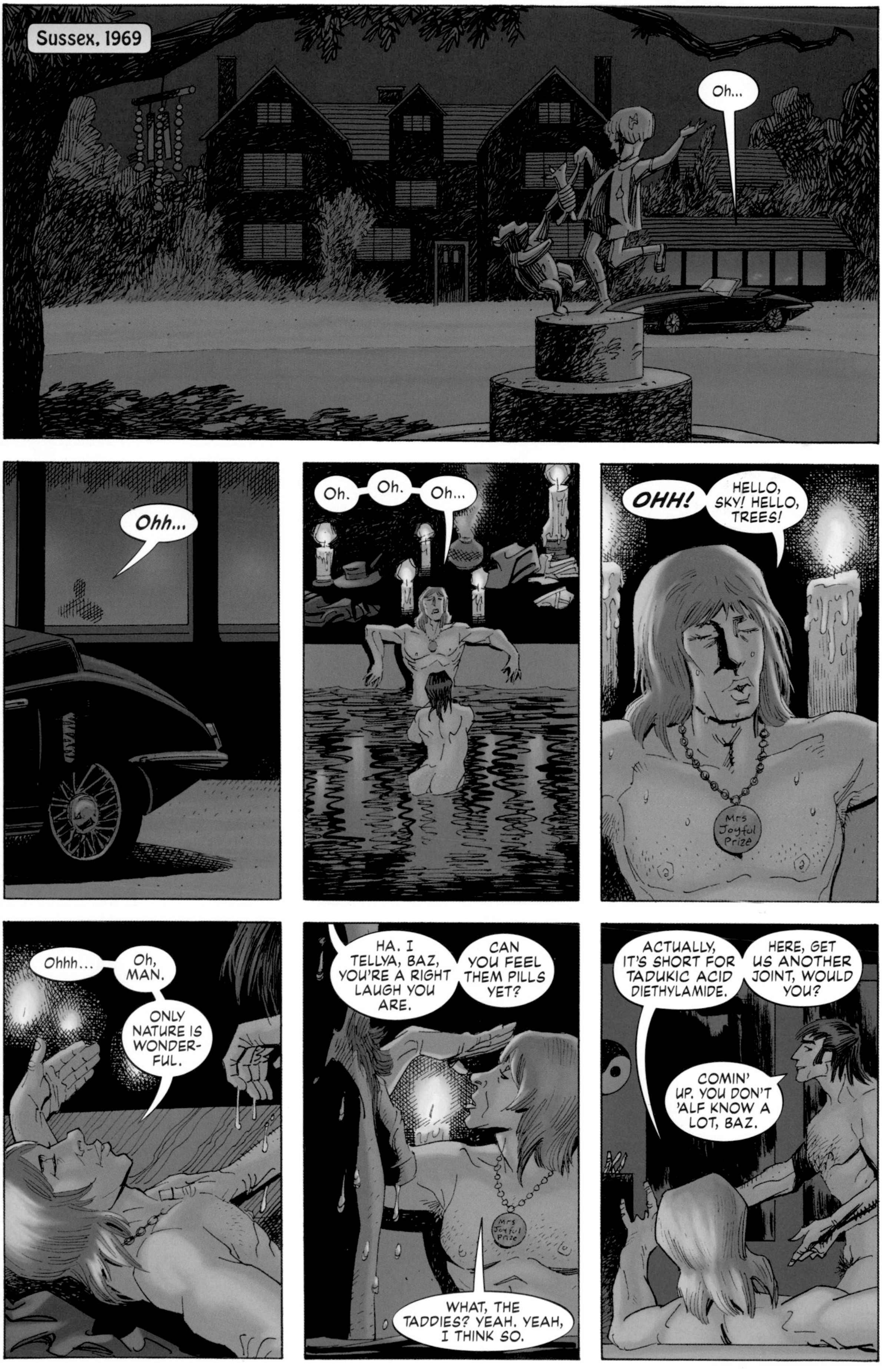
Sussex, 1969
Oh...
Ohh...
Oh.
Oh.
Oh...
OHH!
HELLO, SKY! HELLO, TREES!
Mrs Joyful Prize
Ohhh...
Oh, MAN.
ONLY NATURE IS WONDER-FUL.
HA. I TELLYA, BAZ, YOU'RE A RIGHT LAUGH YOU ARE.
CAN YOU FEEL THEM PILLS YET?
Mrs Joyful Prize
WHAT, THE TADDIES? YEAH. YEAH, I THINK SO.
ACTUALLY, IT'S SHORT FOR TADUKIC ACID DIETHYLAMIDE.
HERE, GET US ANOTHER JOINT, WOULD YOU?
COMIN' UP. YOU DON'T 'ALF KNOW A LOT, BAZ.

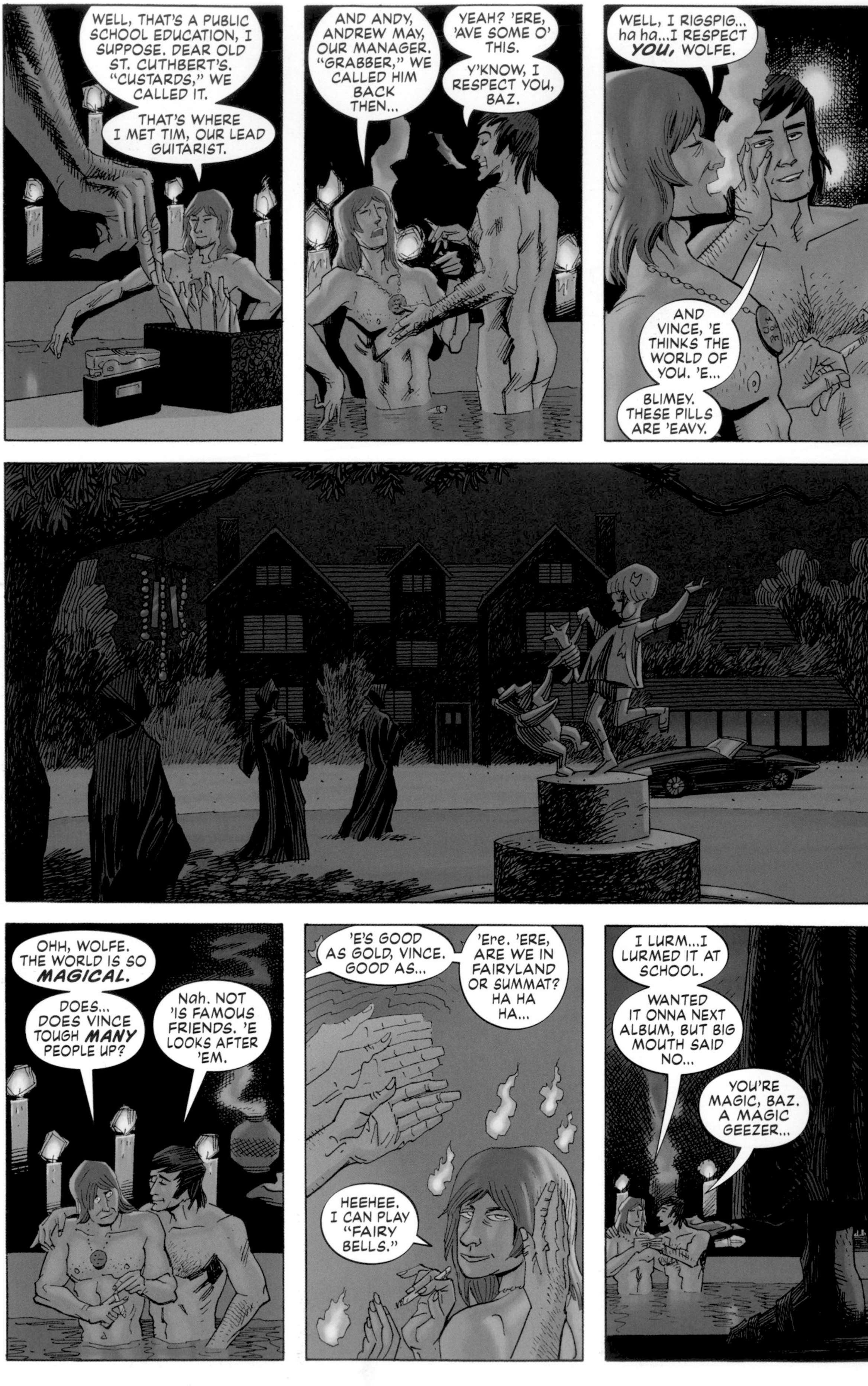
WELL, THAT'S A PUBLIC SCHOOL EDUCATION, I SUPPOSE. DEAR OLD ST. CUTHBERT'S. "CUSTARDS," WE CALLED IT.
THAT'S WHERE I MET TIM, OUR LEAD GUITARIST.
AND ANDY, ANDREW MAY, OUR MANAGER. "GRABBER," WE CALLED HIM BACK THEN...
YEAH? 'ERE, 'AVE SOME O' THIS.
Y'KNOW, I RESPECT YOU, BAZ.
WELL, I RIGSPIG... ha ha...I RESPECT YOU, WOLFE.
AND VINCE, 'E THINKS THE WORLD OF YOU. 'E...
BLIMEY. THESE PILLS ARE 'EAVY.
OHH, WOLFE. THE WORLD IS SO MAGICAL.
DOES... DOES VINCE TOUGH MANY PEOPLE UP?
Nah. NOT 'IS FAMOUS FRIENDS. 'E LOOKS AFTER 'EM.
'E'S GOOD AS GOLD, VINCE. GOOD AS...
'Ere. 'ERE, ARE WE IN FAIRYLAND OR SUMMAT? HA HA HA...
HEEHEE. I CAN PLAY "FAIRY BELLS."
I LURM...I LURMED IT AT SCHOOL.
WANTED IT ONNA NEXT ALBUM, BUT BIG MOUTH SAID NO...
YOU'RE MAGIC, BAZ. A MAGIC GEEZER...

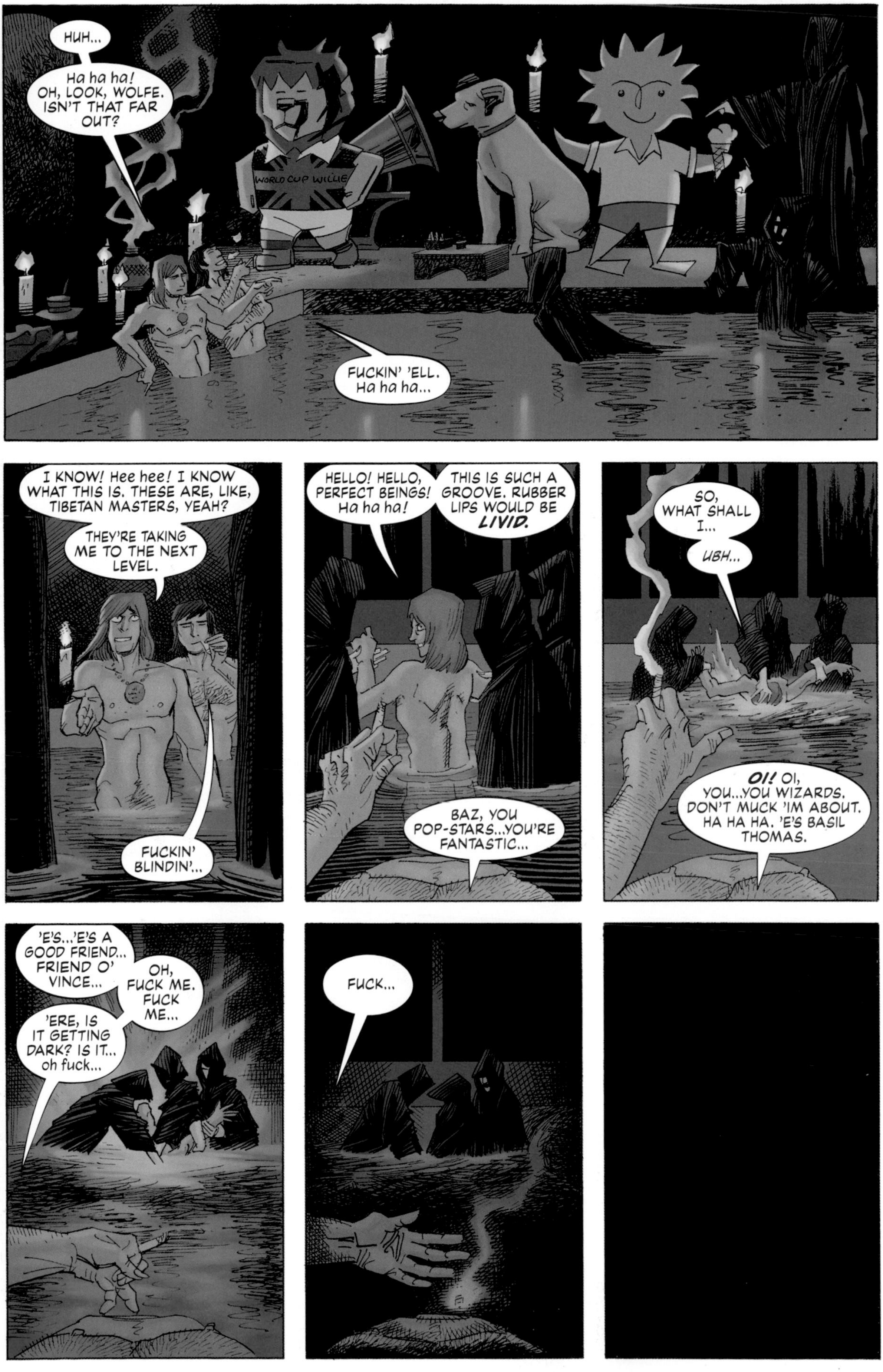
HUH...
Ha ha ha! OH, LOOK, WOLFE. ISN'T THAT FAR OUT?
WORLD CUP WILLIE
FUCKIN' 'ELL. Ha ha ha...
I KNOW! Hee hee! I KNOW WHAT THIS IS. THESE ARE, LIKE, TIBETAN MASTERS, YEAH?
THEY'RE TAKING ME TO THE NEXT LEVEL.
FUCKIN' BLINDIN'...
HELLO! HELLO, PERFECT BEINGS! Ha ha ha!
THIS IS SUCH A GROOVE. RUBBER LIPS WOULD BE LIVID.
BAZ, YOU POP-STARS...YOU'RE FANTASTIC...
SO, WHAT SHALL I...
UBH...
OI! OI, YOU...YOU WIZARDS. DON'T MUCK 'IM ABOUT. HA HA HA. 'E'S BASIL THOMAS.
'E'S...'E'S A GOOD FRIEND... FRIEND O' VINCE...
OH, FUCK ME. FUCK ME...
'ERE, IS IT GETTING DARK? IS IT... oh fuck...
FUCK...

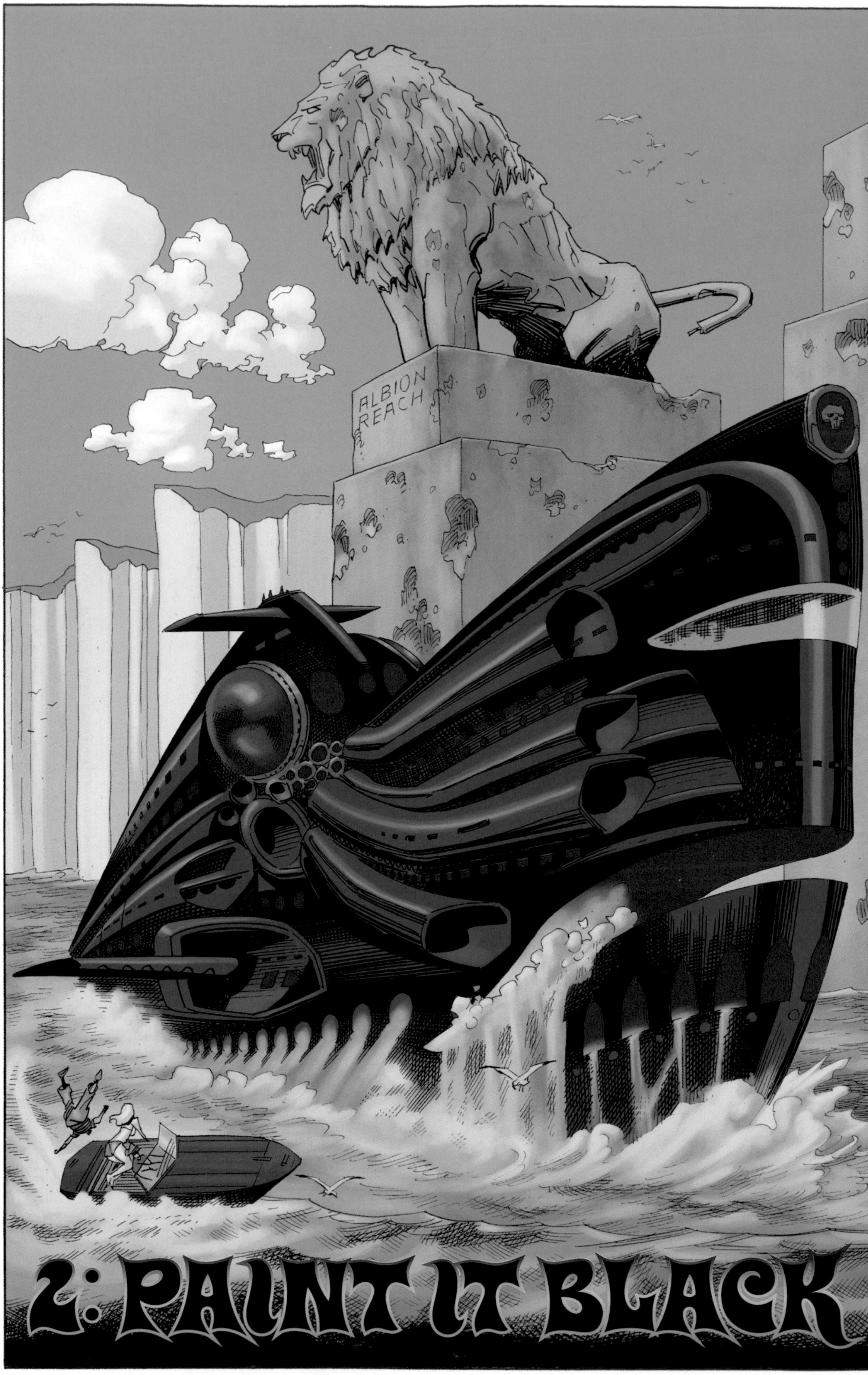
ALBION REACH
2: PAINT IT BLACK

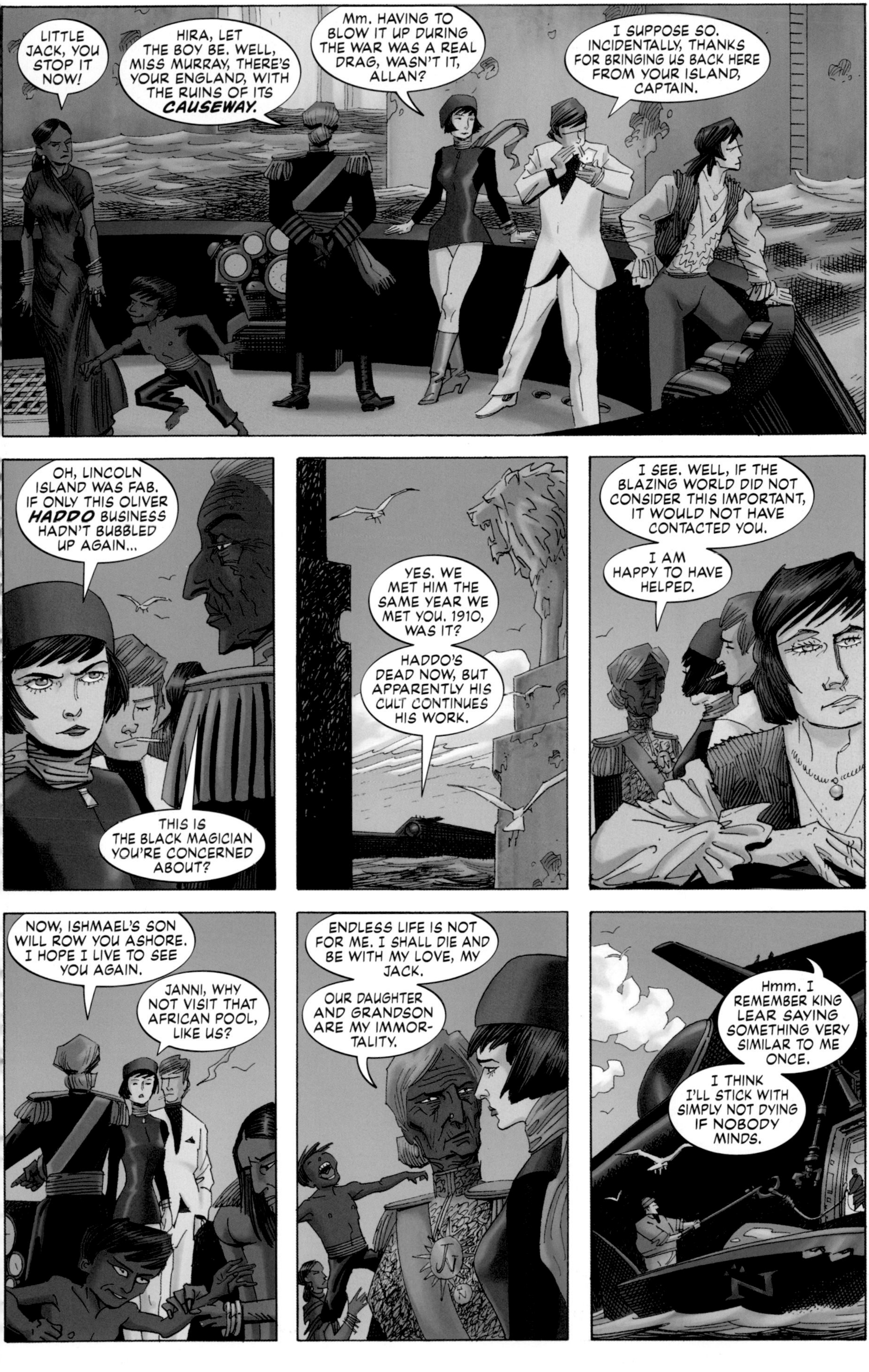
LITTLE JACK, YOU STOP IT NOW!
HIRA, LET THE BOY BE. WELL, MISS MURRAY, THERE'S YOUR ENGLAND, WITH THE RUINS OF ITS CAUSEWAY.
Mm. HAVING TO BLOW IT UP DURING THE WAR WAS A REAL DRAG, WASN'T IT, ALLAN?
I SUPPOSE SO. INCIDENTALLY, THANKS FOR BRINGING US BACK HERE FROM YOUR ISLAND, CAPTAIN.
OH, LINCOLN ISLAND WAS FAB. IF ONLY THIS OLIVER HADDO BUSINESS HADN'T BUBBLED UP AGAIN...
THIS IS THE BLACK MAGICIAN YOU'RE CONCERNED ABOUT?
YES. WE MET HIM THE SAME YEAR WE MET YOU. 1910, WAS IT?
HADDO'S DEAD NOW, BUT APPARENTLY HIS CULT CONTINUES HIS WORK.
I SEE. WELL, IF THE BLAZING WORLD DID NOT CONSIDER THIS IMPORTANT, IT WOULD NOT HAVE CONTACTED YOU.
I AM HAPPY TO HAVE HELPED.
NOW, ISHMAEL'S SON WILL ROW YOU ASHORE. I HOPE I LIVE TO SEE YOU AGAIN.
JANNI, WHY NOT VISIT THAT AFRICAN POOL, LIKE US?
ENDLESS LIFE IS NOT FOR ME. I SHALL DIE AND BE WITH MY LOVE, MY JACK.
OUR DAUGHTER AND GRANDSON ARE MY IMMORTALITY.
Hmm. I REMEMBER KING LEAR SAYING SOMETHING VERY SIMILAR TO ME ONCE.
I THINK I'LL STICK WITH SIMPLY NOT DYING IF NOBODY MINDS.

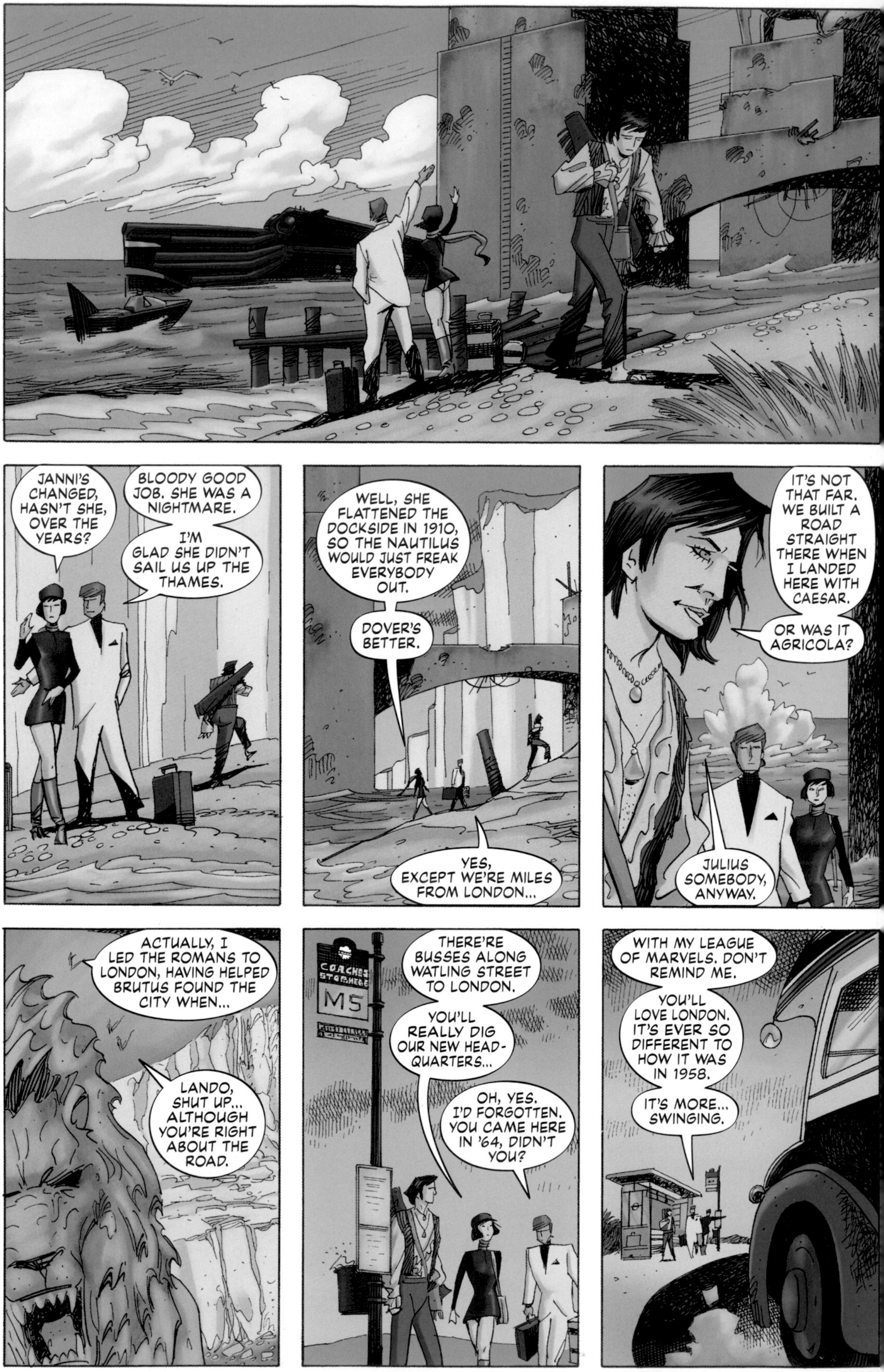
JANNI'S CHANGED, HASN'T SHE, OVER THE YEARS?
BLOODY GOOD JOB. SHE WAS A NIGHTMARE.
I'M GLAD SHE DIDN'T SAIL US UP THE THAMES.
WELL, SHE FLATTENED THE DOCKSIDE IN 1910, SO THE NAUTILUS WOULD JUST FREAK EVERYBODY OUT.
DOVER'S BETTER.
YES, EXCEPT WE'RE MILES FROM LONDON...
IT'S NOT THAT FAR. WE BUILT A ROAD STRAIGHT THERE WHEN I LANDED HERE WITH CAESAR.
OR WAS IT AGRICOLA?
JULIUS SOMEBODY, ANYWAY.
ACTUALLY, I LED THE ROMANS TO LONDON, HAVING HELPED BRUTUS FOUND THE CITY WHEN...
LANDO, SHUT UP... ALTHOUGH YOU'RE RIGHT ABOUT THE ROAD.
M5
THERE'RE BUSSES ALONG WATLING STREET TO LONDON.
YOU'LL REALLY DIG OUR NEW HEAD-QUARTERS...
OH, YES. I'D FORGOTTEN. YOU CAME HERE IN '64, DIDN'T YOU?
WITH MY LEAGUE OF MARVELS. DON'T REMIND ME.
YOU'LL LOVE LONDON. IT'S EVER SO DIFFERENT TO HOW IT WAS IN 1958.
IT'S MORE... SWINGING.

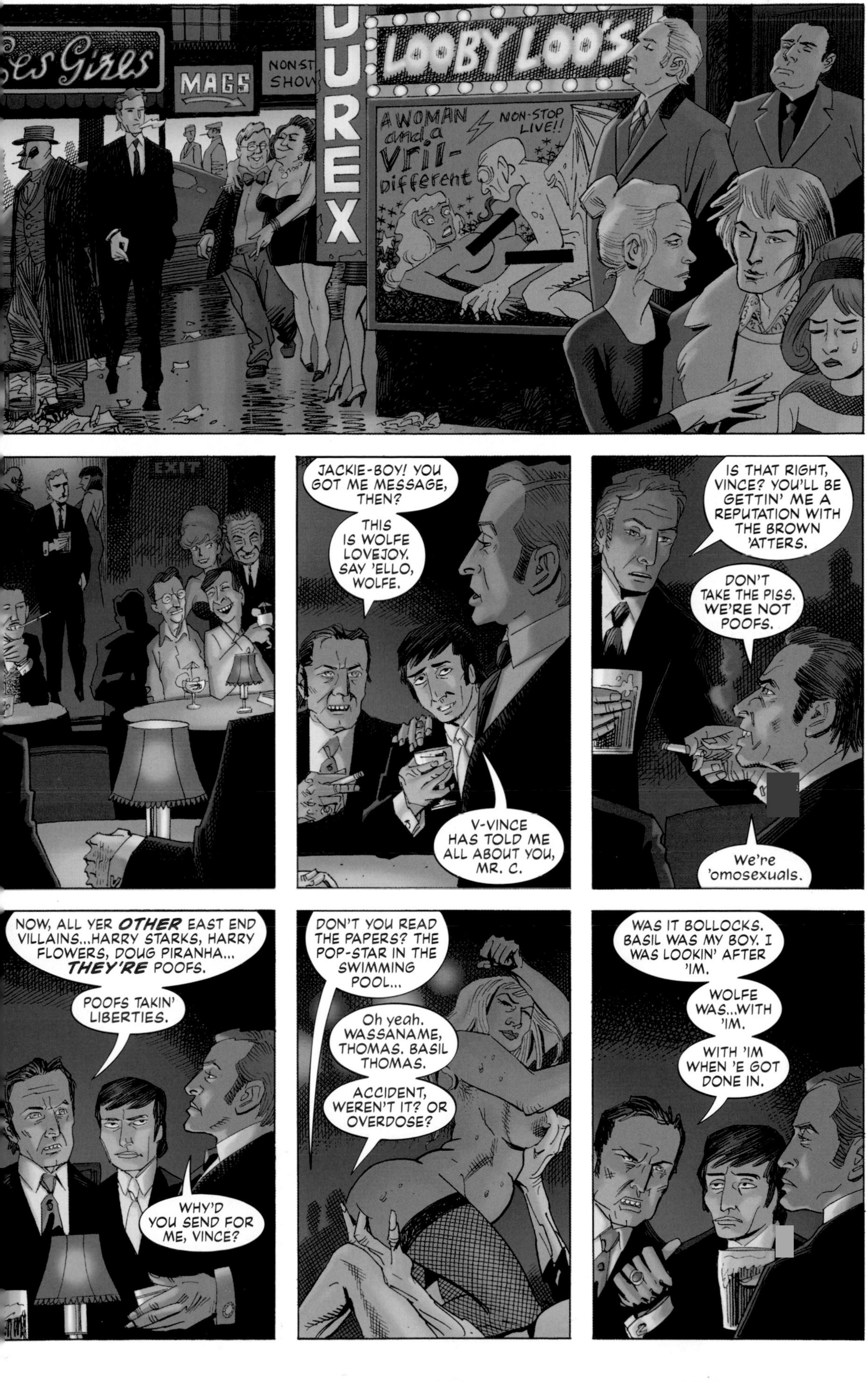
Les Girls
MAGS
NON ST
SHOW
UREX
LOOBY LOO'S
A WOMAN and a Vril-different
NON-STOP LIVE!!
EXIT
JACKIE-BOY! YOU GOT ME MESSAGE, THEN?
THIS IS WOLFE LOVEJOY. SAY 'ELLO, WOLFE.
V-VINCE HAS TOLD ME ALL ABOUT YOU, MR. C.
IS THAT RIGHT, VINCE? YOU'LL BE GETTIN' ME A REPUTATION WITH THE BROWN 'ATTERS.
DON'T TAKE THE PISS. WE'RE NOT POOFS.
We're 'omosexuals.
NOW, ALL YER OTHER EAST END VILLAINS...HARRY STARKS, HARRY FLOWERS, DOUG PIRANHA... THEY'RE POOFS.
POOFS TAKIN' LIBERTIES.
WHY'D YOU SEND FOR ME, VINCE?
DON'T YOU READ THE PAPERS? THE POP-STAR IN THE SWIMMING POOL...
Oh yeah. WASSANAME, THOMAS. BASIL THOMAS.
ACCIDENT, WEREN'T IT? OR OVERDOSE?
WAS IT BOLLOCKS. BASIL WAS MY BOY. I WAS LOOKIN' AFTER 'IM.
WOLFE WAS...WITH 'IM.
WITH 'IM WHEN 'E GOT DONE IN.

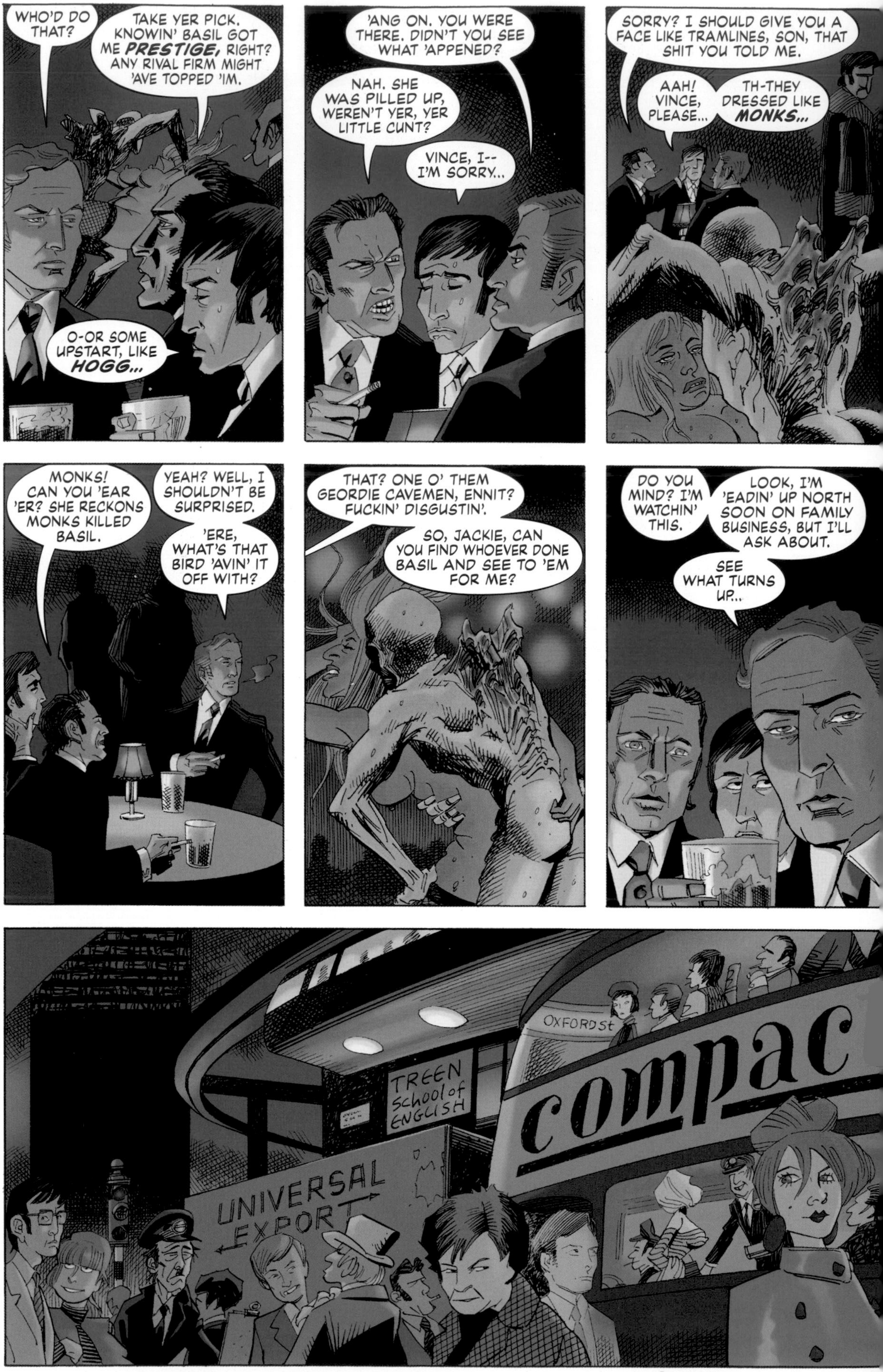
WHO'D DO THAT?
TAKE YER PICK. KNOWIN' BASIL GOT ME PRESTIGE, RIGHT? ANY RIVAL FIRM MIGHT 'AVE TOPPED 'IM.
O-OR SOME UPSTART, LIKE HOGG...
'ANG ON. YOU WERE THERE. DIDN'T YOU SEE WHAT 'APPENED?
NAH. SHE WAS PILLED UP, WEREN'T YER, YER LITTLE CUNT?
VINCE, I-- I'M SORRY...
SORRY? I SHOULD GIVE YOU A FACE LIKE TRAMLINES, SON, THAT SHIT YOU TOLD ME.
AAH! VINCE, PLEASE...
TH-THEY DRESSED LIKE MONKS...
MONKS! CAN YOU 'EAR 'ER? SHE RECKONS MONKS KILLED BASIL.
YEAH? WELL, I SHOULDN'T BE SURPRISED.
'ERE, WHAT'S THAT BIRD 'AVIN' IT OFF WITH?
THAT? ONE O' THEM GEORDIE CAVEMEN, ENNIT? FUCKIN' DISGUSTIN'.
SO, JACKIE, CAN YOU FIND WHOEVER DONE BASIL AND SEE TO 'EM FOR ME?
DO YOU MIND? I'M WATCHIN' THIS.
LOOK, I'M 'EADIN' UP NORTH SOON ON FAMILY BUSINESS, BUT I'LL ASK ABOUT.
SEE WHAT TURNS UP...
OXFORD St
compac
TREEN School of ENGLISH
UNIVERSAL EXPORT

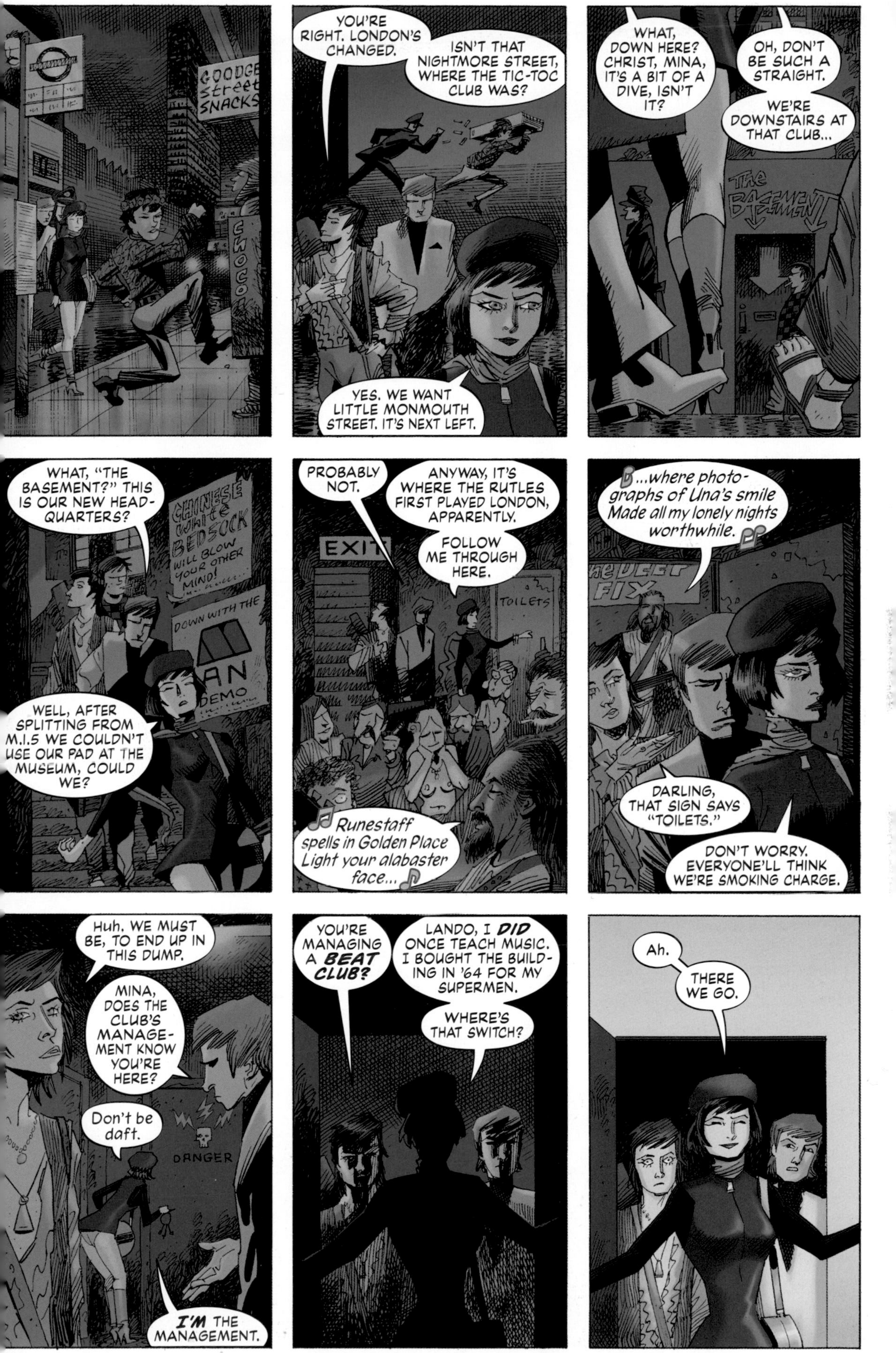
GOODGE Street SNACKS
YOU'RE RIGHT. LONDON'S CHANGED.
ISN'T THAT NIGHTMORE STREET, WHERE THE TIC-TOC CLUB WAS?
YES. WE WANT LITTLE MONMOUTH STREET. IT'S NEXT LEFT.
WHAT, DOWN HERE? CHRIST, MINA, IT'S A BIT OF A DIVE, ISN'T IT?
OH, DON'T BE SUCH A STRAIGHT.
WE'RE DOWNSTAIRS AT THAT CLUB...
The BASEMENT
WHAT, "THE BASEMENT?" THIS IS OUR NEW HEAD-QUARTERS?
CHINESE White BEDSOCK WILL BLOW YOUR OTHER MIND!
DOWN WITH THE
DEMO
WELL, AFTER SPLITTING FROM M.I.5 WE COULDN'T USE OUR PAD AT THE MUSEUM, COULD WE?
PROBABLY NOT.
ANYWAY, IT'S WHERE THE RUTLES FIRST PLAYED LONDON, APPARENTLY.
FOLLOW ME THROUGH HERE.
EXIT
TOILETS
Runestaff spells in Golden Place Light your alabaster face...
...where photo-graphs of Una's smile Made all my lonely nights worthwhile.
FIX
DARLING, THAT SIGN SAYS "TOILETS."
DON'T WORRY. EVERYONE'LL THINK WE'RE SMOKING CHARGE.
Huh. WE MUST BE, TO END UP IN THIS DUMP.
MINA, DOES THE CLUB'S MANAGE-MENT KNOW YOU'RE HERE?
Don't be daft.
DANGER
I'M THE MANAGEMENT.
YOU'RE MANAGING A BEAT CLUB?
LANDO, I DID ONCE TEACH MUSIC. I BOUGHT THE BUILD-ING IN '64 FOR MY SUPERMEN.
WHERE'S THAT SWITCH?
Ah.
THERE WE GO.

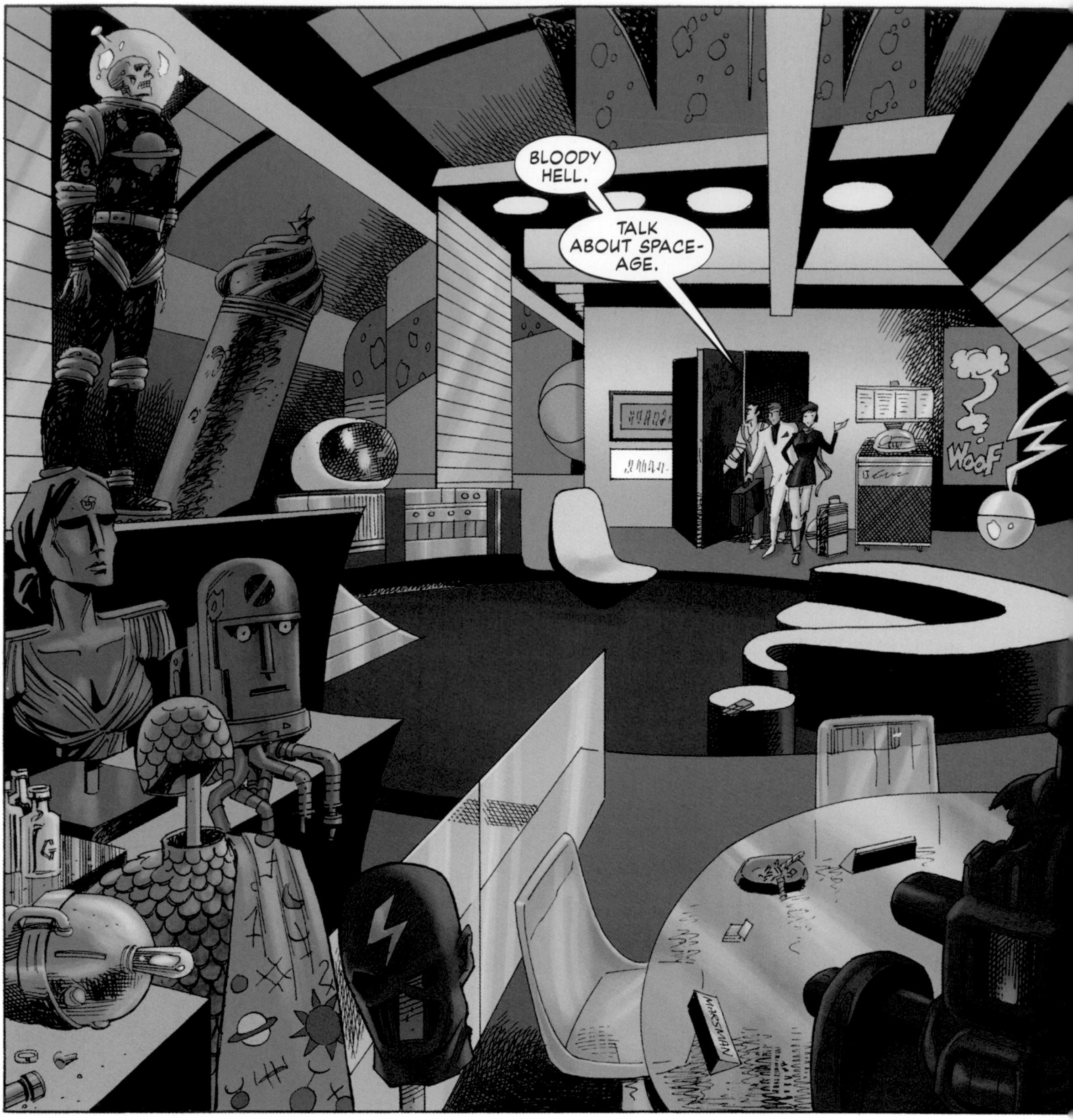
BLOODY HELL.
TALK ABOUT SPACE-AGE.
WOOF

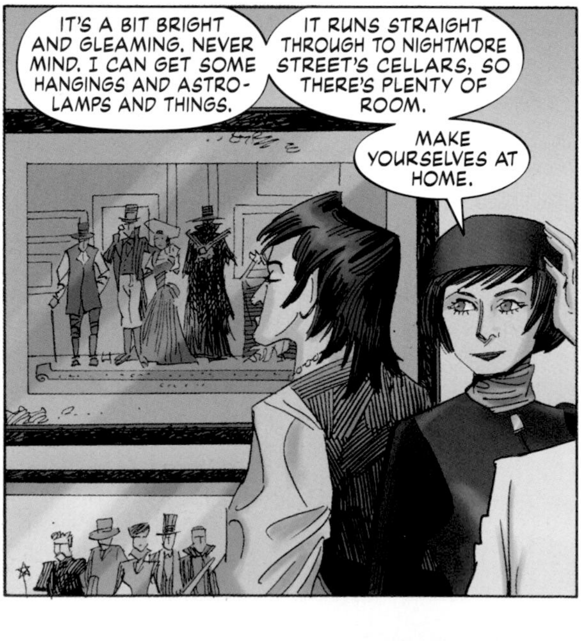
IT'S A BIT BRIGHT AND GLEAMING. NEVER MIND. I CAN GET SOME HANGINGS AND ASTRO-LAMPS AND THINGS.
IT RUNS STRAIGHT THROUGH TO NIGHTMORE STREET'S CELLARS, SO THERE'S PLENTY OF ROOM.
MAKE YOURSELVES AT HOME.

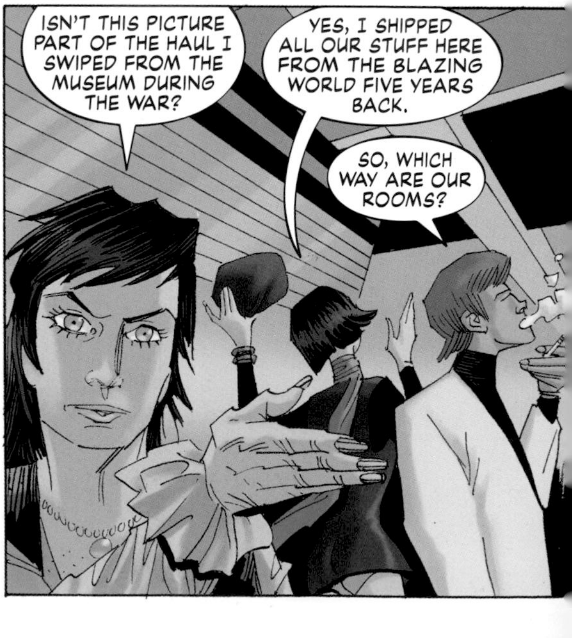
ISN'T THIS PICTURE PART OF THE HAUL I SWIPED FROM THE MUSEUM DURING THE WAR?
YES, I SHIPPED ALL OUR STUFF HERE FROM THE BLAZING WORLD FIVE YEARS BACK.
SO, WHICH WAY ARE OUR ROOMS?

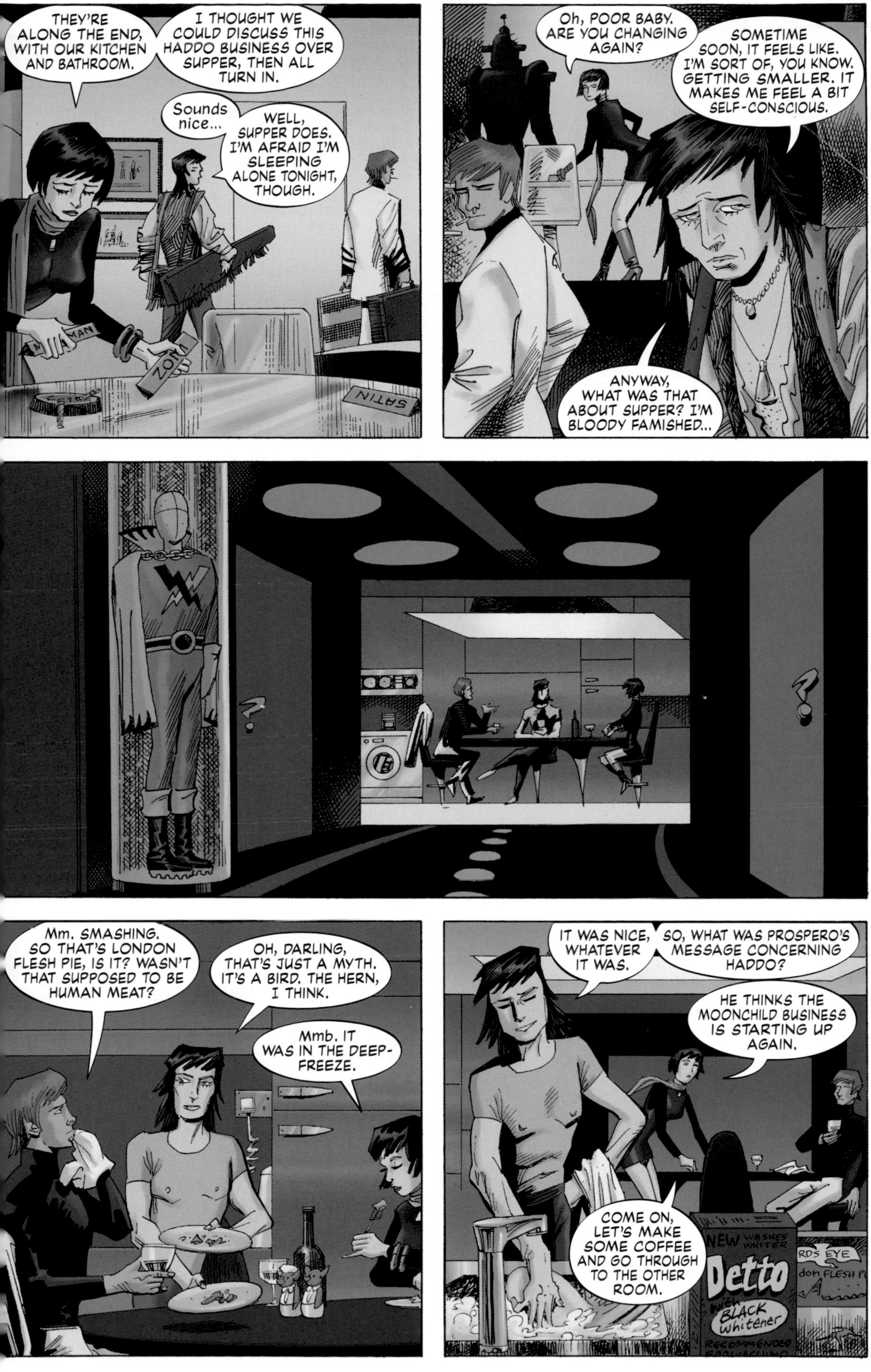
THEY'RE ALONG THE END, WITH OUR KITCHEN AND BATHROOM.
I THOUGHT WE COULD DISCUSS THIS HADDO BUSINESS OVER SUPPER, THEN ALL TURN IN.
Sounds nice...
WELL, SUPPER DOES. I'M AFRAID I'M SLEEPING ALONE TONIGHT, THOUGH.
ZOM
SATIN
Oh, POOR BABY. ARE YOU CHANGING AGAIN?
SOMETIME SOON, IT FEELS LIKE. I'M SORT OF, YOU KNOW. GETTING SMALLER. IT MAKES ME FEEL A BIT SELF-CONSCIOUS.
ANYWAY, WHAT WAS THAT ABOUT SUPPER? I'M BLOODY FAMISHED...
Mm. SMASHING. SO THAT'S LONDON FLESH PIE, IS IT? WASN'T THAT SUPPOSED TO BE HUMAN MEAT?
OH, DARLING, THAT'S JUST A MYTH. IT'S A BIRD. THE HERN, I THINK.
Mmb. IT WAS IN THE DEEP-FREEZE.
IT WAS NICE, WHATEVER IT WAS.
SO, WHAT WAS PROSPERO'S MESSAGE CONCERNING HADDO?
HE THINKS THE MOONCHILD BUSINESS IS STARTING UP AGAIN.
COME ON, LET'S MAKE SOME COFFEE AND GO THROUGH TO THE OTHER ROOM.
NEW
Detto
with BLACK whitener
RECOMMENDED

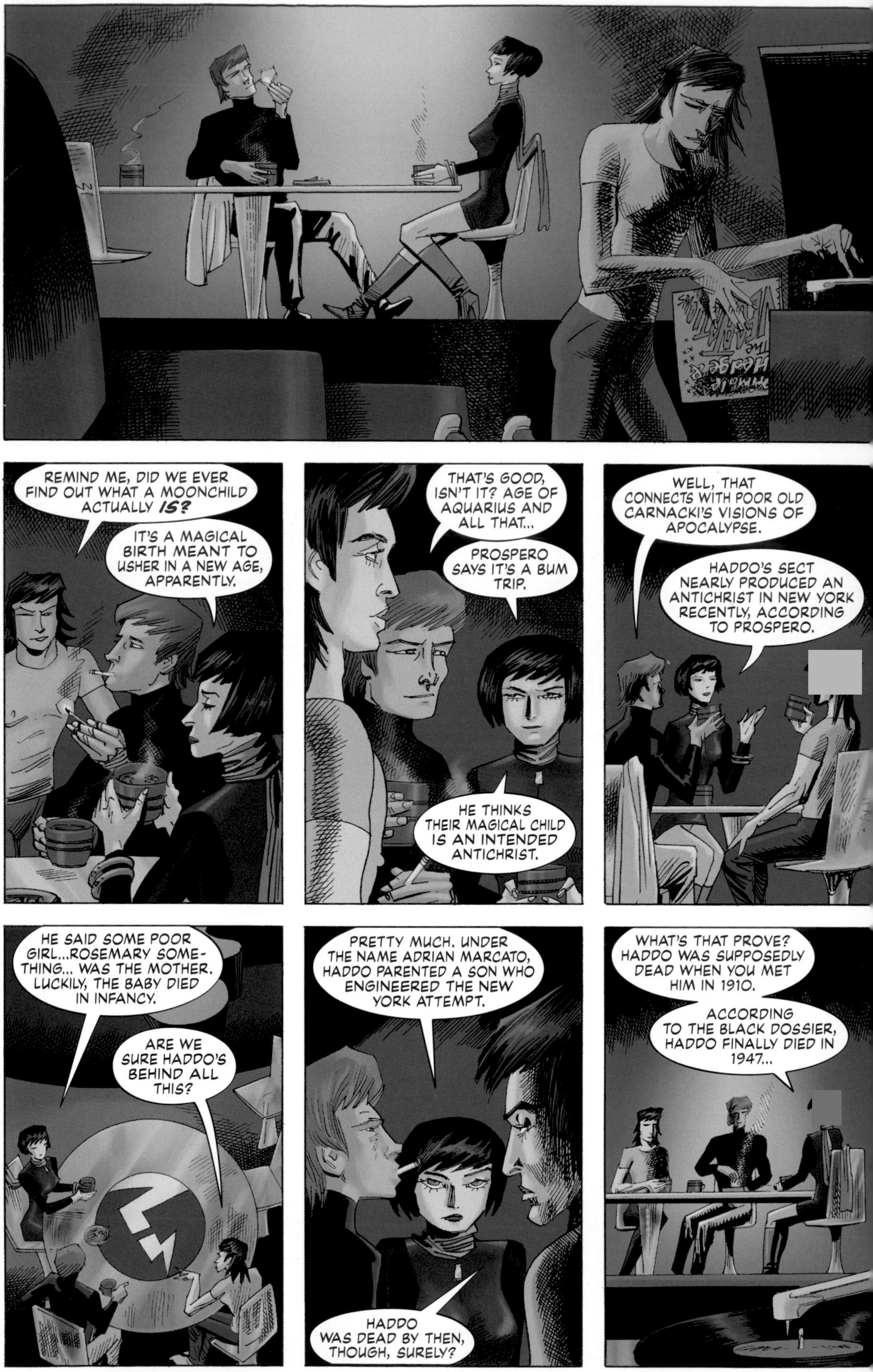

REMIND ME, DID WE EVER FIND OUT WHAT A MOONCHILD ACTUALLY *IS?*
IT'S A MAGICAL BIRTH MEANT TO USHER IN A NEW AGE, APPARENTLY.
THAT'S GOOD, ISN'T IT? AGE OF AQUARIUS AND ALL THAT...
PROSPERO SAYS IT'S A BUM TRIP.
HE THINKS THEIR MAGICAL CHILD IS AN INTENDED ANTICHRIST.
WELL, THAT CONNECTS WITH POOR OLD CARNACKI'S VISIONS OF APOCALYPSE.
HADDO'S SECT NEARLY PRODUCED AN ANTICHRIST IN NEW YORK RECENTLY, ACCORDING TO PROSPERO.
HE SAID SOME POOR GIRL...ROSEMARY SOME-THING... WAS THE MOTHER. LUCKILY, THE BABY DIED IN INFANCY.
ARE WE SURE HADDO'S BEHIND ALL THIS?
PRETTY MUCH. UNDER THE NAME ADRIAN MARCATO, HADDO PARENTED A SON WHO ENGINEERED THE NEW YORK ATTEMPT.
HADDO WAS DEAD BY THEN, THOUGH, SURELY?
WHAT'S THAT PROVE? HADDO WAS SUPPOSEDLY DEAD WHEN YOU MET HIM IN 1910.
ACCORDING TO THE BLACK DOSSIER, HADDO FINALLY DIED IN 1947...

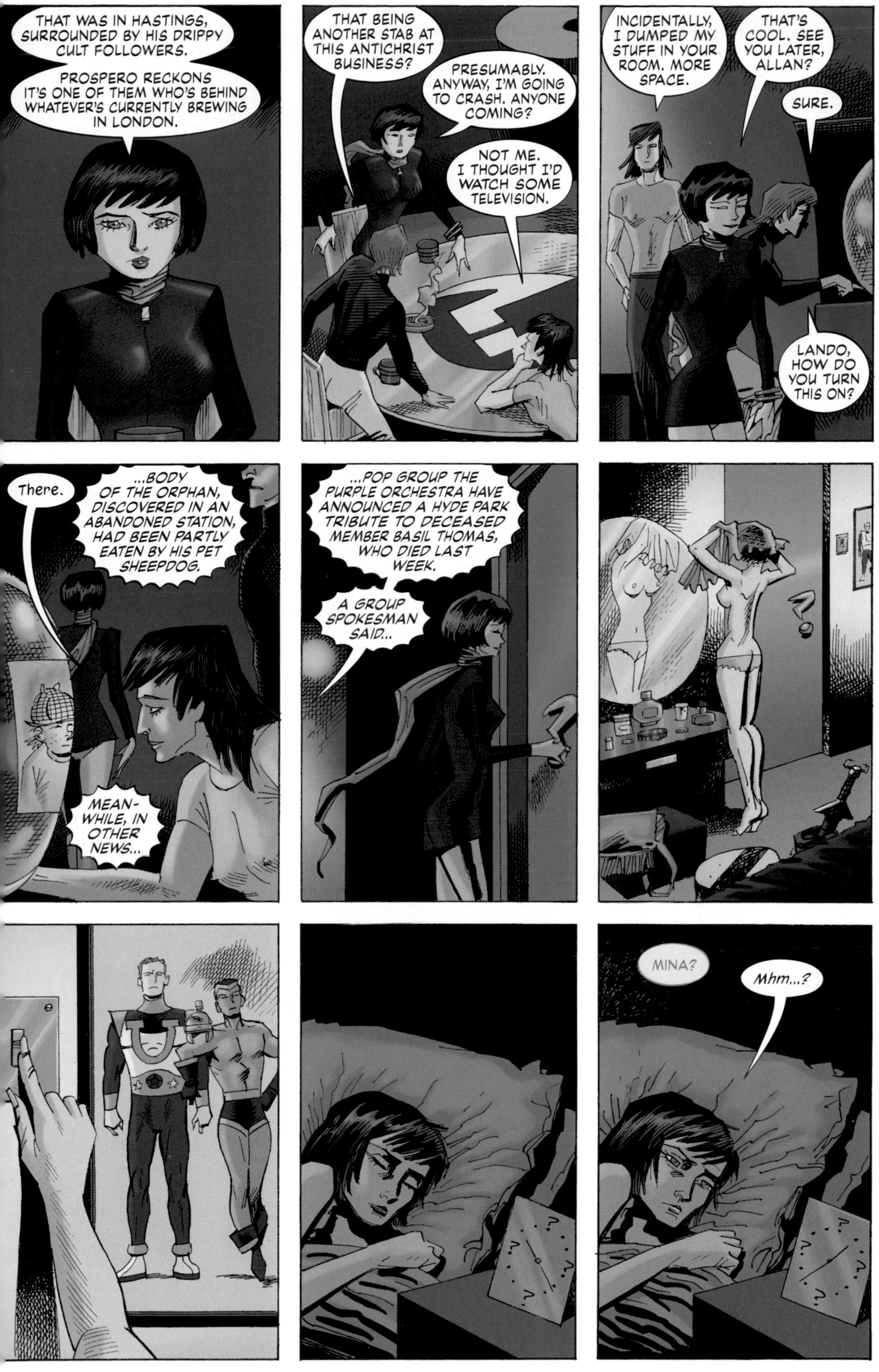
THAT WAS IN HASTINGS, SURROUNDED BY HIS DRIPPY CULT FOLLOWERS.
PROSPERO RECKONS IT'S ONE OF THEM WHO'S BEHIND WHATEVER'S CURRENTLY BREWING IN LONDON.
THAT BEING ANOTHER STAB AT THIS ANTICHRIST BUSINESS?
PRESUMABLY. ANYWAY, I'M GOING TO CRASH. ANYONE COMING?
NOT ME. I THOUGHT I'D WATCH SOME TELEVISION.
INCIDENTALLY, I DUMPED MY STUFF IN YOUR ROOM. MORE SPACE.
THAT'S COOL. SEE YOU LATER, ALLAN?
SURE.
LANDO, HOW DO YOU TURN THIS ON?
There.
...BODY OF THE ORPHAN, DISCOVERED IN AN ABANDONED STATION, HAD BEEN PARTLY EATEN BY HIS PET SHEEPDOG.
MEAN-WHILE, IN OTHER NEWS...
...POP GROUP THE PURPLE ORCHESTRA HAVE ANNOUNCED A HYDE PARK TRIBUTE TO DECEASED MEMBER BASIL THOMAS, WHO DIED LAST WEEK.
A GROUP SPOKESMAN SAID...
MINA?
Mhm...?

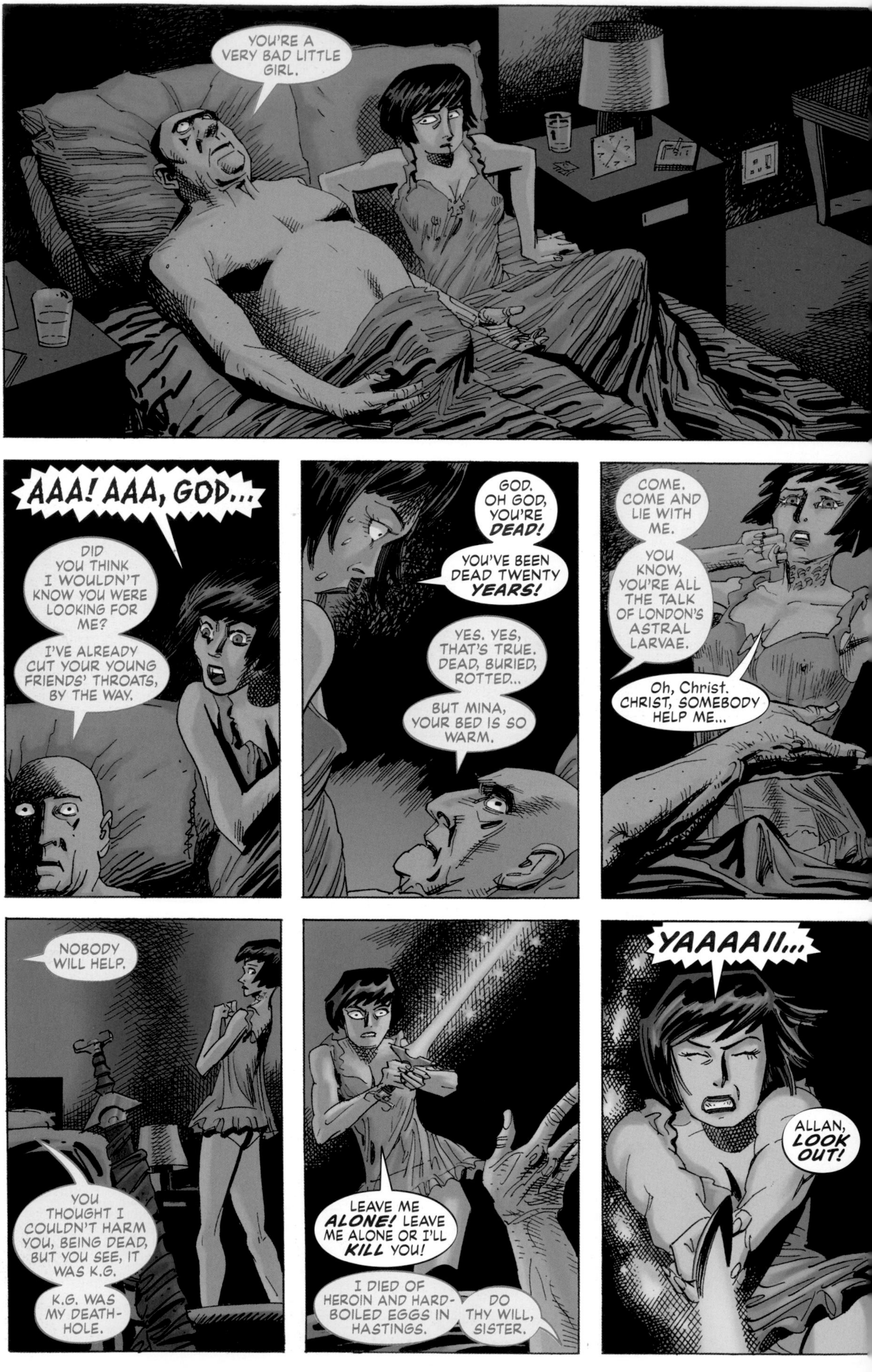
YOU'RE A VERY BAD LITTLE GIRL.
AAA! AAA, GOD...
DID YOU THINK I WOULDN'T KNOW YOU WERE LOOKING FOR ME?
I'VE ALREADY CUT YOUR YOUNG FRIENDS' THROATS, BY THE WAY.
GOD. OH GOD, YOU'RE DEAD!
YOU'VE BEEN DEAD TWENTY YEARS!
YES. YES, THAT'S TRUE. DEAD, BURIED, ROTTED...
BUT MINA, YOUR BED IS SO WARM.
COME. COME AND LIE WITH ME.
YOU KNOW, YOU'RE ALL THE TALK OF LONDON'S ASTRAL LARVAE.
Oh, Christ. CHRIST, SOMEBODY HELP ME...
NOBODY WILL HELP.
YOU THOUGHT I COULDN'T HARM YOU, BEING DEAD, BUT YOU SEE, IT WAS K.G.
K.G. WAS MY DEATH-HOLE.
LEAVE ME ALONE! LEAVE ME ALONE OR I'LL KILL YOU!
I DIED OF HEROIN AND HARD-BOILED EGGS IN HASTINGS.
DO THY WILL, SISTER.
YAAAAII...
ALLAN, LOOK OUT!

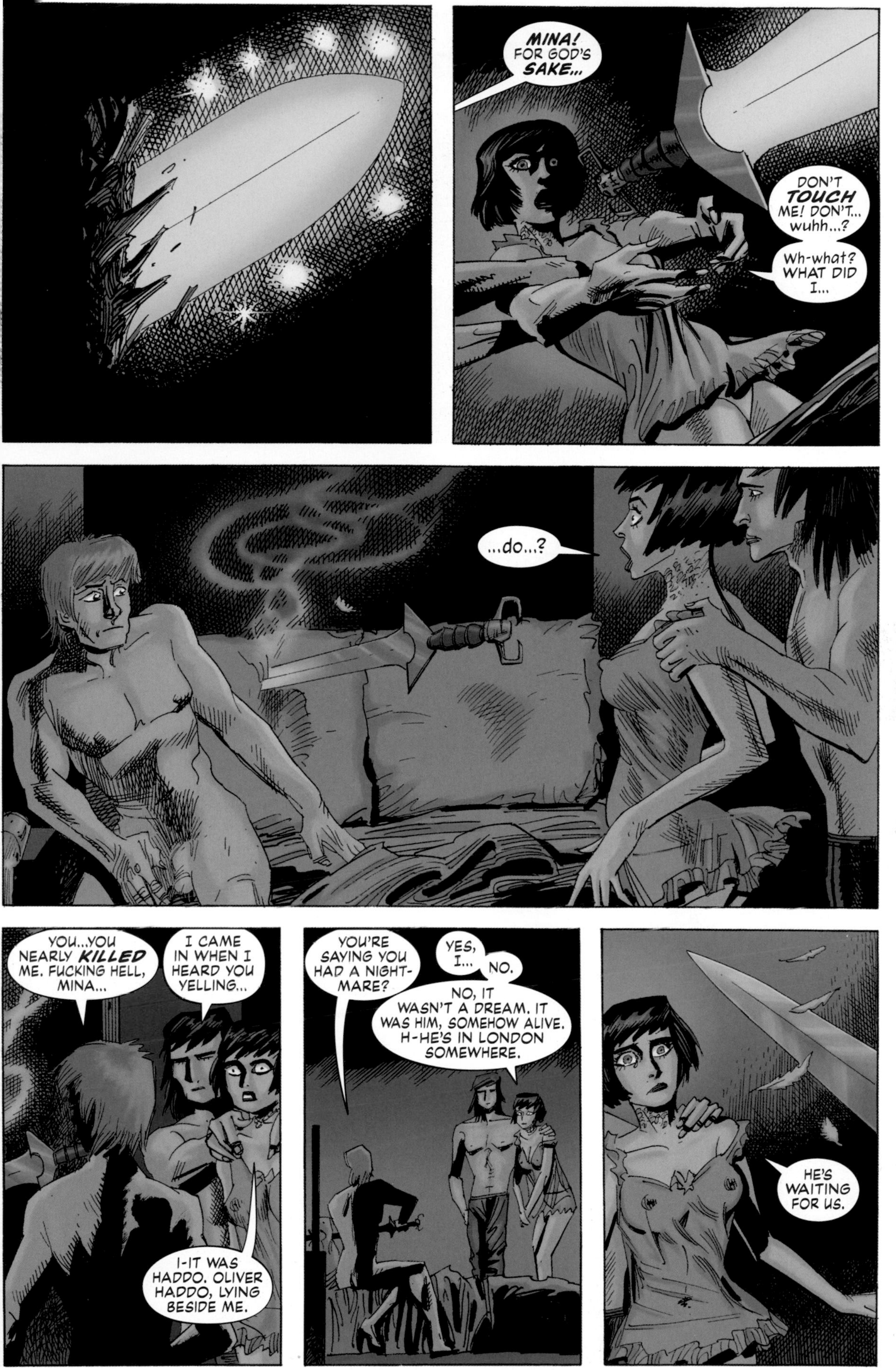
MINA! FOR GOD'S SAKE...
DON'T TOUCH ME! DON'T... wuhh...?
Wh-what? WHAT DID I...
...do...?
YOU...YOU NEARLY KILLED ME. FUCKING HELL, MINA...
I CAME IN WHEN I HEARD YOU YELLING...
I-IT WAS HADDO. OLIVER HADDO, LYING BESIDE ME.
YOU'RE SAYING YOU HAD A NIGHT-MARE?
YES, I...
NO.
NO, IT WASN'T A DREAM. IT WAS HIM, SOMEHOW ALIVE. H-HE'S IN LONDON SOMEWHERE.
HE'S WAITING FOR US.

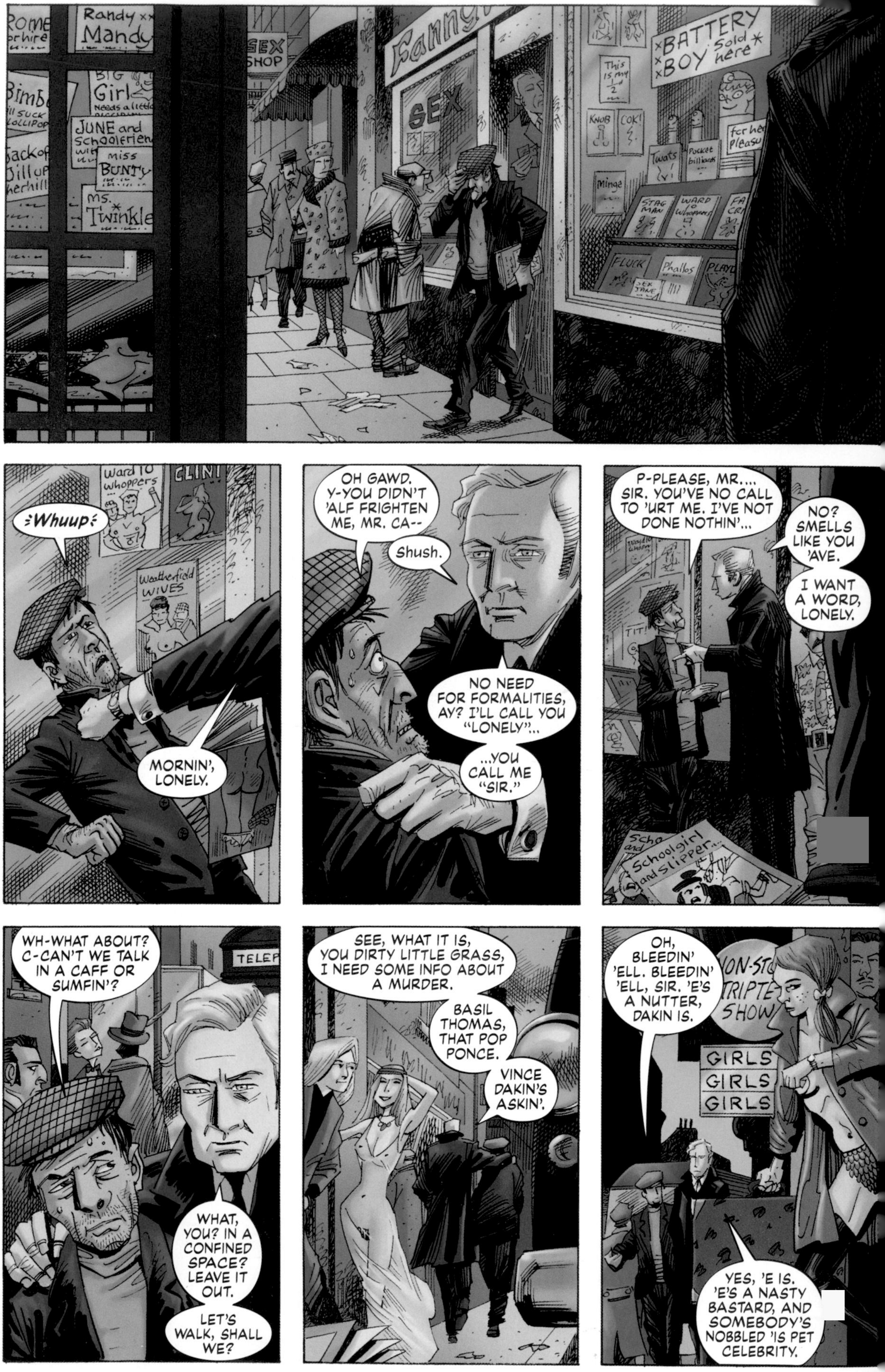
Randy xx Mandy
SEX SHOP
SEX
BATTERY BOY Sold here
Ward 10 whoppers
Weatherfield WIVES
Whuup
MORNIN', LONELY.
OH GAWD. Y-YOU DIDN'T 'ALF FRIGHTEN ME, MR. CA--
Shush.
NO NEED FOR FORMALITIES, AY? I'LL CALL YOU "LONELY"...
...YOU CALL ME "SIR."
P-PLEASE, MR.... SIR. YOU'VE NO CALL TO 'URT ME. I'VE NOT DONE NOTHIN'...
NO? SMELLS LIKE YOU 'AVE.
I WANT A WORD, LONELY.
Schoolgirl and Slipper...
WH-WHAT ABOUT? C-CAN'T WE TALK IN A CAFF OR SUMFIN'?
WHAT, YOU? IN A CONFINED SPACE? LEAVE IT OUT.
LET'S WALK, SHALL WE?
SEE, WHAT IT IS, YOU DIRTY LITTLE GRASS, I NEED SOME INFO ABOUT A MURDER.
BASIL THOMAS, THAT POP PONCE.
VINCE DAKIN'S ASKIN'.
OH, BLEEDIN' 'ELL. BLEEDIN' 'ELL, SIR. 'E'S A NUTTER, DAKIN IS.
GIRLS
GIRLS
GIRLS
YES, 'E IS. 'E'S A NASTY BASTARD, AND SOMEBODY'S NOBBLED 'IS PET CELEBRITY.

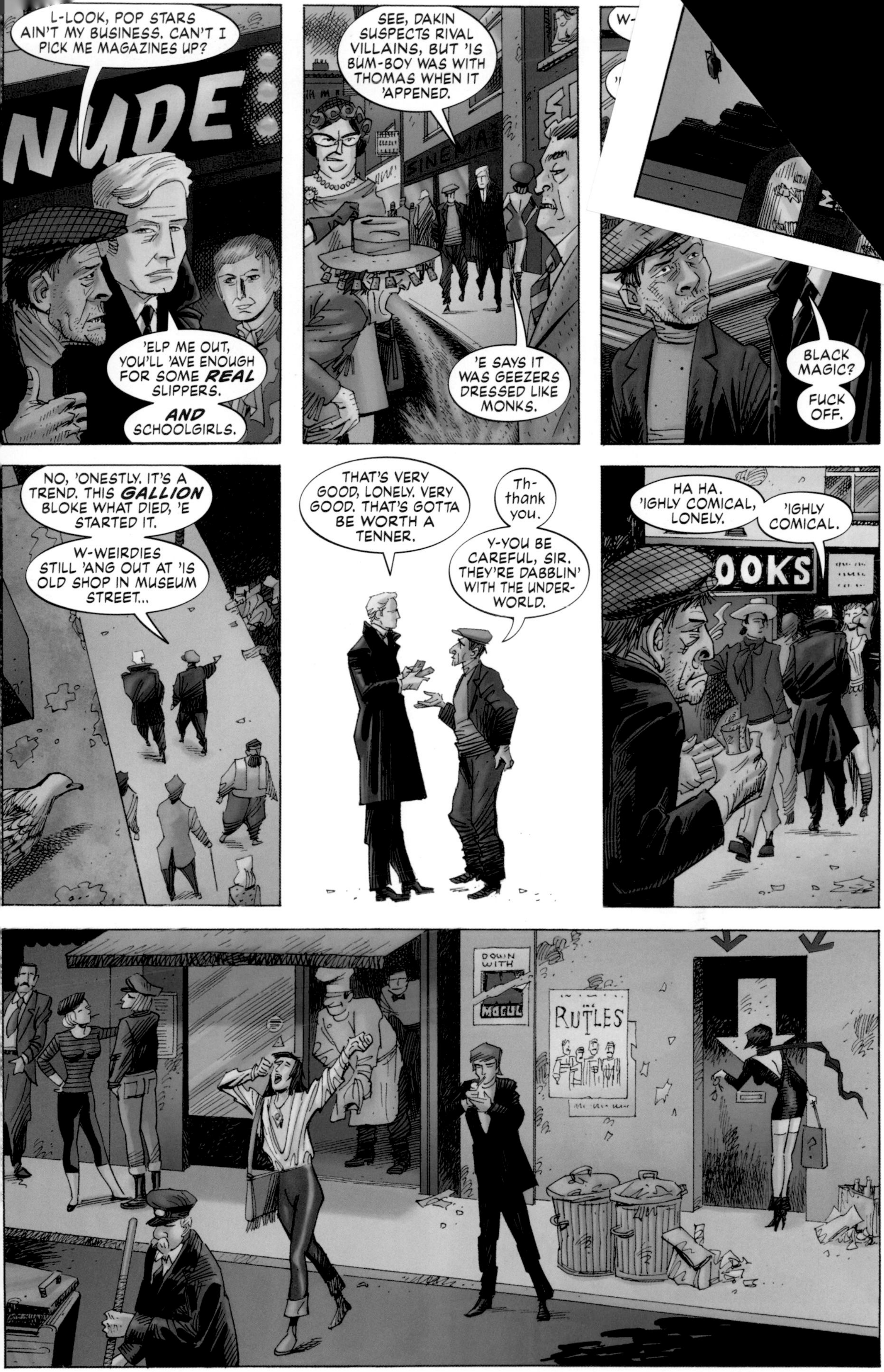
L-LOOK, POP STARS AIN'T MY BUSINESS. CAN'T I PICK ME MAGAZINES UP?
NUDE
'ELP ME OUT, YOU'LL 'AVE ENOUGH FOR SOME **REAL** SLIPPERS.
AND SCHOOLGIRLS.
SEE, DAKIN SUSPECTS RIVAL VILLAINS, BUT 'IS BUM-BOY WAS WITH THOMAS WHEN IT 'APPENED.
'E SAYS IT WAS GEEZERS DRESSED LIKE MONKS.
BLACK MAGIC?
FUCK OFF.
NO, 'ONESTLY. IT'S A TREND. THIS **GALLION** BLOKE WHAT DIED, 'E STARTED IT.
W-WEIRDIES STILL 'ANG OUT AT 'IS OLD SHOP IN MUSEUM STREET...
THAT'S VERY GOOD, LONELY. VERY GOOD. THAT'S GOTTA BE WORTH A TENNER.
Th-thank you.
Y-YOU BE CAREFUL, SIR. THEY'RE DABBLIN' WITH THE UNDER-WORLD.
HA HA. 'IGHLY COMICAL, LONELY.
'IGHLY COMICAL.
OOKS
DOWN WITH
RUTLES

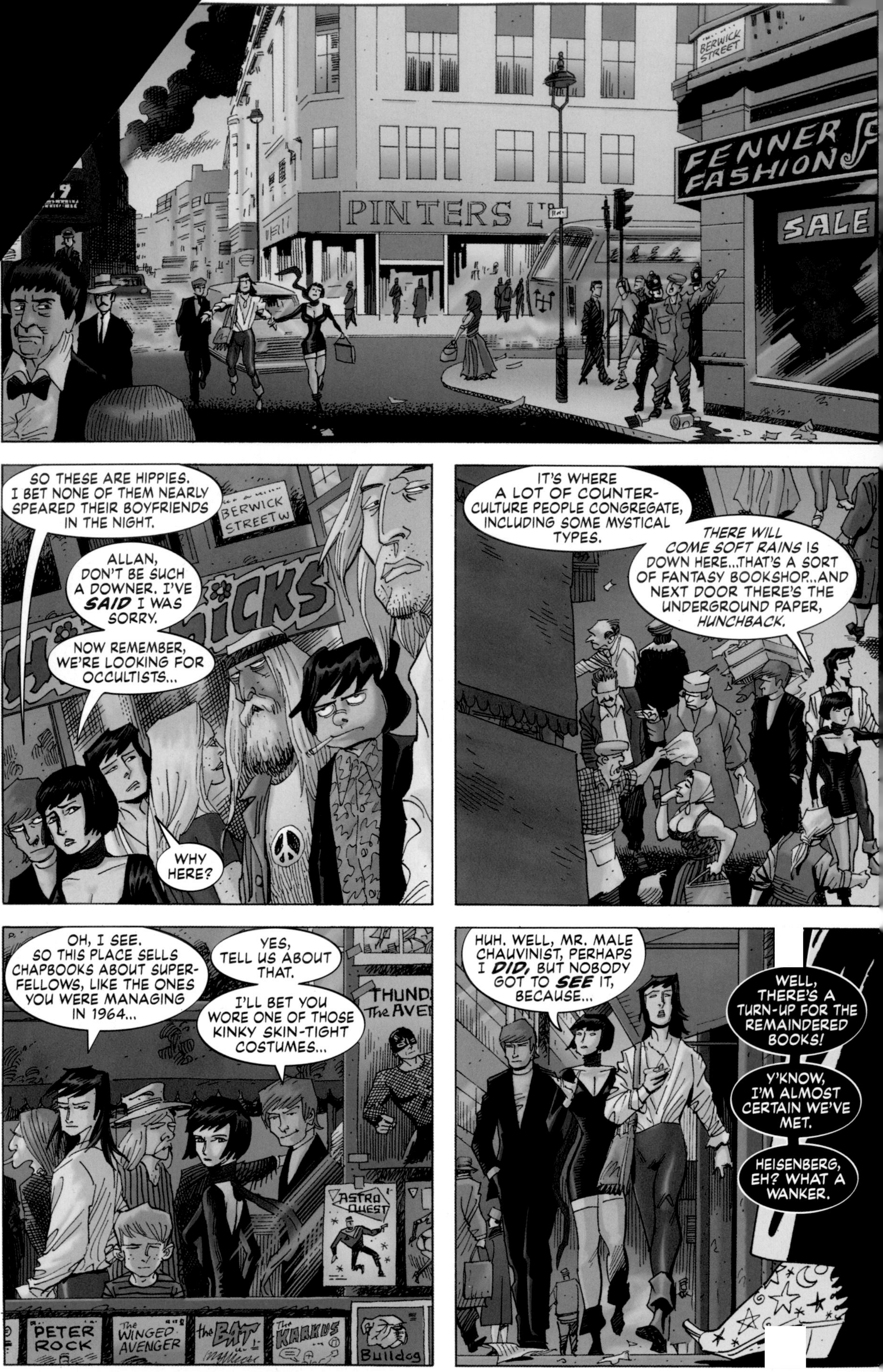
BERWICK STREET
FENNER FASHION
SALE
PINTERS
SO THESE ARE HIPPIES. I BET NONE OF THEM NEARLY SPEARED THEIR BOYFRIENDS IN THE NIGHT.
BERWICK STREET W
ALLAN, DON'T BE SUCH A DOWNER. I'VE ***SAID*** I WAS SORRY.
NOW REMEMBER, WE'RE LOOKING FOR OCCULTISTS...
WHY HERE?
IT'S WHERE A LOT OF COUNTER-CULTURE PEOPLE CONGREGATE, INCLUDING SOME MYSTICAL TYPES.
THERE WILL COME SOFT RAINS IS DOWN HERE...THAT'S A SORT OF FANTASY BOOKSHOP...AND NEXT DOOR THERE'S THE UNDERGROUND PAPER, *HUNCHBACK.*
OH, I SEE. SO THIS PLACE SELLS CHAPBOOKS ABOUT SUPER-FELLOWS, LIKE THE ONES YOU WERE MANAGING IN 1964...
YES, TELL US ABOUT THAT.
I'LL BET YOU WORE ONE OF THOSE KINKY SKIN-TIGHT COSTUMES...
ASTRA QUEST
PETER ROCK
The WINGED AVENGER
the BAT
The KARKUS
Bulldog
HUH. WELL, MR. MALE CHAUVINIST, PERHAPS I ***DID,*** BUT NOBODY GOT TO ***SEE*** IT, BECAUSE...
WELL, THERE'S A TURN-UP FOR THE REMAINDERED BOOKS!
Y'KNOW, I'M ALMOST CERTAIN WE'VE MET.
HEISENBERG, EH? WHAT A WANKER.

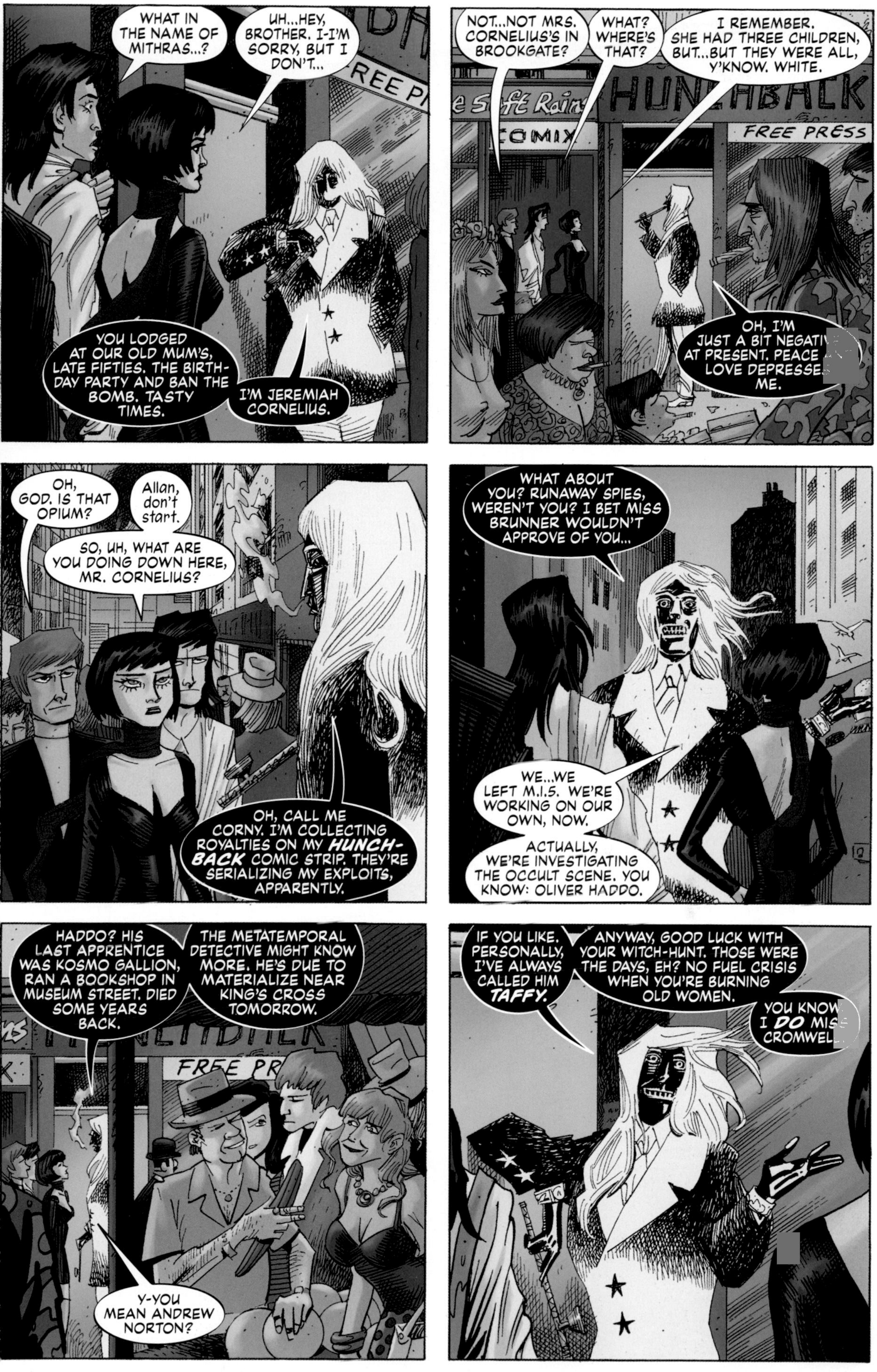
WHAT IN THE NAME OF MITHRAS...?
UH...HEY, BROTHER. I-I'M SORRY, BUT I DON'T...
YOU LODGED AT OUR OLD MUM'S, LATE FIFTIES. THE BIRTHDAY PARTY AND BAN THE BOMB. TASTY TIMES.
I'M JEREMIAH CORNELIUS.
NOT...NOT MRS. CORNELIUS'S IN BROOKGATE?
WHAT? WHERE'S THAT?
I REMEMBER. SHE HAD THREE CHILDREN, BUT...BUT THEY WERE ALL, Y'KNOW. WHITE.
HUNCHBACK
FREE PRESS
COMIX
OH, I'M JUST A BIT NEGATIV AT PRESENT. PEACE LOVE DEPRESSE ME.
OH, GOD. IS THAT OPIUM?
Allan, don't start.
SO, UH, WHAT ARE YOU DOING DOWN HERE, MR. CORNELIUS?
OH, CALL ME CORNY. I'M COLLECTING ROYALTIES ON MY ***HUNCHBACK*** COMIC STRIP. THEY'RE SERIALIZING MY EXPLOITS, APPARENTLY.
WHAT ABOUT YOU? RUNAWAY SPIES, WEREN'T YOU? I BET MISS BRUNNER WOULDN'T APPROVE OF YOU...
WE...WE LEFT M.I.5. WE'RE WORKING ON OUR OWN, NOW.
ACTUALLY, WE'RE INVESTIGATING THE OCCULT SCENE. YOU KNOW: OLIVER HADDO.
HADDO? HIS LAST APPRENTICE WAS KOSMO GALLION, RAN A BOOKSHOP IN MUSEUM STREET. DIED SOME YEARS BACK.
THE METATEMPORAL DETECTIVE MIGHT KNOW MORE. HE'S DUE TO MATERIALIZE NEAR KING'S CROSS TOMORROW.
FREE PR
Y-YOU MEAN ANDREW NORTON?
IF YOU LIKE. PERSONALLY, I'VE ALWAYS CALLED HIM ***TAFFY.***
ANYWAY, GOOD LUCK WITH YOUR WITCH-HUNT. THOSE WERE THE DAYS, EH? NO FUEL CRISIS WHEN YOU'RE BURNING OLD WOMEN.
YOU KNOW I ***DO*** MIS CROMWEL

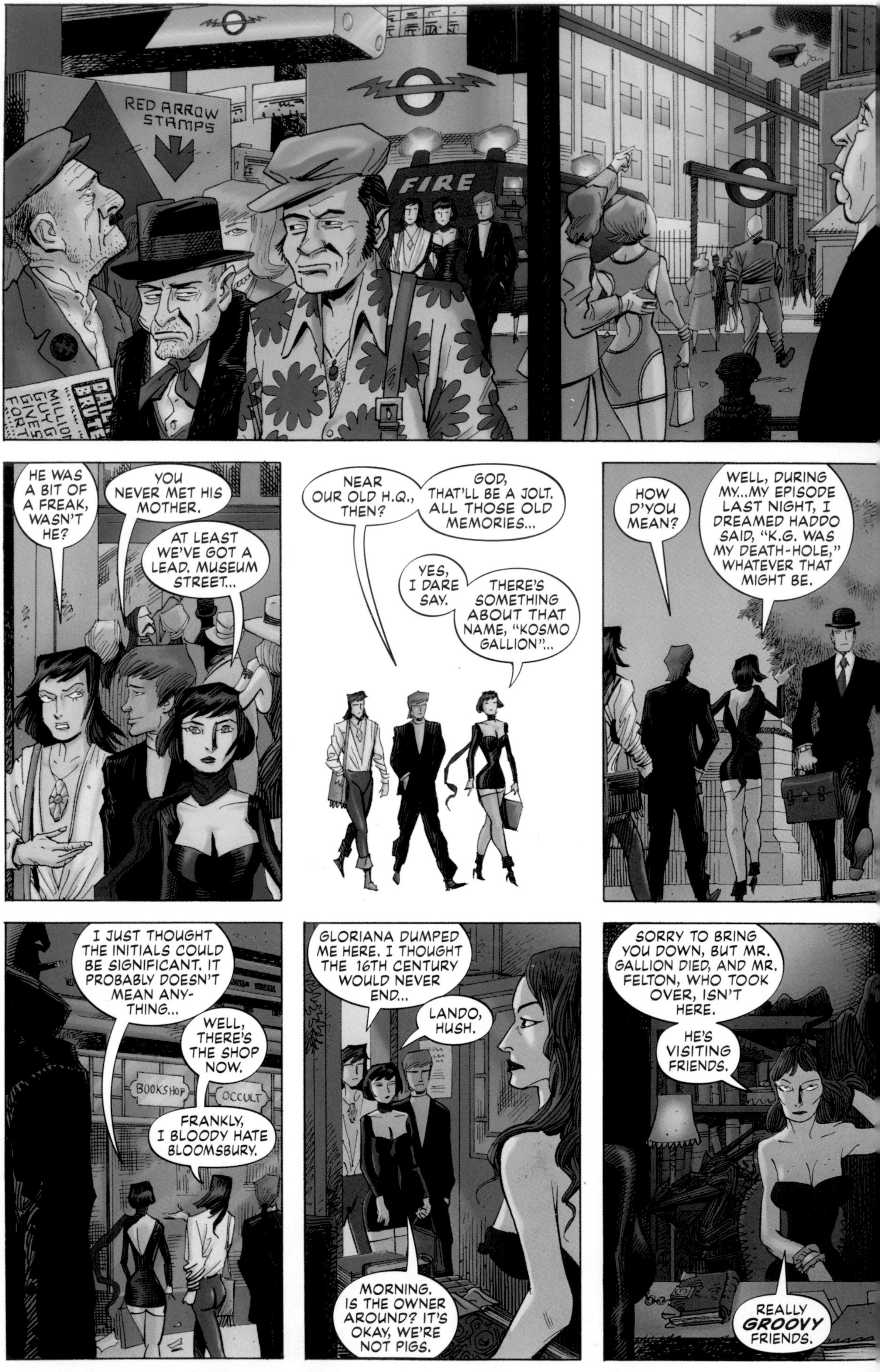
RED ARROW STAMPS
FIRE
HE WAS A BIT OF A FREAK, WASN'T HE?
YOU NEVER MET HIS MOTHER.
AT LEAST WE'VE GOT A LEAD. MUSEUM STREET...
NEAR OUR OLD H.Q., THEN?
GOD, THAT'LL BE A JOLT. ALL THOSE OLD MEMORIES...
YES, I DARE SAY.
THERE'S SOMETHING ABOUT THAT NAME, "KOSMO GALLION"...
HOW D'YOU MEAN?
WELL, DURING MY...MY EPISODE LAST NIGHT, I DREAMED HADDO SAID, "K.G. WAS MY DEATH-HOLE," WHATEVER THAT MIGHT BE.
I JUST THOUGHT THE INITIALS COULD BE SIGNIFICANT. IT PROBABLY DOESN'T MEAN ANY-THING...
WELL, THERE'S THE SHOP NOW.
BOOKSHOP
OCCULT
FRANKLY, I BLOODY HATE BLOOMSBURY.
GLORIANA DUMPED ME HERE. I THOUGHT THE 16TH CENTURY WOULD NEVER END...
LANDO, HUSH.
MORNING. IS THE OWNER AROUND? IT'S OKAY, WE'RE NOT PIGS.
SORRY TO BRING YOU DOWN, BUT MR. GALLION DIED, AND MR. FELTON, WHO TOOK OVER, ISN'T HERE.
HE'S VISITING FRIENDS.
REALLY GROOVY FRIENDS.

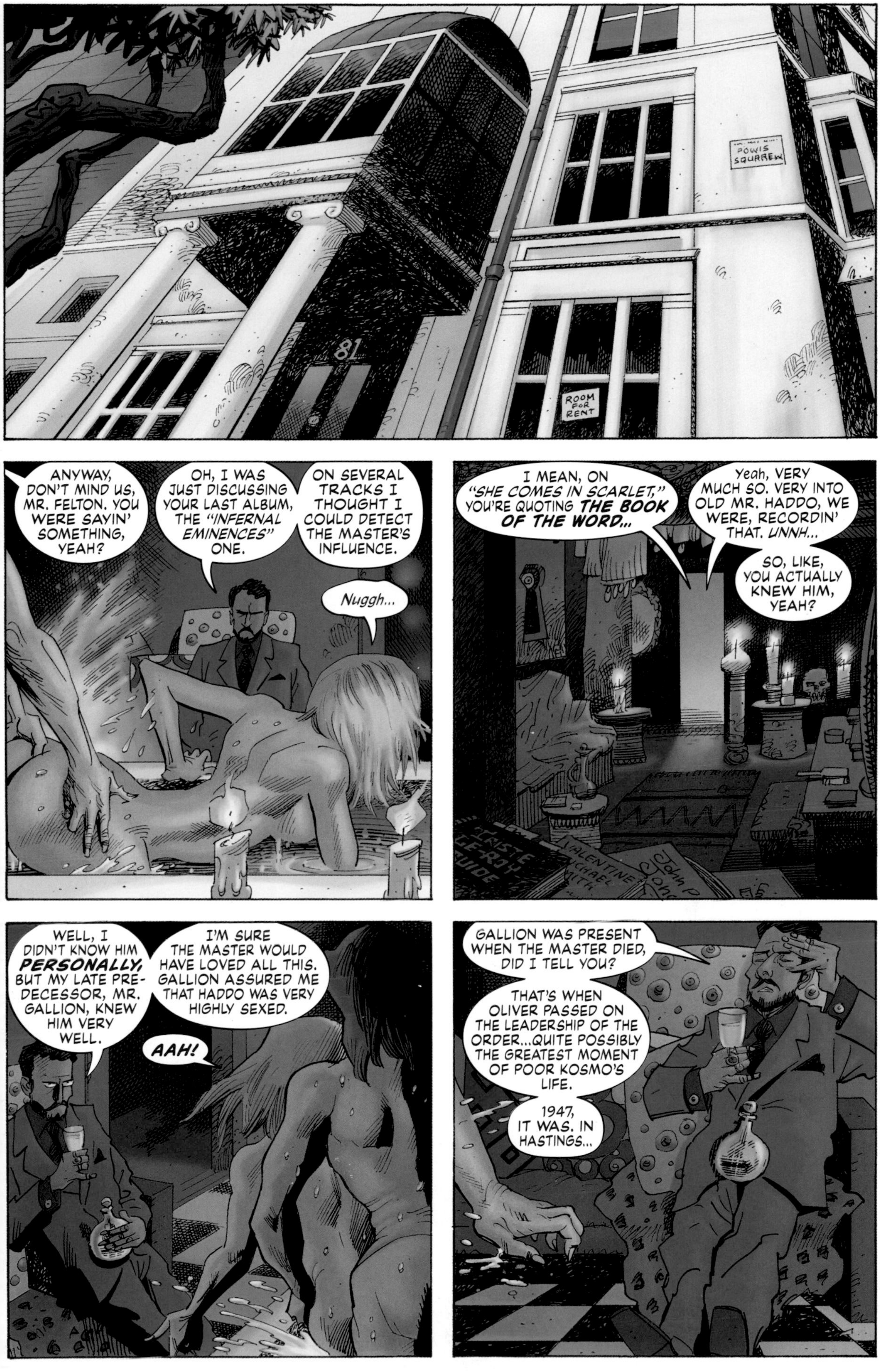
POWIS SQUARE W
81
ROOM FOR RENT
ANYWAY, DON'T MIND US, MR. FELTON. YOU WERE SAYIN' SOMETHING, YEAH?
OH, I WAS JUST DISCUSSING YOUR LAST ALBUM, THE "INFERNAL EMINENCES" ONE.
ON SEVERAL TRACKS I THOUGHT I COULD DETECT THE MASTER'S INFLUENCE.
Nuggh...
I MEAN, ON "SHE COMES IN SCARLET," YOU'RE QUOTING THE BOOK OF THE WORD...
Yeah, VERY MUCH SO. VERY INTO OLD MR. HADDO, WE WERE, RECORDIN' THAT. UNNH...
SO, LIKE, YOU ACTUALLY KNEW HIM, YEAH?
VALENTINE MICHAEL SMITH
WELL, I DIDN'T KNOW HIM PERSONALLY, BUT MY LATE PRE-DECESSOR, MR. GALLION, KNEW HIM VERY WELL.
I'M SURE THE MASTER WOULD HAVE LOVED ALL THIS. GALLION ASSURED ME THAT HADDO WAS VERY HIGHLY SEXED.
AAH!
GALLION WAS PRESENT WHEN THE MASTER DIED, DID I TELL YOU?
THAT'S WHEN OLIVER PASSED ON THE LEADERSHIP OF THE ORDER...QUITE POSSIBLY THE GREATEST MOMENT OF POOR KOSMO'S LIFE.
1947, IT WAS. IN HASTINGS...

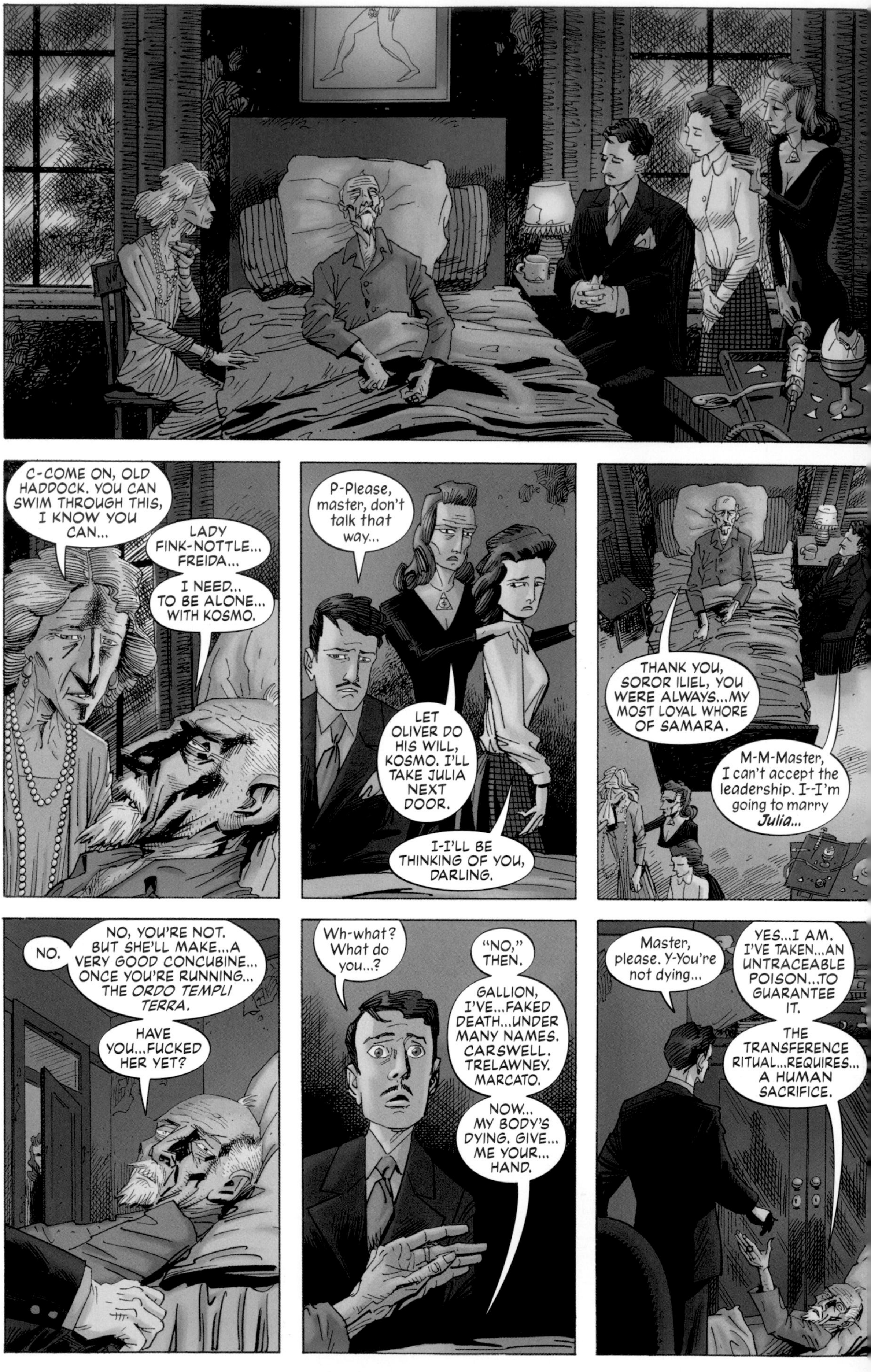
C-COME ON, OLD HADDOCK. YOU CAN SWIM THROUGH THIS, I KNOW YOU CAN...
LADY FINK-NOTTLE... FREIDA...
I NEED... TO BE ALONE... WITH KOSMO.
P-Please, master, don't talk that way...
LET OLIVER DO HIS WILL, KOSMO. I'LL TAKE JULIA NEXT DOOR.
I-I'LL BE THINKING OF YOU, DARLING.
THANK YOU, SOROR ILIEL, YOU WERE ALWAYS...MY MOST LOYAL WHORE OF SAMARA.
M-M-Master, I can't accept the leadership. I--I'm going to marry *Julia*...
NO.
NO, YOU'RE NOT. BUT SHE'LL MAKE...A VERY GOOD CONCUBINE... ONCE YOU'RE RUNNING... THE *ORDO TEMPLI TERRA*.
HAVE YOU...FUCKED HER YET?
Wh-what? What do you...?
"NO," THEN.
GALLION, I'VE...FAKED DEATH...UNDER MANY NAMES. CARSWELL. TRELAWNEY. MARCATO.
NOW... MY BODY'S DYING. GIVE... ME YOUR... HAND.
Master, please. Y-You're not dying...
YES...I AM. I'VE TAKEN...AN UNTRACEABLE POISON...TO GUARANTEE IT.
THE TRANSFERENCE RITUAL...REQUIRES... A HUMAN SACRIFICE.

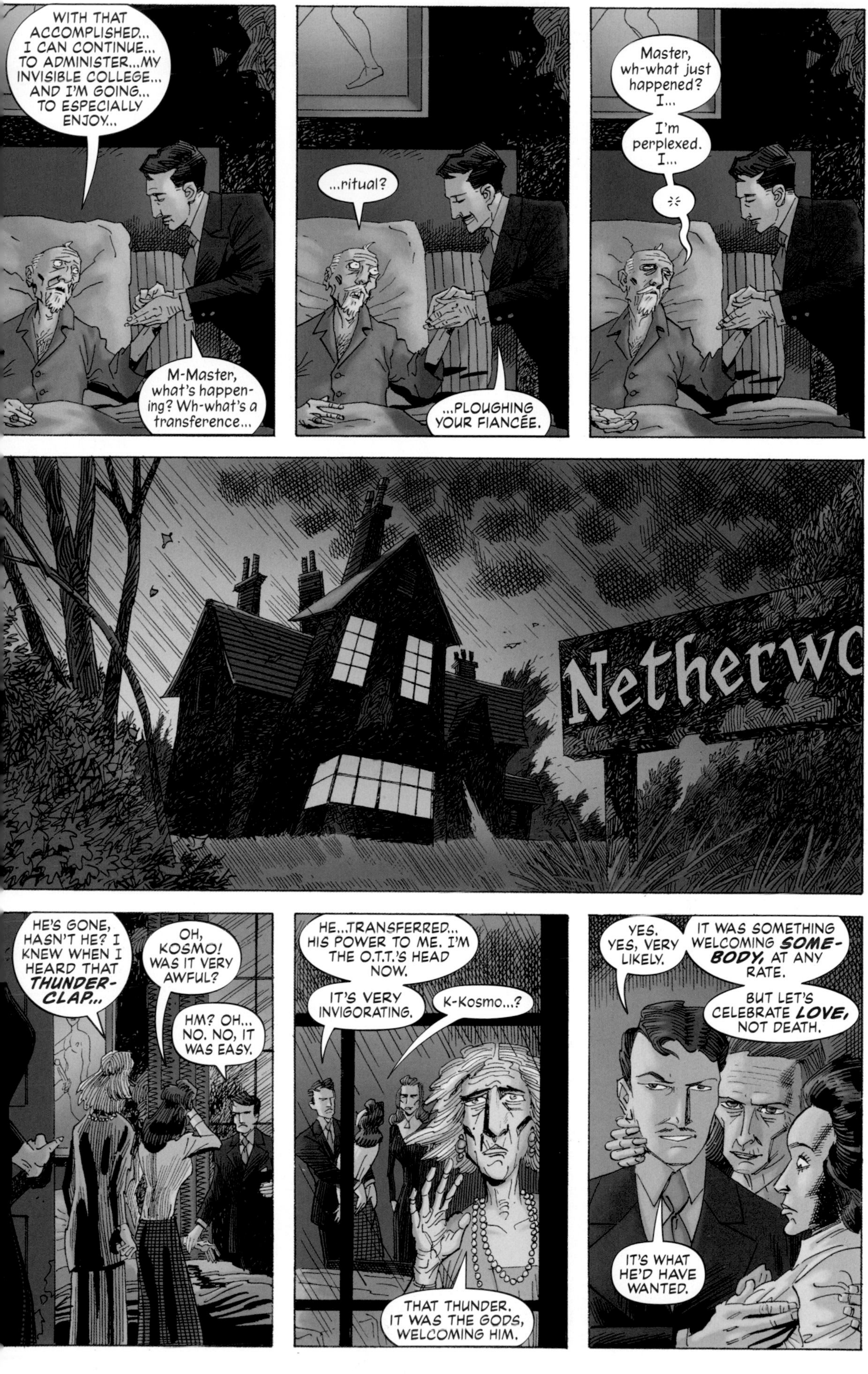
WITH THAT ACCOMPLISHED... I CAN CONTINUE... TO ADMINISTER...MY INVISIBLE COLLEGE... AND I'M GOING... TO ESPECIALLY ENJOY...
M-Master, what's happening? Wh-what's a transference...
...ritual?
...PLOUGHING YOUR FIANCÉE.
Master, wh-what just happened? I...
I'm perplexed. I...
Netherwo
HE'S GONE, HASN'T HE? I KNEW WHEN I HEARD THAT THUNDER-CLAP...
OH, KOSMO! WAS IT VERY AWFUL?
HM? OH... NO. NO, IT WAS EASY.
HE...TRANSFERRED... HIS POWER TO ME. I'M THE O.T.T.'S HEAD NOW.
IT'S VERY INVIGORATING.
K-Kosmo...?
THAT THUNDER. IT WAS THE GODS, WELCOMING HIM.
YES. YES, VERY LIKELY.
IT WAS SOMETHING WELCOMING SOME-BODY, AT ANY RATE.
BUT LET'S CELEBRATE LOVE, NOT DEATH.
IT'S WHAT HE'D HAVE WANTED.

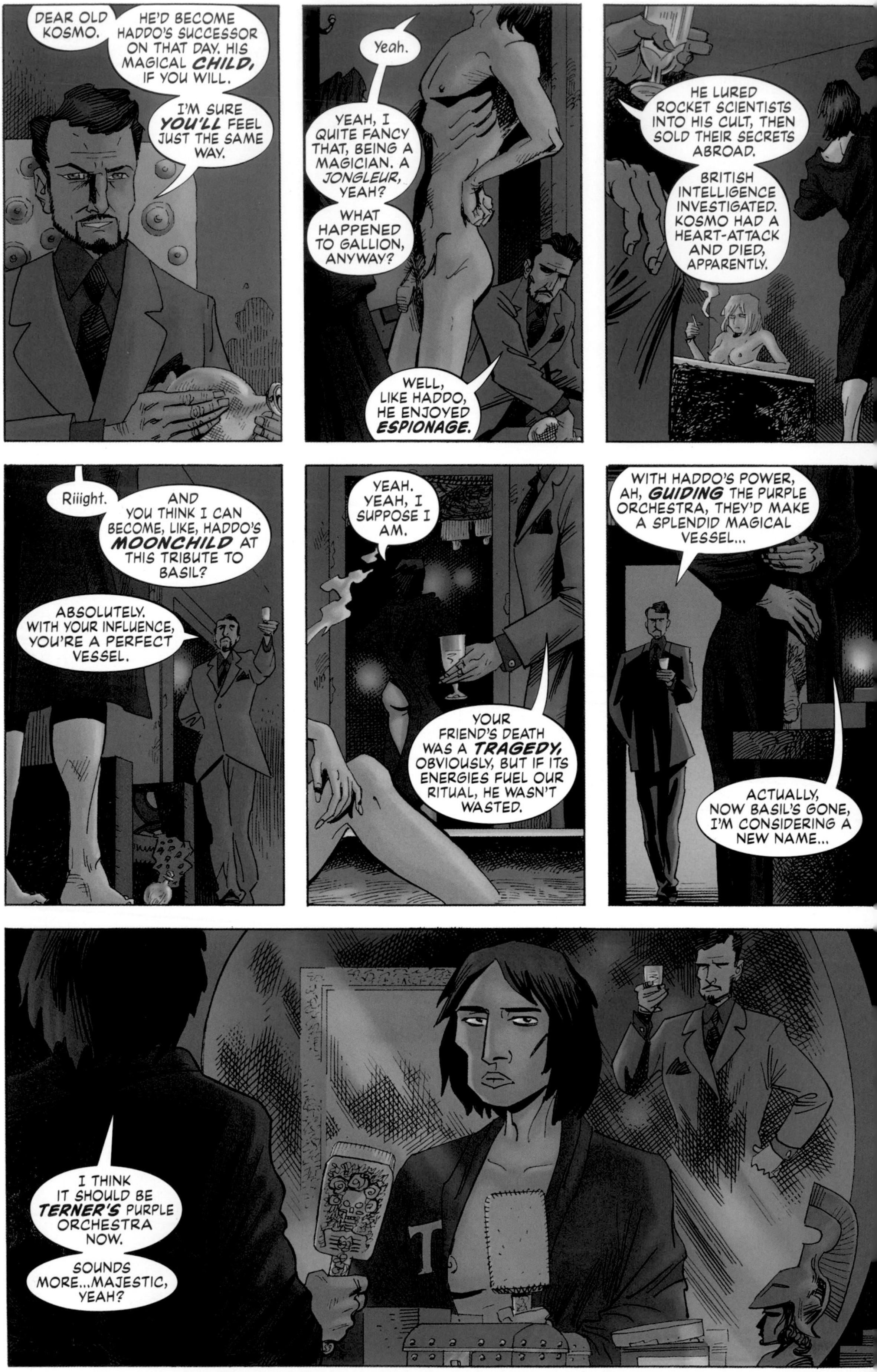
DEAR OLD KOSMO.
HE'D BECOME HADDO'S SUCCESSOR ON THAT DAY. HIS MAGICAL CHILD, IF YOU WILL.
I'M SURE YOU'LL FEEL JUST THE SAME WAY.
Yeah.
YEAH, I QUITE FANCY THAT, BEING A MAGICIAN. A JONGLEUR, YEAH?
WHAT HAPPENED TO GALLION, ANYWAY?
WELL, LIKE HADDO, HE ENJOYED ESPIONAGE.
HE LURED ROCKET SCIENTISTS INTO HIS CULT, THEN SOLD THEIR SECRETS ABROAD.
BRITISH INTELLIGENCE INVESTIGATED. KOSMO HAD A HEART-ATTACK AND DIED, APPARENTLY.
Riiight.
AND YOU THINK I CAN BECOME, LIKE, HADDO'S MOONCHILD AT THIS TRIBUTE TO BASIL?
ABSOLUTELY. WITH YOUR INFLUENCE, YOU'RE A PERFECT VESSEL.
YEAH. YEAH, I SUPPOSE I AM.
YOUR FRIEND'S DEATH WAS A TRAGEDY, OBVIOUSLY, BUT IF ITS ENERGIES FUEL OUR RITUAL, HE WASN'T WASTED.
WITH HADDO'S POWER, AH, GUIDING THE PURPLE ORCHESTRA, THEY'D MAKE A SPLENDID MAGICAL VESSEL...
ACTUALLY, NOW BASIL'S GONE, I'M CONSIDERING A NEW NAME...
I THINK IT SHOULD BE TERNER'S PURPLE ORCHESTRA NOW.
SOUNDS MORE...MAJESTIC, YEAH?

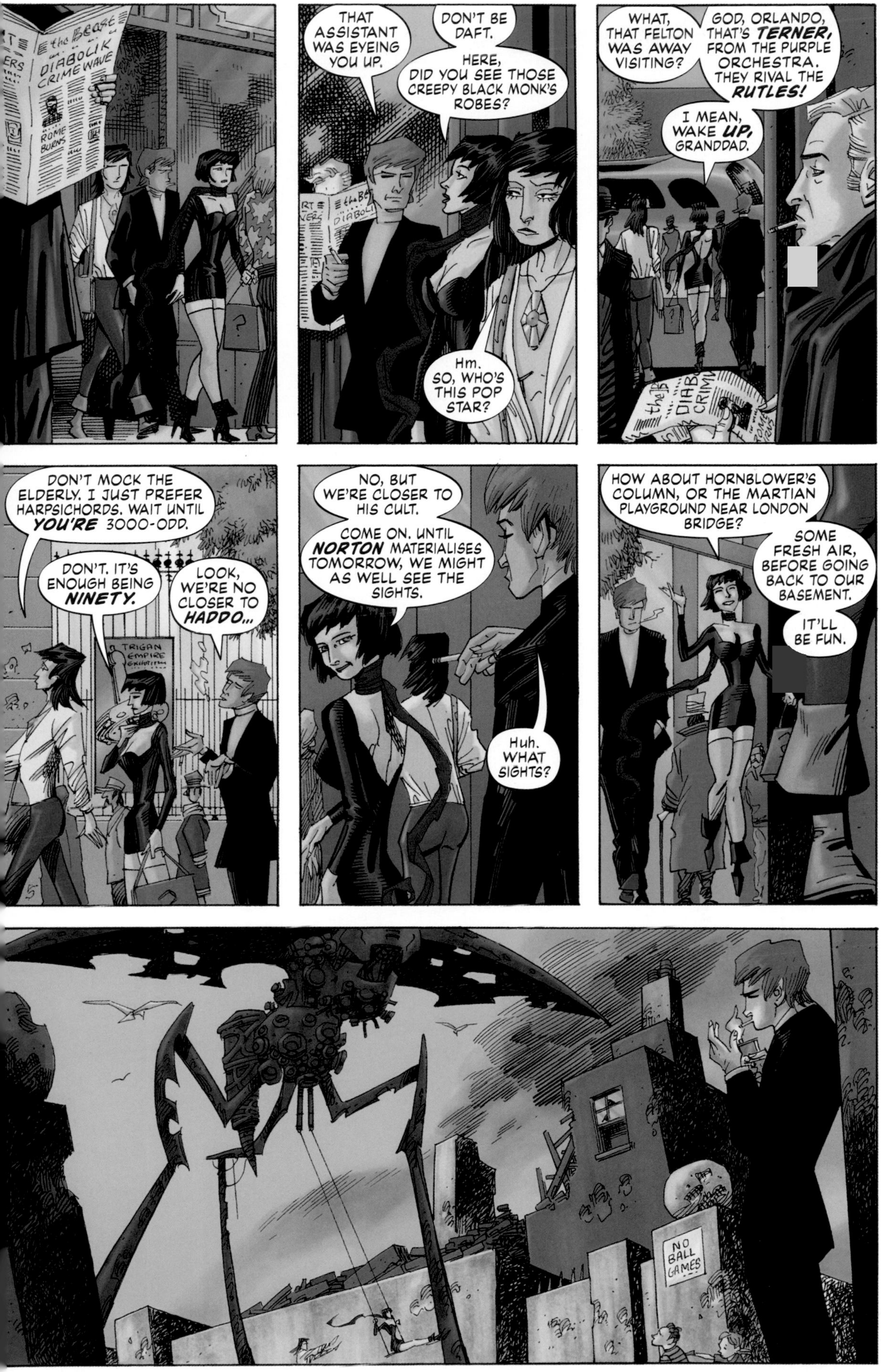
the Beast
DIABOLIK CRIME WAVE
ROME BURNS
THAT ASSISTANT WAS EYEING YOU UP.
DON'T BE DAFT.
HERE, DID YOU SEE THOSE CREEPY BLACK MONK'S ROBES?
Hm. SO, WHO'S THIS POP STAR?
WHAT, THAT FELTON WAS AWAY VISITING?
GOD, ORLANDO, THAT'S TERNER, FROM THE PURPLE ORCHESTRA. THEY RIVAL THE RUTLES!
I MEAN, WAKE UP, GRANDDAD.
DON'T MOCK THE ELDERLY. I JUST PREFER HARPSICHORDS. WAIT UNTIL YOU'RE 3000-ODD.
DON'T. IT'S ENOUGH BEING NINETY.
LOOK, WE'RE NO CLOSER TO HADDO...
TRIGAN EMPIRE
NO, BUT WE'RE CLOSER TO HIS CULT.
COME ON. UNTIL NORTON MATERIALISES TOMORROW, WE MIGHT AS WELL SEE THE SIGHTS.
Huh. WHAT SIGHTS?
HOW ABOUT HORNBLOWER'S COLUMN, OR THE MARTIAN PLAYGROUND NEAR LONDON BRIDGE?
SOME FRESH AIR, BEFORE GOING BACK TO OUR BASEMENT.
IT'LL BE FUN.
NO BALL GAMES

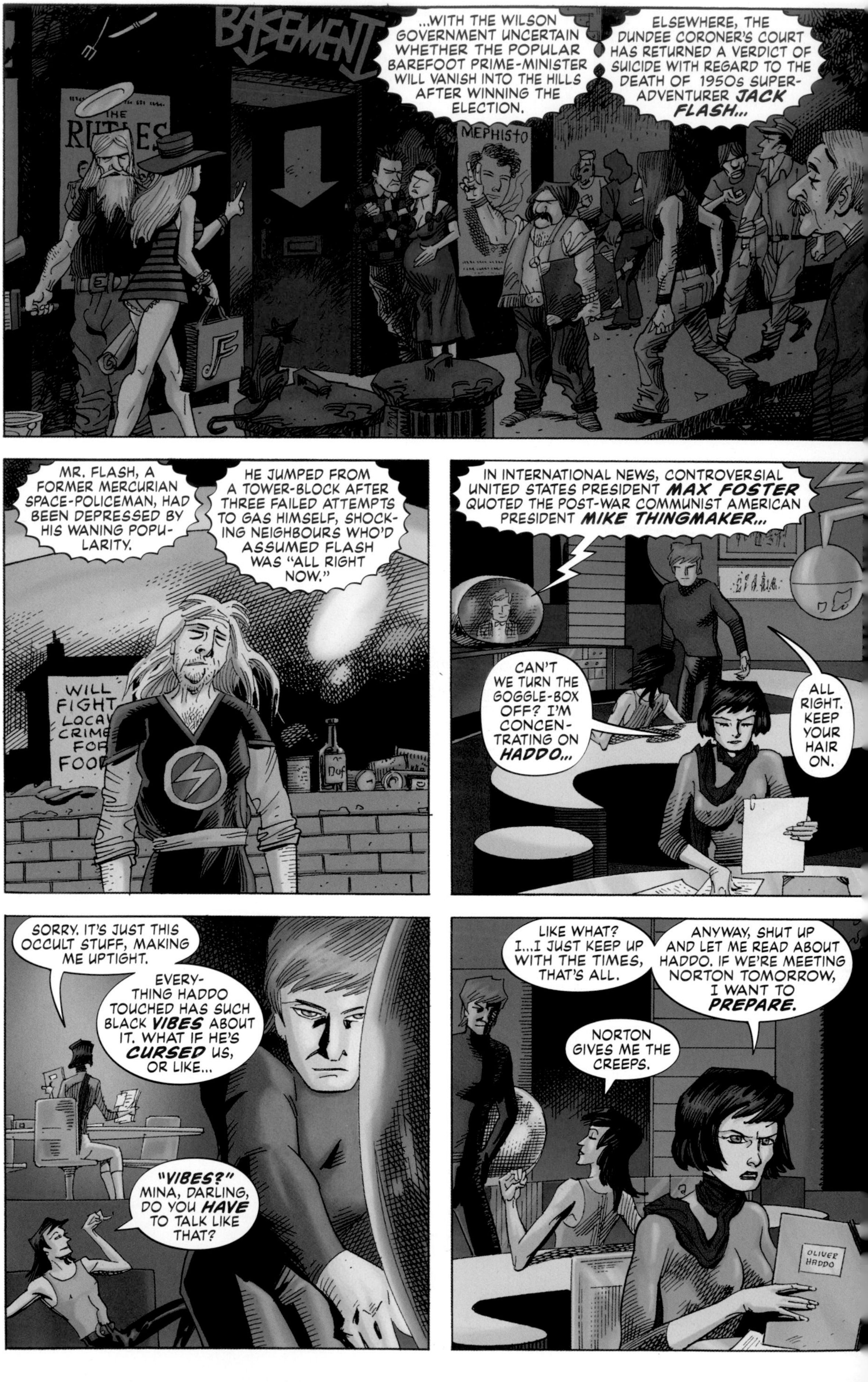
BASEMENT
...WITH THE WILSON GOVERNMENT UNCERTAIN WHETHER THE POPULAR BAREFOOT PRIME-MINISTER WILL VANISH INTO THE HILLS AFTER WINNING THE ELECTION.
ELSEWHERE, THE DUNDEE CORONER'S COURT HAS RETURNED A VERDICT OF SUICIDE WITH REGARD TO THE DEATH OF 1950s SUPER-ADVENTURER **JACK FLASH...**
THE
MEPHISTO
MR. FLASH, A FORMER MERCURIAN SPACE-POLICEMAN, HAD BEEN DEPRESSED BY HIS WANING POPULARITY.
HE JUMPED FROM A TOWER-BLOCK AFTER THREE FAILED ATTEMPTS TO GAS HIMSELF, SHOCKING NEIGHBOURS WHO'D ASSUMED FLASH WAS "ALL RIGHT NOW."
WILL FIGHT
IN INTERNATIONAL NEWS, CONTROVERSIAL UNITED STATES PRESIDENT **MAX FOSTER** QUOTED THE POST-WAR COMMUNIST AMERICAN PRESIDENT **MIKE THINGMAKER...**
CAN'T WE TURN THE GOGGLE-BOX OFF? I'M CONCENTRATING ON **HADDO...**
ALL RIGHT. KEEP YOUR HAIR ON.
SORRY. IT'S JUST THIS OCCULT STUFF, MAKING ME UPTIGHT.
EVERYTHING HADDO TOUCHED HAS SUCH BLACK **VIBES** ABOUT IT. WHAT IF HE'S **CURSED** US, OR LIKE...
"VIBES?" MINA, DARLING, DO YOU **HAVE** TO TALK LIKE THAT?
LIKE WHAT? I...I JUST KEEP UP WITH THE TIMES, THAT'S ALL.
ANYWAY, SHUT UP AND LET ME READ ABOUT HADDO. IF WE'RE MEETING NORTON TOMORROW, I WANT TO **PREPARE.**
NORTON GIVES ME THE CREEPS.
OLIVER HADDO

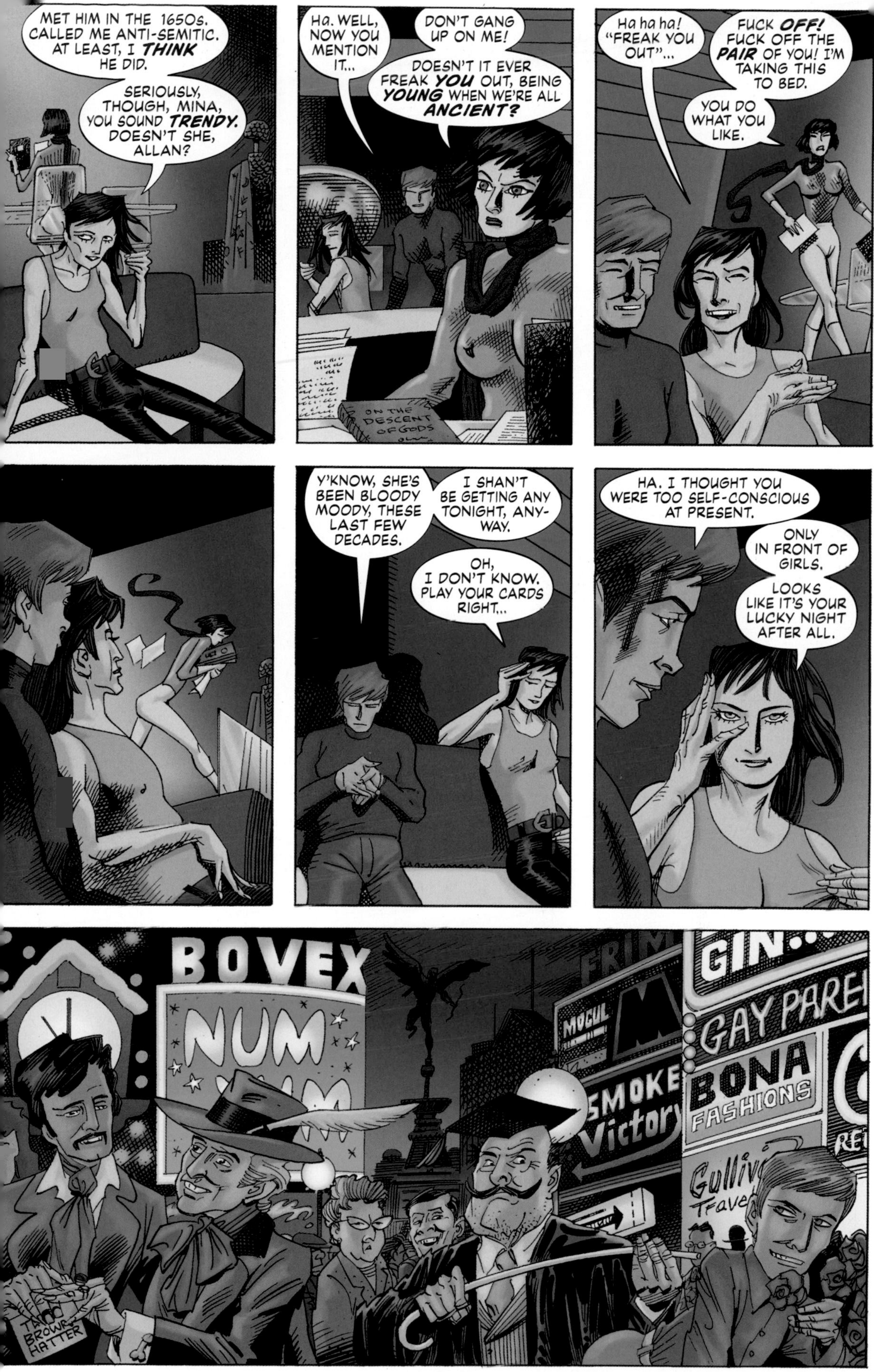
MET HIM IN THE 1650s. CALLED ME ANTI-SEMITIC. AT LEAST, I **THINK** HE DID.
SERIOUSLY, THOUGH, MINA, YOU SOUND **TRENDY.** DOESN'T SHE, ALLAN?
Ha. WELL, NOW YOU MENTION IT...
DON'T GANG UP ON ME!
DOESN'T IT EVER FREAK **YOU** OUT, BEING **YOUNG** WHEN WE'RE ALL **ANCIENT?**
ON THE DESCENT OF GODS
Ha ha ha! "FREAK YOU OUT"...
FUCK **OFF!** FUCK OFF THE **PAIR** OF YOU! I'M TAKING THIS TO BED.
YOU DO WHAT YOU LIKE.
Y'KNOW, SHE'S BEEN BLOODY MOODY, THESE LAST FEW DECADES.
I SHAN'T BE GETTING ANY TONIGHT, ANY-WAY.
OH, I DON'T KNOW. PLAY YOUR CARDS RIGHT...
HA. I THOUGHT YOU WERE TOO SELF-CONSCIOUS AT PRESENT.
ONLY IN FRONT OF GIRLS.
LOOKS LIKE IT'S YOUR LUCKY NIGHT AFTER ALL.
BOVEX
NUM
MOGUL
SMOKE
Victory
BONA
FASHIONS
HATTER

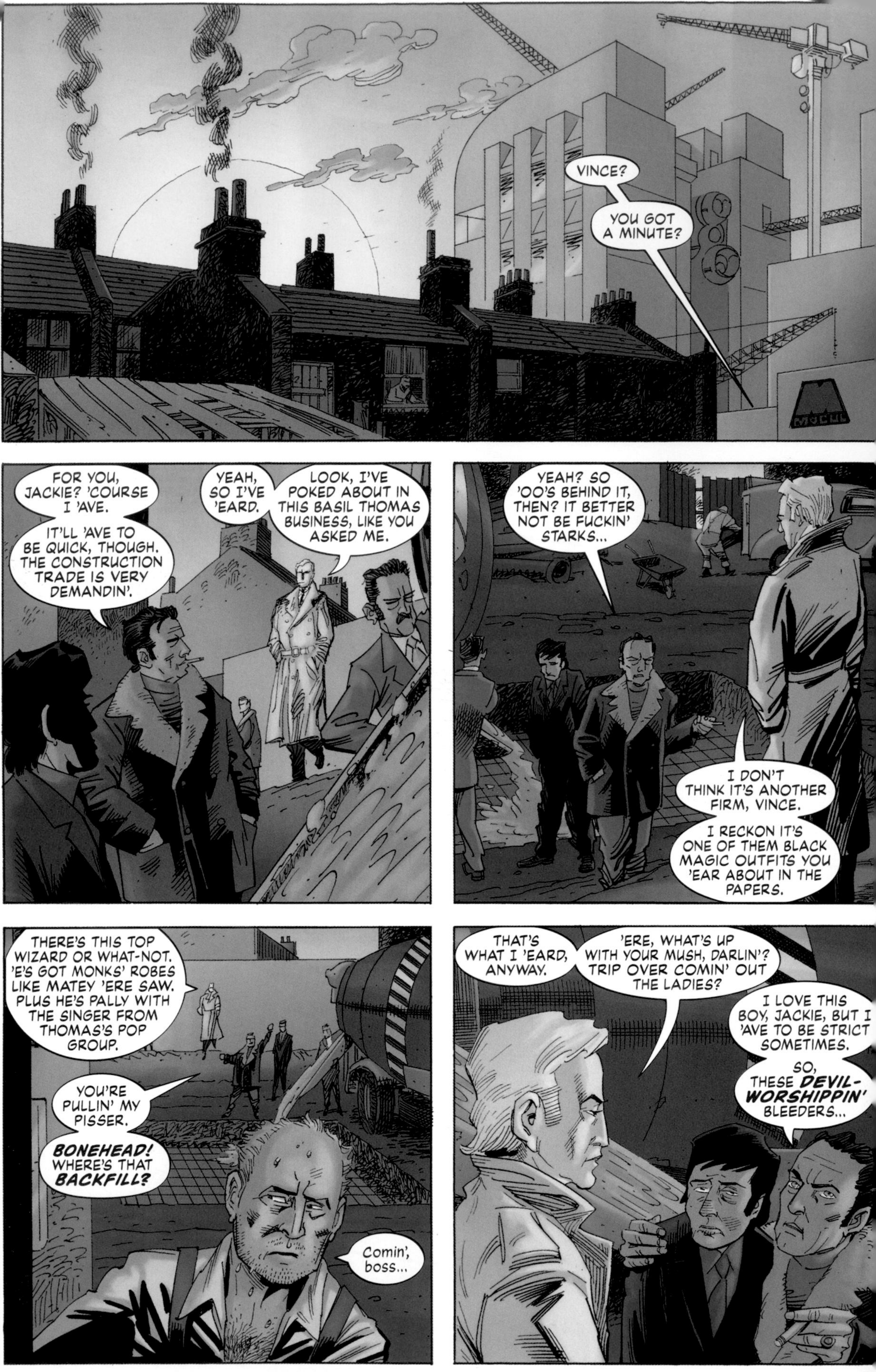
VINCE?
YOU GOT A MINUTE?
FOR YOU, JACKIE? 'COURSE I 'AVE.
IT'LL 'AVE TO BE QUICK, THOUGH. THE CONSTRUCTION TRADE IS VERY DEMANDIN'.
YEAH, SO I'VE 'EARD.
LOOK, I'VE POKED ABOUT IN THIS BASIL THOMAS BUSINESS, LIKE YOU ASKED ME.
YEAH? SO 'OO'S BEHIND IT, THEN? IT BETTER NOT BE FUCKIN' STARKS...
I DON'T THINK IT'S ANOTHER FIRM, VINCE.
I RECKON IT'S ONE OF THEM BLACK MAGIC OUTFITS YOU 'EAR ABOUT IN THE PAPERS.
THERE'S THIS TOP WIZARD OR WHAT-NOT. 'E'S GOT MONKS' ROBES LIKE MATEY 'ERE SAW. PLUS HE'S PALLY WITH THE SINGER FROM THOMAS'S POP GROUP.
YOU'RE PULLIN' MY PISSER.
BONEHEAD! WHERE'S THAT **BACKFILL?**
Comin', boss...
THAT'S WHAT I 'EARD, ANYWAY.
'ERE, WHAT'S UP WITH YOUR MUSH, DARLIN'? TRIP OVER COMIN' OUT THE LADIES?
I LOVE THIS BOY, JACKIE, BUT I 'AVE TO BE STRICT SOMETIMES.
SO, THESE **DEVIL-WORSHIPPIN'** BLEEDERS...

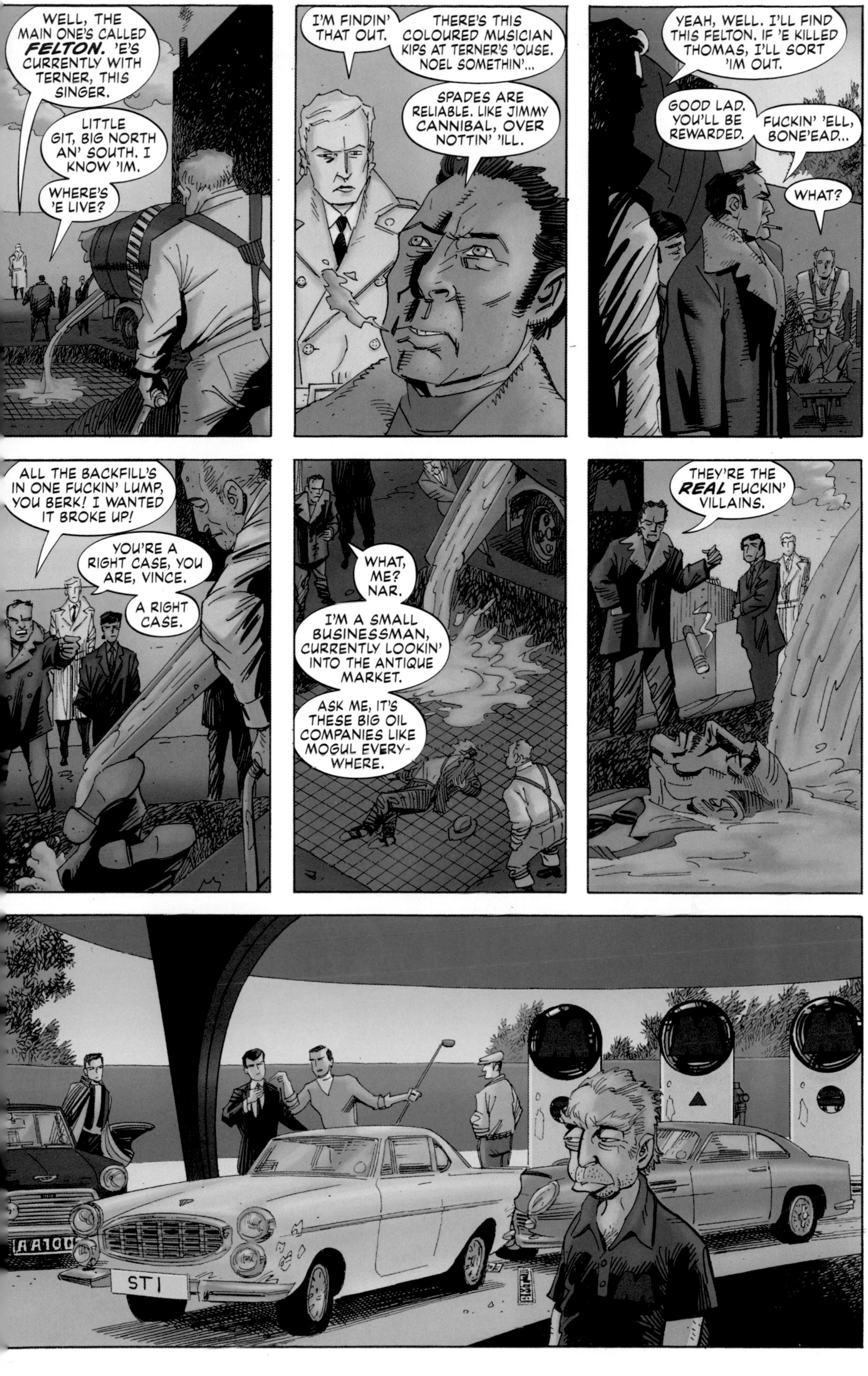
WELL, THE MAIN ONE'S CALLED FELTON. 'E'S CURRENTLY WITH TERNER, THIS SINGER.
LITTLE GIT, BIG NORTH AN' SOUTH. I KNOW 'IM.
WHERE'S 'E LIVE?
I'M FINDIN' THAT OUT.
THERE'S THIS COLOURED MUSICIAN KIPS AT TERNER'S 'OUSE. NOEL SOMETHIN'...
SPADES ARE RELIABLE. LIKE JIMMY CANNIBAL, OVER NOTTIN' 'ILL.
YEAH, WELL. I'LL FIND THIS FELTON. IF 'E KILLED THOMAS, I'LL SORT 'IM OUT.
GOOD LAD. YOU'LL BE REWARDED.
FUCKIN' 'ELL, BONE'EAD...
WHAT?
ALL THE BACKFILL'S IN ONE FUCKIN' LUMP, YOU BERK! I WANTED IT BROKE UP!
YOU'RE A RIGHT CASE, YOU ARE, VINCE.
A RIGHT CASE.
WHAT, ME? NAR.
I'M A SMALL BUSINESSMAN, CURRENTLY LOOKIN' INTO THE ANTIQUE MARKET.
ASK ME, IT'S THESE BIG OIL COMPANIES LIKE MOGUL EVERY-WHERE.
THEY'RE THE REAL FUCKIN' VILLAINS.
AA 100
ST 1

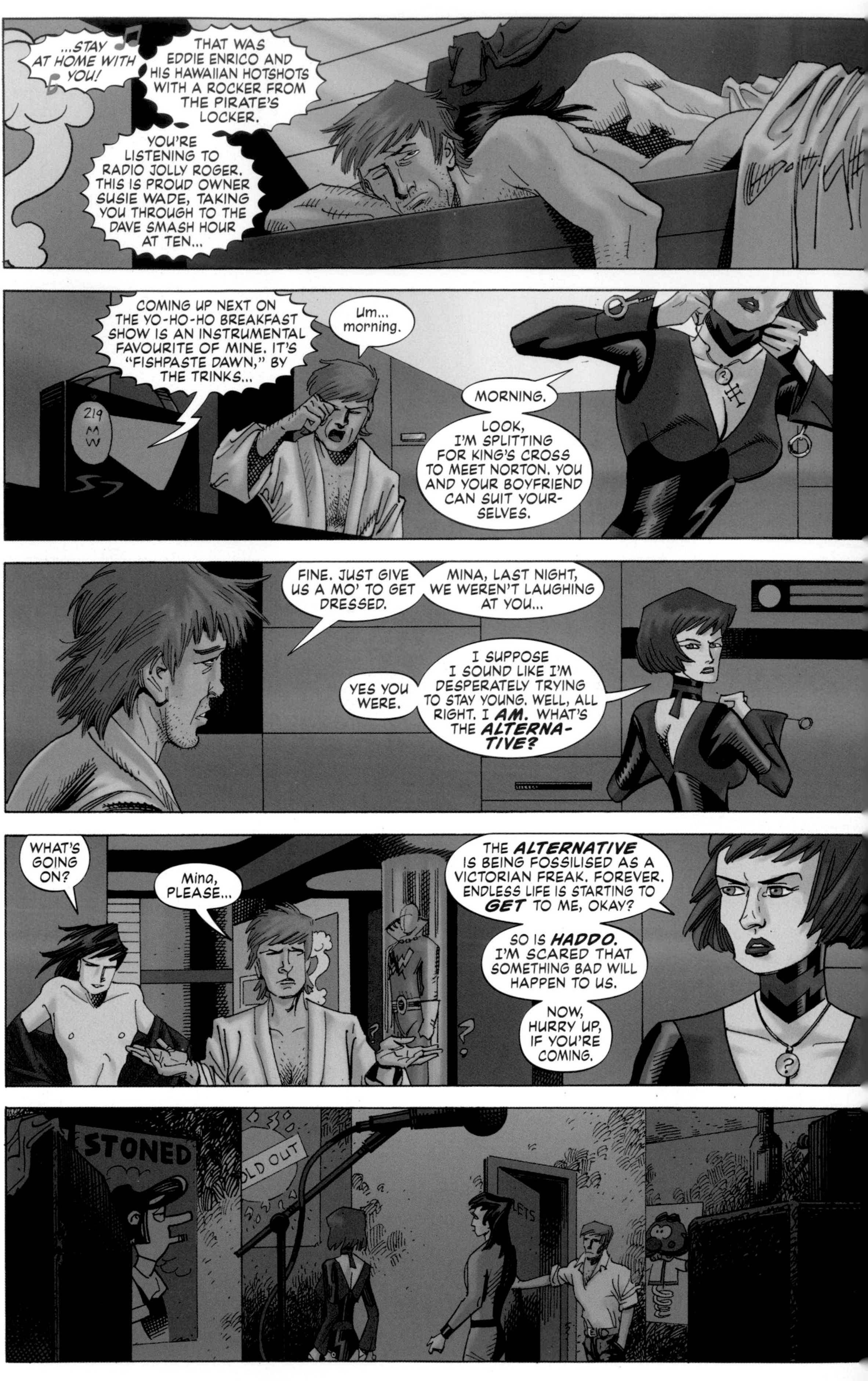
...STAY AT HOME WITH YOU!
THAT WAS EDDIE ENRICO AND HIS HAWAIIAN HOTSHOTS WITH A ROCKER FROM THE PIRATE'S LOCKER.
YOU'RE LISTENING TO RADIO JOLLY ROGER. THIS IS PROUD OWNER SUSIE WADE, TAKING YOU THROUGH TO THE DAVE SMASH HOUR AT TEN...
COMING UP NEXT ON THE YO-HO-HO BREAKFAST SHOW IS AN INSTRUMENTAL FAVOURITE OF MINE. IT'S "FISHPASTE DAWN," BY THE TRINKS...
219 MW
Um... morning.
MORNING.
LOOK, I'M SPLITTING FOR KING'S CROSS TO MEET NORTON. YOU AND YOUR BOYFRIEND CAN SUIT YOUR-SELVES.
FINE. JUST GIVE US A MO' TO GET DRESSED.
MINA, LAST NIGHT, WE WEREN'T LAUGHING AT YOU...
YES YOU WERE.
I SUPPOSE I SOUND LIKE I'M DESPERATELY TRYING TO STAY YOUNG. WELL, ALL RIGHT. I AM. WHAT'S THE ALTERNA-TIVE?
WHAT'S GOING ON?
Mina, PLEASE...
THE ALTERNATIVE IS BEING FOSSILISED AS A VICTORIAN FREAK. FOREVER. ENDLESS LIFE IS STARTING TO GET TO ME, OKAY?
SO IS HADDO. I'M SCARED THAT SOMETHING BAD WILL HAPPEN TO US.
NOW, HURRY UP, IF YOU'RE COMING.
STONED
OLD OUT
LETS

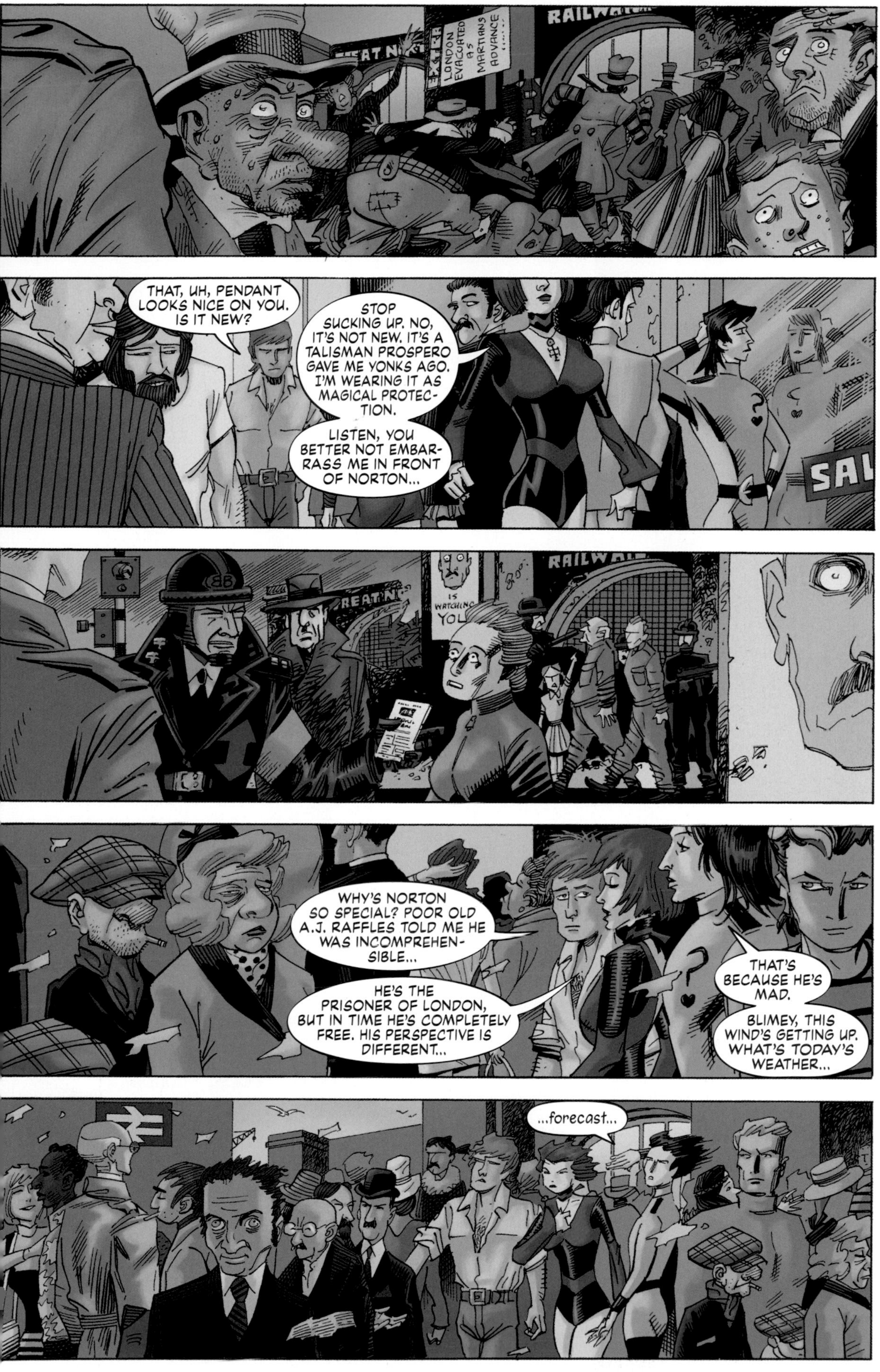
EXTRA
LONDON EVACUATED AS MARTIANS ADVANCE
RAILWAY
THAT, UH, PENDANT LOOKS NICE ON YOU. IS IT NEW?
STOP SUCKING UP. NO, IT'S NOT NEW. IT'S A TALISMAN PROSPERO GAVE ME YONKS AGO. I'M WEARING IT AS MAGICAL PROTECTION.
LISTEN, YOU BETTER NOT EMBARRASS ME IN FRONT OF NORTON...
IS WATCHING YOU
WHY'S NORTON SO SPECIAL? POOR OLD A.J. RAFFLES TOLD ME HE WAS INCOMPREHENSIBLE...
HE'S THE PRISONER OF LONDON, BUT IN TIME HE'S COMPLETELY FREE. HIS PERSPECTIVE IS DIFFERENT...
THAT'S BECAUSE HE'S MAD.
BLIMEY, THIS WIND'S GETTING UP. WHAT'S TODAY'S WEATHER...
...forecast...

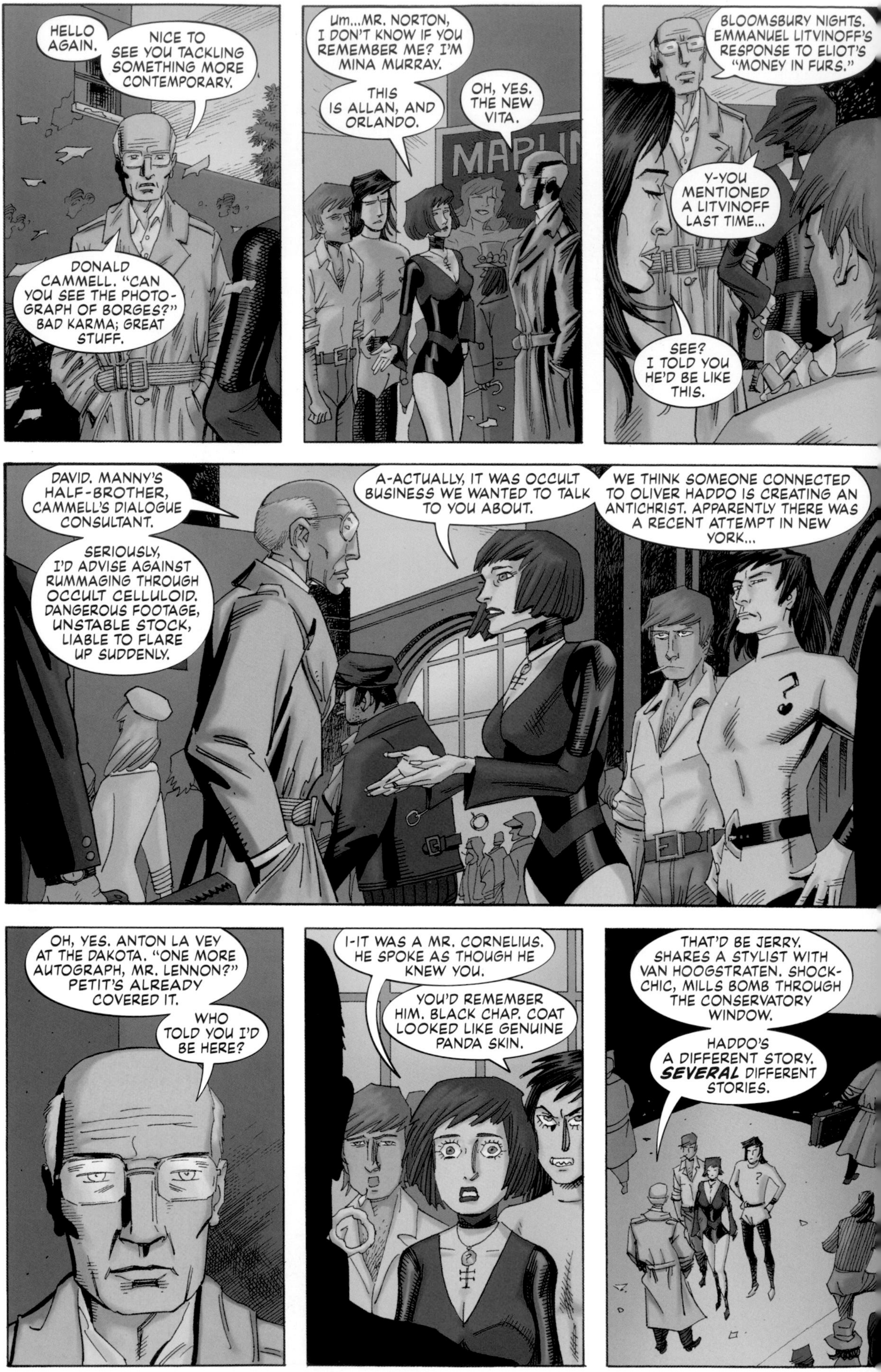
HELLO AGAIN.
NICE TO SEE YOU TACKLING SOMETHING MORE CONTEMPORARY.
DONALD CAMMELL. "CAN YOU SEE THE PHOTOGRAPH OF BORGES?" BAD KARMA; GREAT STUFF.
Um...MR. NORTON, I DON'T KNOW IF YOU REMEMBER ME? I'M MINA MURRAY.
THIS IS ALLAN, AND ORLANDO.
OH, YES. THE NEW VITA.
MAPLIN
BLOOMSBURY NIGHTS. EMMANUEL LITVINOFF'S RESPONSE TO ELIOT'S "MONEY IN FURS."
Y-YOU MENTIONED A LITVINOFF LAST TIME...
SEE? I TOLD YOU HE'D BE LIKE THIS.
DAVID. MANNY'S HALF-BROTHER, CAMMELL'S DIALOGUE CONSULTANT.
SERIOUSLY, I'D ADVISE AGAINST RUMMAGING THROUGH OCCULT CELLULOID. DANGEROUS FOOTAGE, UNSTABLE STOCK, LIABLE TO FLARE UP SUDDENLY.
A-ACTUALLY, IT WAS OCCULT BUSINESS WE WANTED TO TALK TO YOU ABOUT.
WE THINK SOMEONE CONNECTED TO OLIVER HADDO IS CREATING AN ANTICHRIST. APPARENTLY THERE WAS A RECENT ATTEMPT IN NEW YORK...
OH, YES. ANTON LA VEY AT THE DAKOTA. "ONE MORE AUTOGRAPH, MR. LENNON?" PETIT'S ALREADY COVERED IT.
WHO TOLD YOU I'D BE HERE?
I-IT WAS A MR. CORNELIUS. HE SPOKE AS THOUGH HE KNEW YOU.
YOU'D REMEMBER HIM. BLACK CHAP. COAT LOOKED LIKE GENUINE PANDA SKIN.
THAT'D BE JERRY. SHARES A STYLIST WITH VAN HOOGSTRATEN. SHOCK-CHIC, MILLS BOMB THROUGH THE CONSERVATORY WINDOW.
HADDO'S A DIFFERENT STORY. SEVERAL DIFFERENT STORIES.

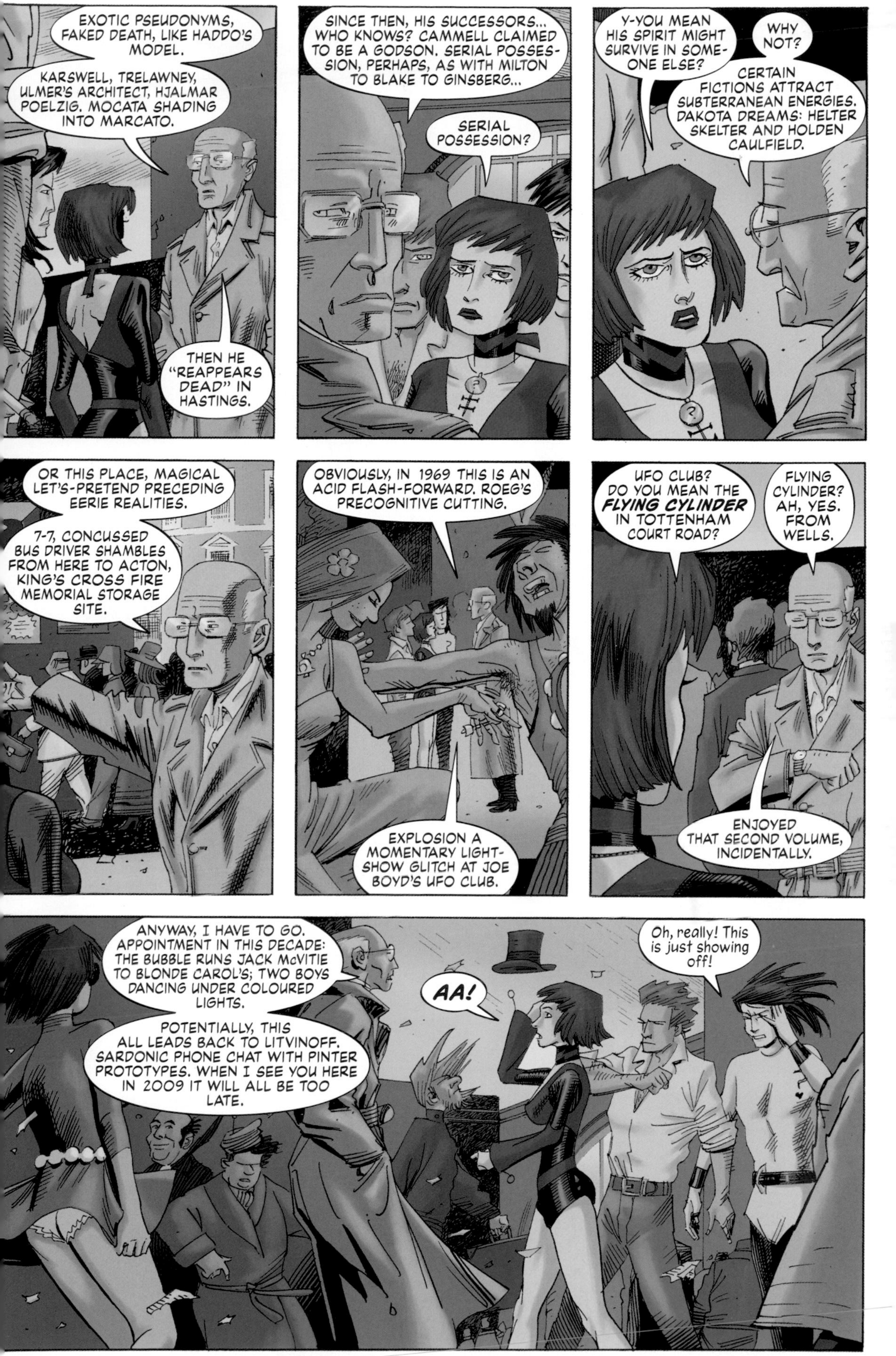
EXOTIC PSEUDONYMS, FAKED DEATH, LIKE HADDO'S MODEL.
KARSWELL, TRELAWNEY, ULMER'S ARCHITECT, HJALMAR POELZIG. MOCATA SHADING INTO MARCATO.
THEN HE "REAPPEARS DEAD" IN HASTINGS.
SINCE THEN, HIS SUCCESSORS... WHO KNOWS? CAMMELL CLAIMED TO BE A GODSON. SERIAL POSSESSION, PERHAPS, AS WITH MILTON TO BLAKE TO GINSBERG...
SERIAL POSSESSION?
Y-YOU MEAN HIS SPIRIT MIGHT SURVIVE IN SOMEONE ELSE?
WHY NOT?
CERTAIN FICTIONS ATTRACT SUBTERRANEAN ENERGIES. DAKOTA DREAMS: HELTER SKELTER AND HOLDEN CAULFIELD.
OR THIS PLACE, MAGICAL LET'S-PRETEND PRECEDING EERIE REALITIES.
7-7, CONCUSSED BUS DRIVER SHAMBLES FROM HERE TO ACTON, KING'S CROSS FIRE MEMORIAL STORAGE SITE.
OBVIOUSLY, IN 1969 THIS IS AN ACID FLASH-FORWARD. ROEG'S PRECOGNITIVE CUTTING.
EXPLOSION A MOMENTARY LIGHT-SHOW GLITCH AT JOE BOYD'S UFO CLUB.
UFO CLUB? DO YOU MEAN THE FLYING CYLINDER IN TOTTENHAM COURT ROAD?
FLYING CYLINDER? AH, YES. FROM WELLS.
ENJOYED THAT SECOND VOLUME, INCIDENTALLY.
ANYWAY, I HAVE TO GO. APPOINTMENT IN THIS DECADE: THE BUBBLE RUNS JACK McVITIE TO BLONDE CAROL'S; TWO BOYS DANCING UNDER COLOURED LIGHTS.
POTENTIALLY, THIS ALL LEADS BACK TO LITVINOFF. SARDONIC PHONE CHAT WITH PINTER PROTOTYPES. WHEN I SEE YOU HERE IN 2009 IT WILL ALL BE TOO LATE.
AA!
Oh, really! This is just showing off!

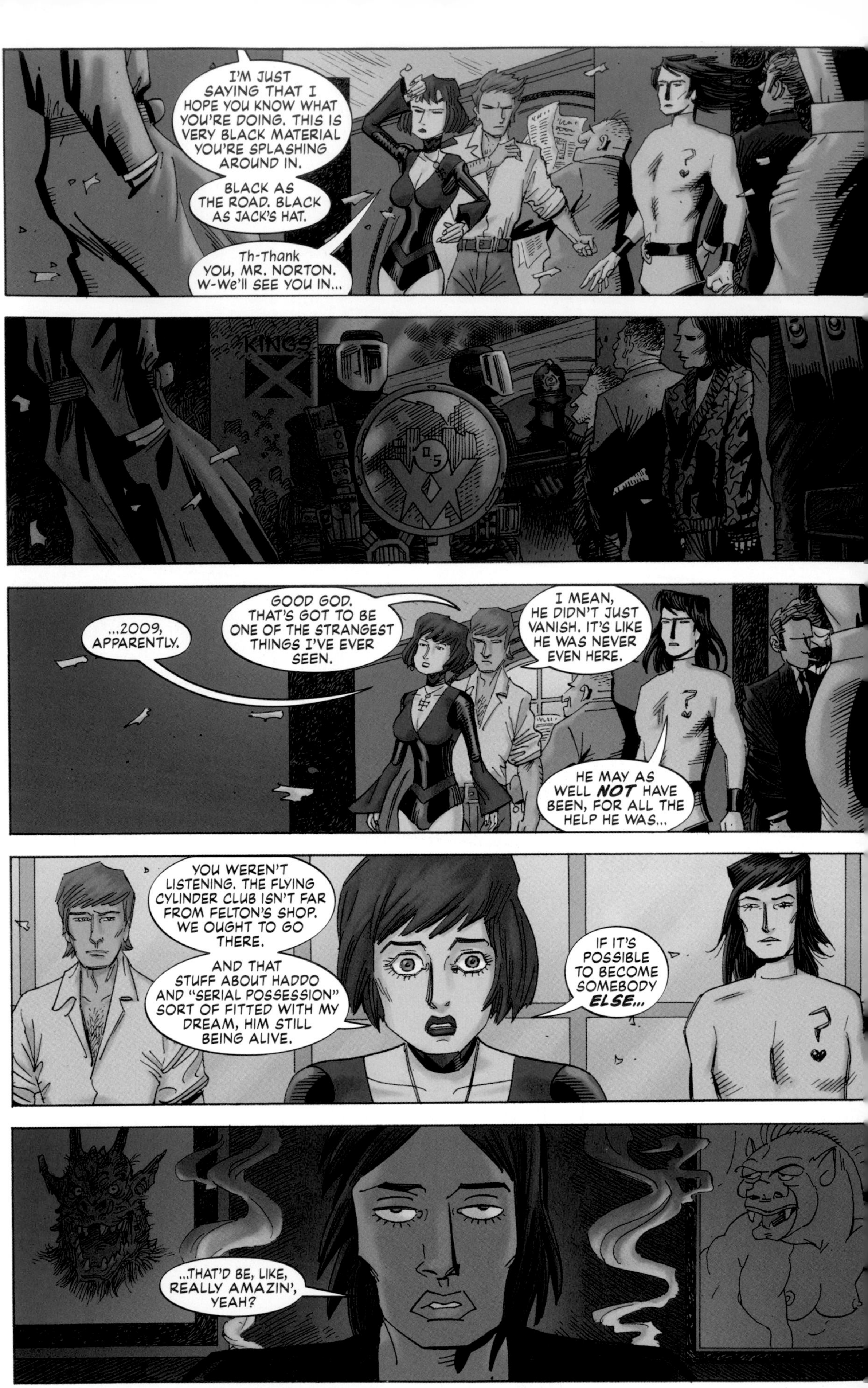
I'M JUST SAYING THAT I HOPE YOU KNOW WHAT YOU'RE DOING. THIS IS VERY BLACK MATERIAL YOU'RE SPLASHING AROUND IN.
BLACK AS THE ROAD. BLACK AS JACK'S HAT.
Th-Thank YOU, MR. NORTON. W-We'll SEE YOU IN...
KINGS
...2009, APPARENTLY.
GOOD GOD. THAT'S GOT TO BE ONE OF THE STRANGEST THINGS I'VE EVER SEEN.
I MEAN, HE DIDN'T JUST VANISH. IT'S LIKE HE WAS NEVER EVEN HERE.
HE MAY AS WELL NOT HAVE BEEN, FOR ALL THE HELP HE WAS...
YOU WEREN'T LISTENING. THE FLYING CYLINDER CLUB ISN'T FAR FROM FELTON'S SHOP. WE OUGHT TO GO THERE.
AND THAT STUFF ABOUT HADDO AND "SERIAL POSSESSION" SORT OF FITTED WITH MY DREAM, HIM STILL BEING ALIVE.
IF IT'S POSSIBLE TO BECOME SOMEBODY ELSE...
...THAT'D BE, LIKE, REALLY AMAZIN', YEAH?

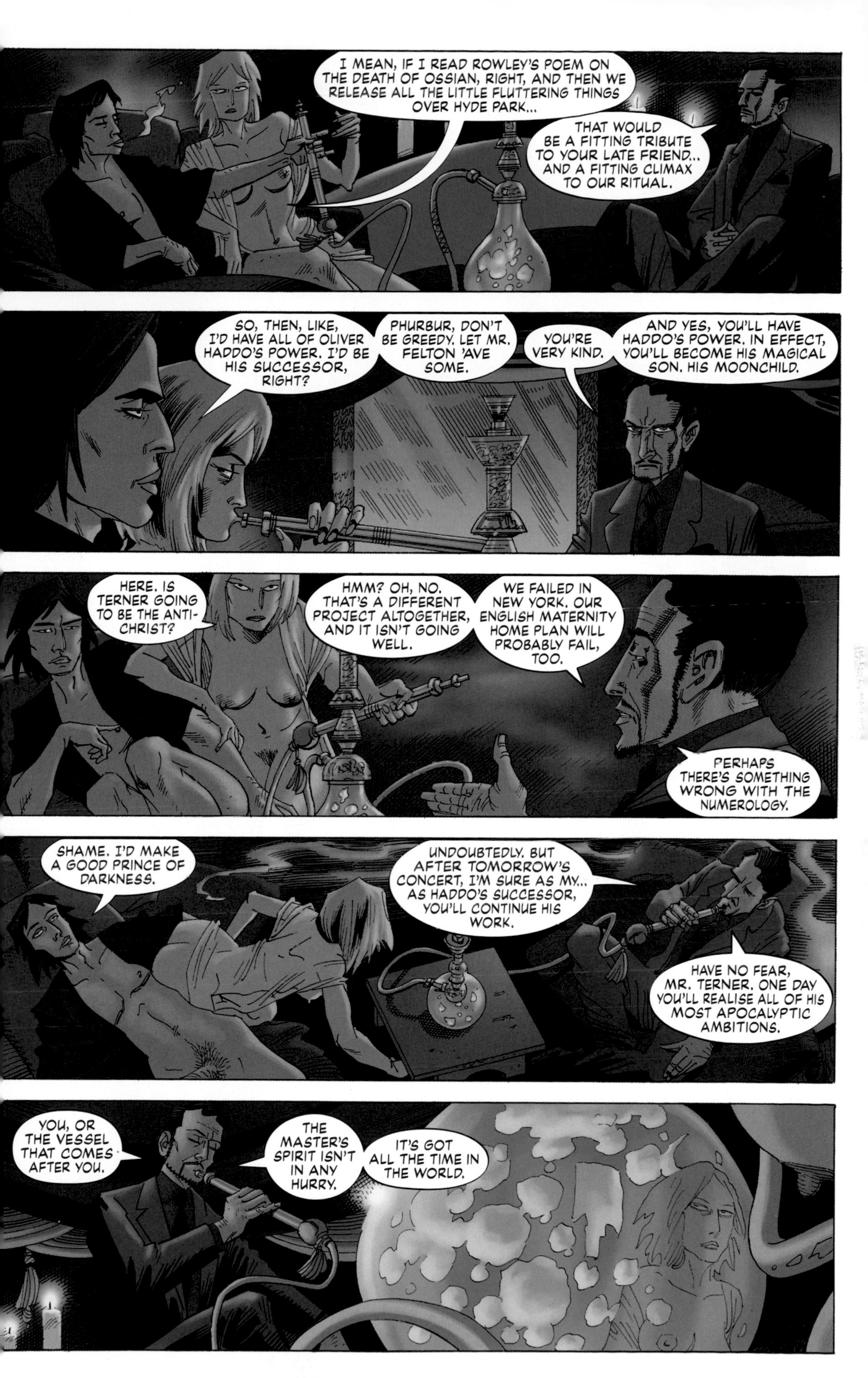
I MEAN, IF I READ ROWLEY'S POEM ON THE DEATH OF OSSIAN, RIGHT, AND THEN WE RELEASE ALL THE LITTLE FLUTTERING THINGS OVER HYDE PARK...
THAT WOULD BE A FITTING TRIBUTE TO YOUR LATE FRIEND... AND A FITTING CLIMAX TO OUR RITUAL.
SO, THEN, LIKE, I'D HAVE ALL OF OLIVER HADDO'S POWER. I'D BE HIS SUCCESSOR, RIGHT?
PHURBUR, DON'T BE GREEDY. LET MR. FELTON 'AVE SOME.
YOU'RE VERY KIND.
AND YES, YOU'LL HAVE HADDO'S POWER. IN EFFECT, YOU'LL BECOME HIS MAGICAL SON. HIS MOONCHILD.
HERE. IS TERNER GOING TO BE THE ANTI-CHRIST?
HMM? OH, NO. THAT'S A DIFFERENT PROJECT ALTOGETHER, AND IT ISN'T GOING WELL.
WE FAILED IN NEW YORK. OUR ENGLISH MATERNITY HOME PLAN WILL PROBABLY FAIL, TOO.
PERHAPS THERE'S SOMETHING WRONG WITH THE NUMEROLOGY.
SHAME. I'D MAKE A GOOD PRINCE OF DARKNESS.
UNDOUBTEDLY. BUT AFTER TOMORROW'S CONCERT, I'M SURE AS MY... AS HADDO'S SUCCESSOR, YOU'LL CONTINUE HIS WORK.
HAVE NO FEAR, MR. TERNER. ONE DAY YOU'LL REALISE ALL OF HIS MOST APOCALYPTIC AMBITIONS.
YOU, OR THE VESSEL THAT COMES AFTER YOU.
THE MASTER'S SPIRIT ISN'T IN ANY HURRY.
IT'S GOT ALL THE TIME IN THE WORLD.

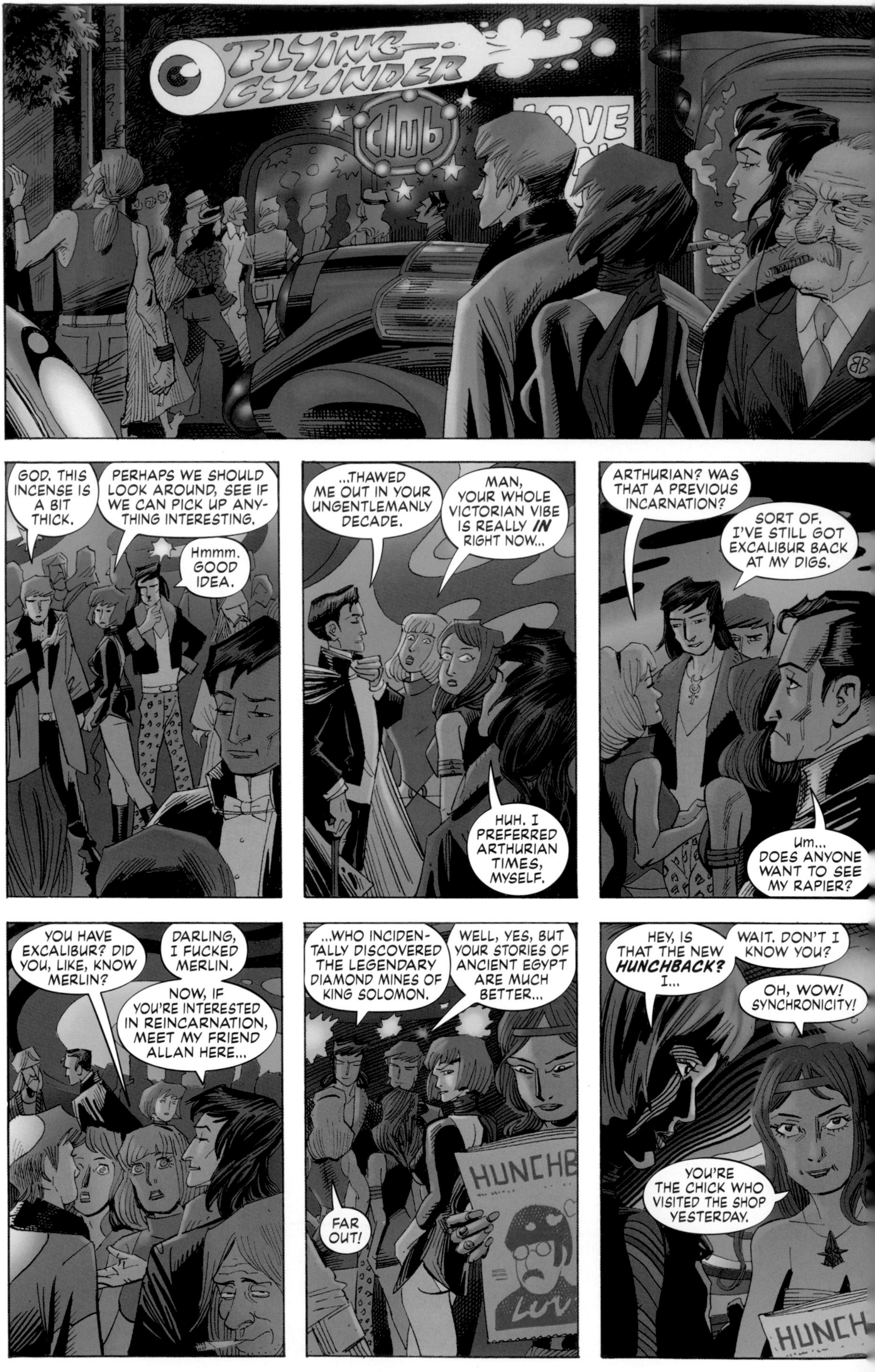
FLYING CYLINDER
club
LOVE
GOD. THIS INCENSE IS A BIT THICK.
PERHAPS WE SHOULD LOOK AROUND, SEE IF WE CAN PICK UP ANYTHING INTERESTING.
Hmmm. GOOD IDEA.
...THAWED ME OUT IN YOUR UNGENTLEMANLY DECADE.
MAN, YOUR WHOLE VICTORIAN VIBE IS REALLY IN RIGHT NOW...
HUH. I PREFERRED ARTHURIAN TIMES, MYSELF.
ARTHURIAN? WAS THAT A PREVIOUS INCARNATION?
SORT OF. I'VE STILL GOT EXCALIBUR BACK AT MY DIGS.
Um... DOES ANYONE WANT TO SEE MY RAPIER?
YOU HAVE EXCALIBUR? DID YOU, LIKE, KNOW MERLIN?
DARLING, I FUCKED MERLIN.
NOW, IF YOU'RE INTERESTED IN REINCARNATION, MEET MY FRIEND ALLAN HERE...
...WHO INCIDENTALLY DISCOVERED THE LEGENDARY DIAMOND MINES OF KING SOLOMON.
WELL, YES, BUT YOUR STORIES OF ANCIENT EGYPT ARE MUCH BETTER...
FAR OUT!
HUNCHB
HEY, IS THAT THE NEW HUNCHBACK? I...
WAIT. DON'T I KNOW YOU?
OH, WOW! SYNCHRONICITY!
YOU'RE THE CHICK WHO VISITED THE SHOP YESTERDAY.
HUNCH

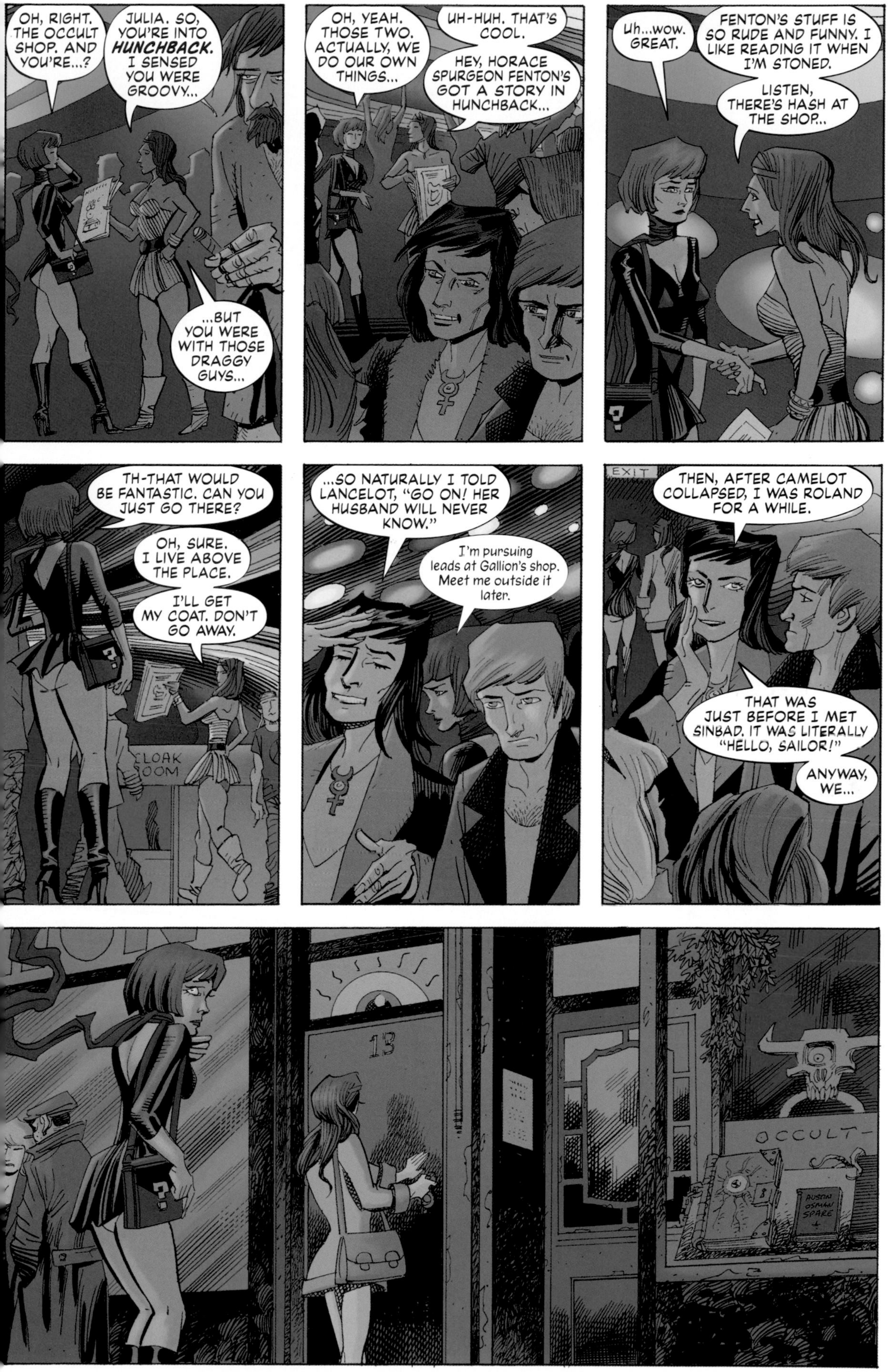

OH, RIGHT. THE OCCULT SHOP. AND YOU'RE...?
JULIA. SO, YOU'RE INTO **HUNCHBACK.** I SENSED YOU WERE GROOVY...
...BUT YOU WERE WITH THOSE DRAGGY GUYS...
OH, YEAH. THOSE TWO. ACTUALLY, WE DO OUR OWN THINGS...
UH-HUH. THAT'S COOL.
HEY, HORACE SPURGEON FENTON'S GOT A STORY IN HUNCHBACK...
Uh...wow. GREAT.
FENTON'S STUFF IS SO RUDE AND FUNNY. I LIKE READING IT WHEN I'M STONED.
LISTEN, THERE'S HASH AT THE SHOP...
TH-THAT WOULD BE FANTASTIC. CAN YOU JUST GO THERE?
OH, SURE. I LIVE ABOVE THE PLACE.
I'LL GET MY COAT. DON'T GO AWAY.
CLOAK ROOM
...SO NATURALLY I TOLD LANCELOT, "GO ON! HER HUSBAND WILL NEVER KNOW."
I'm pursuing leads at Gallion's shop. Meet me outside it later.
EXIT
THEN, AFTER CAMELOT COLLAPSED, I WAS ROLAND FOR A WHILE.
THAT WAS JUST BEFORE I MET SINBAD. IT WAS LITERALLY "HELLO, SAILOR!"
ANYWAY, WE...
13
OCCULT-
AUSTIN OSMAN SPARE

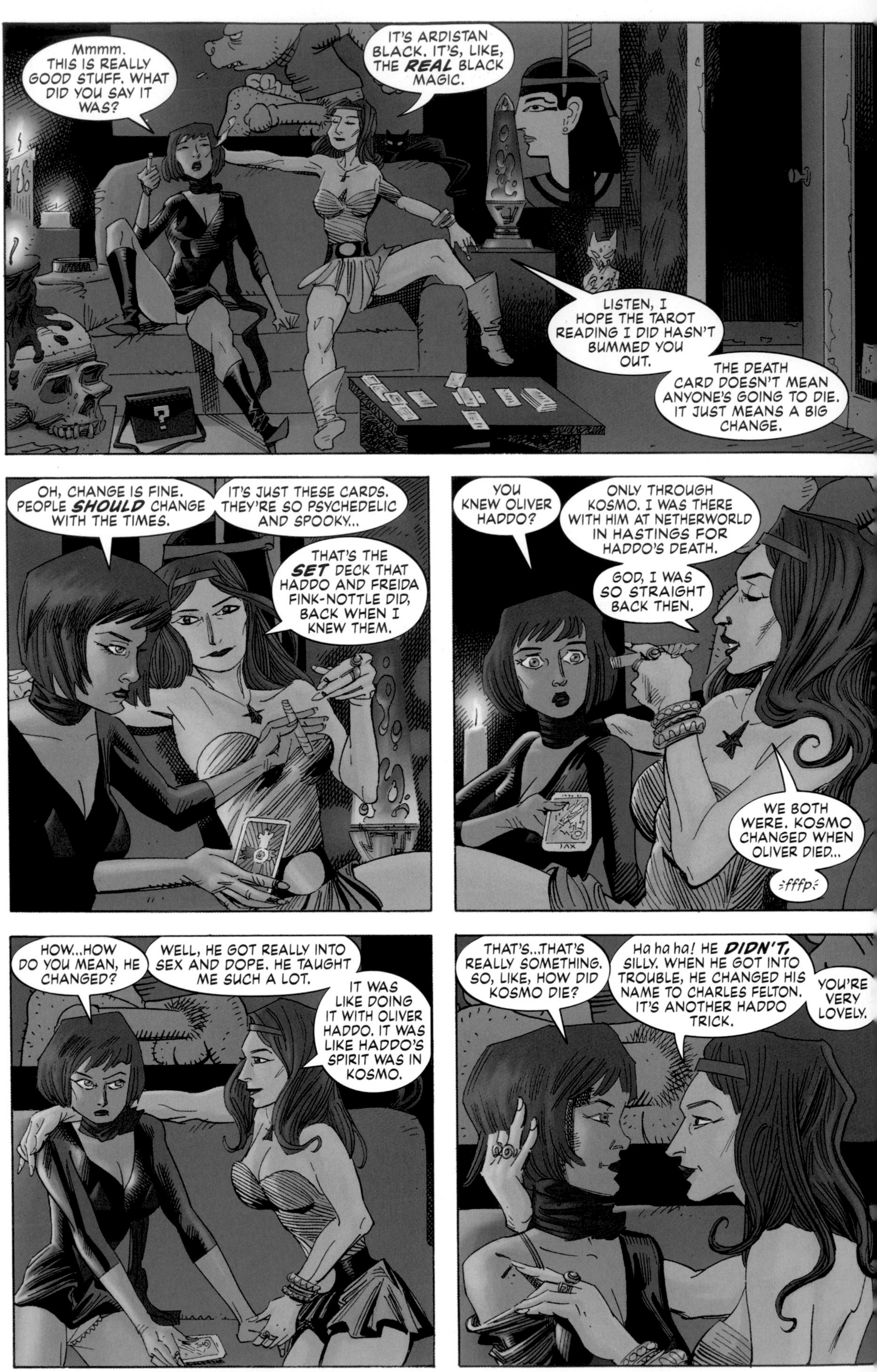
Mmmm. THIS IS REALLY GOOD STUFF. WHAT DID YOU SAY IT WAS?
IT'S ARDISTAN BLACK. IT'S, LIKE, THE *REAL* BLACK MAGIC.
LISTEN, I HOPE THE TAROT READING I DID HASN'T BUMMED YOU OUT.
THE DEATH CARD DOESN'T MEAN ANYONE'S GOING TO DIE. IT JUST MEANS A BIG CHANGE.
OH, CHANGE IS FINE. PEOPLE *SHOULD* CHANGE WITH THE TIMES.
IT'S JUST THESE CARDS. THEY'RE SO PSYCHEDELIC AND SPOOKY...
THAT'S THE *SET* DECK THAT HADDO AND FREIDA FINK-NOTTLE DID, BACK WHEN I KNEW THEM.
YOU KNEW OLIVER HADDO?
ONLY THROUGH KOSMO. I WAS THERE WITH HIM AT NETHERWORLD IN HASTINGS FOR HADDO'S DEATH.
GOD, I WAS SO STRAIGHT BACK THEN.
WE BOTH WERE. KOSMO CHANGED WHEN OLIVER DIED...
fffp
HOW...HOW DO YOU MEAN, HE CHANGED?
WELL, HE GOT REALLY INTO SEX AND DOPE. HE TAUGHT ME SUCH A LOT.
IT WAS LIKE DOING IT WITH OLIVER HADDO. IT WAS LIKE HADDO'S SPIRIT WAS IN KOSMO.
THAT'S...THAT'S REALLY SOMETHING. SO, LIKE, HOW DID KOSMO DIE?
Ha ha ha! HE *DIDN'T*, SILLY. WHEN HE GOT INTO TROUBLE, HE CHANGED HIS NAME TO CHARLES FELTON. IT'S ANOTHER HADDO TRICK.
YOU'RE VERY LOVELY.

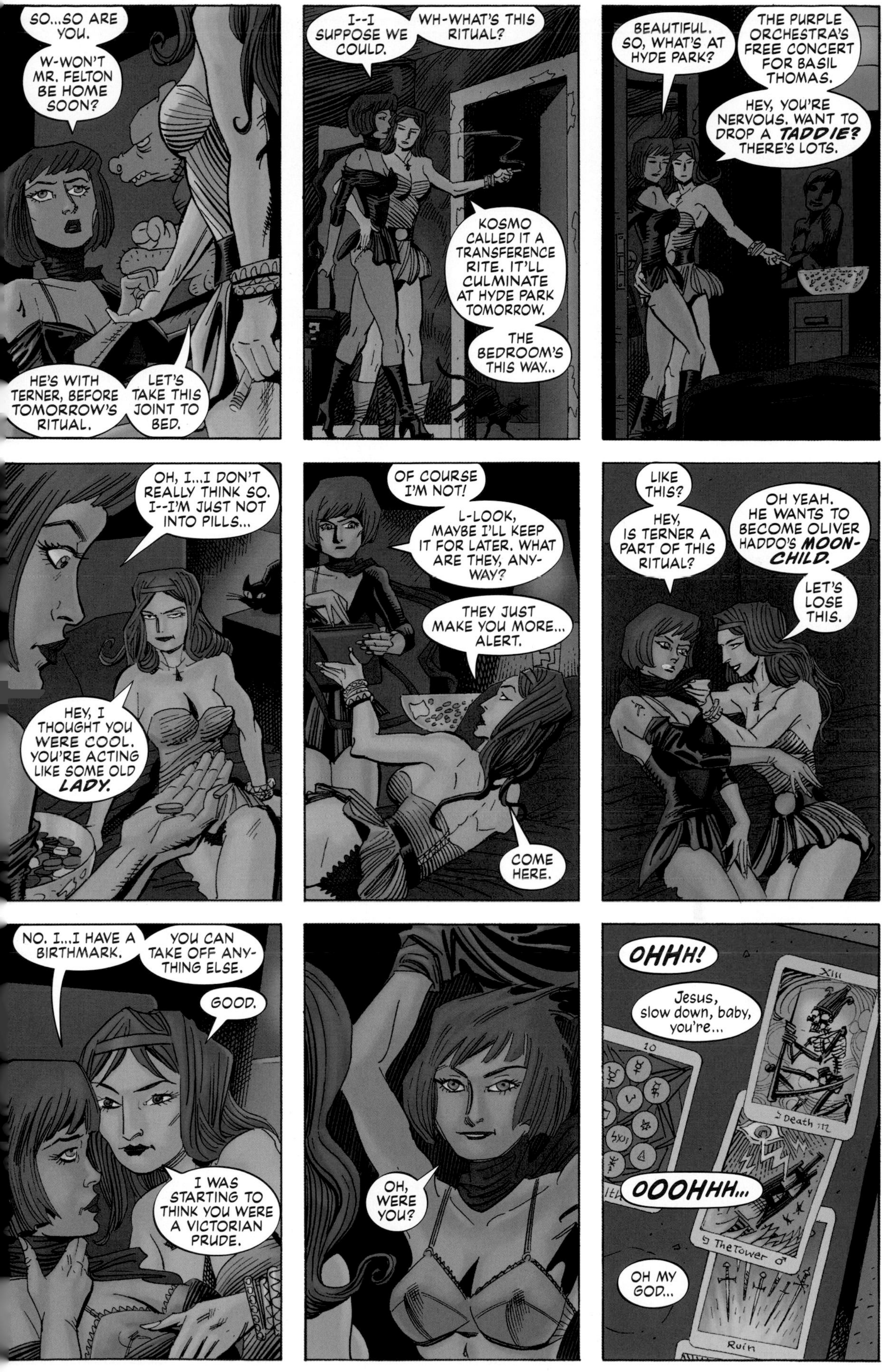
SO...SO ARE YOU.
W-WON'T MR. FELTON BE HOME SOON?
HE'S WITH TERNER, BEFORE TOMORROW'S RITUAL.
LET'S TAKE THIS JOINT TO BED.
I--I SUPPOSE WE COULD.
WH-WHAT'S THIS RITUAL?
KOSMO CALLED IT A TRANSFERENCE RITE. IT'LL CULMINATE AT HYDE PARK TOMORROW.
THE BEDROOM'S THIS WAY...
BEAUTIFUL. SO, WHAT'S AT HYDE PARK?
THE PURPLE ORCHESTRA'S FREE CONCERT FOR BASIL THOMAS.
HEY, YOU'RE NERVOUS. WANT TO DROP A TADDIE? THERE'S LOTS.
OH, I...I DON'T REALLY THINK SO. I--I'M JUST NOT INTO PILLS...
HEY, I THOUGHT YOU WERE COOL. YOU'RE ACTING LIKE SOME OLD LADY.
OF COURSE I'M NOT!
L-LOOK, MAYBE I'LL KEEP IT FOR LATER. WHAT ARE THEY, ANY-WAY?
THEY JUST MAKE YOU MORE... ALERT.
COME HERE.
LIKE THIS?
HEY, IS TERNER A PART OF THIS RITUAL?
OH YEAH. HE WANTS TO BECOME OLIVER HADDO'S MOON-CHILD.
LET'S LOSE THIS.
NO. I...I HAVE A BIRTHMARK.
YOU CAN TAKE OFF ANY-THING ELSE.
GOOD.
I WAS STARTING TO THINK YOU WERE A VICTORIAN PRUDE.
OH, WERE YOU?
OHHH!
Jesus, slow down, baby, you're...
XIII
Death
The Tower
OOOHHH...
OH MY GOD...
Ruin

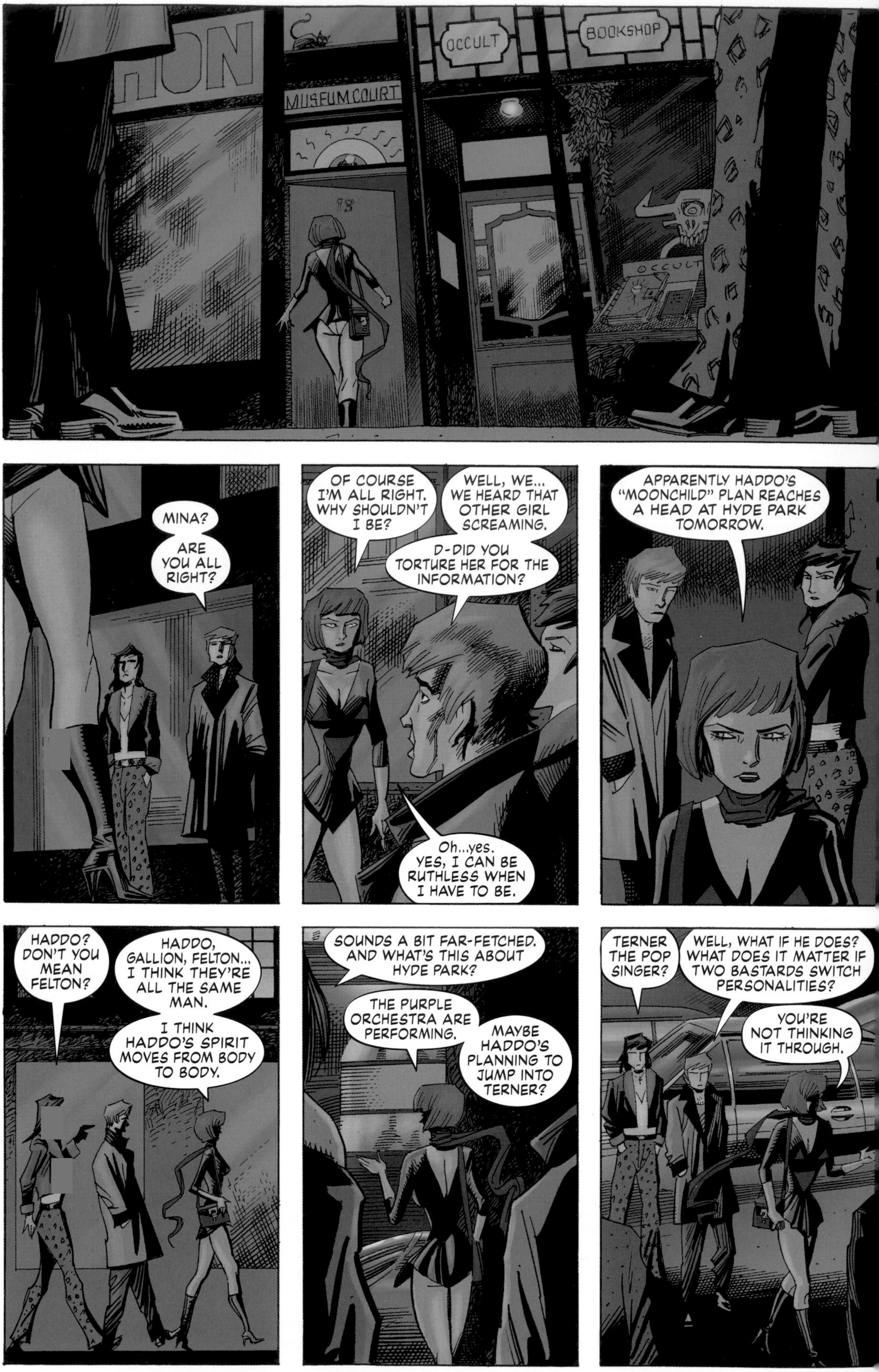
HON
MUSEUM COURT
OCCULT
BOOKSHOP
13
OCCULT
MINA?
ARE YOU ALL RIGHT?
OF COURSE I'M ALL RIGHT. WHY SHOULDN'T I BE?
WELL, WE... WE HEARD THAT OTHER GIRL SCREAMING.
D-DID YOU TORTURE HER FOR THE INFORMATION?
Oh...yes. YES, I CAN BE RUTHLESS WHEN I HAVE TO BE.
APPARENTLY HADDO'S "MOONCHILD" PLAN REACHES A HEAD AT HYDE PARK TOMORROW.
HADDO? DON'T YOU MEAN FELTON?
HADDO, GALLION, FELTON... I THINK THEY'RE ALL THE SAME MAN.
I THINK HADDO'S SPIRIT MOVES FROM BODY TO BODY.
SOUNDS A BIT FAR-FETCHED. AND WHAT'S THIS ABOUT HYDE PARK?
THE PURPLE ORCHESTRA ARE PERFORMING.
MAYBE HADDO'S PLANNING TO JUMP INTO TERNER?
TERNER THE POP SINGER?
WELL, WHAT IF HE DOES? WHAT DOES IT MATTER IF TWO BASTARDS SWITCH PERSONALITIES?
YOU'RE NOT THINKING IT THROUGH.

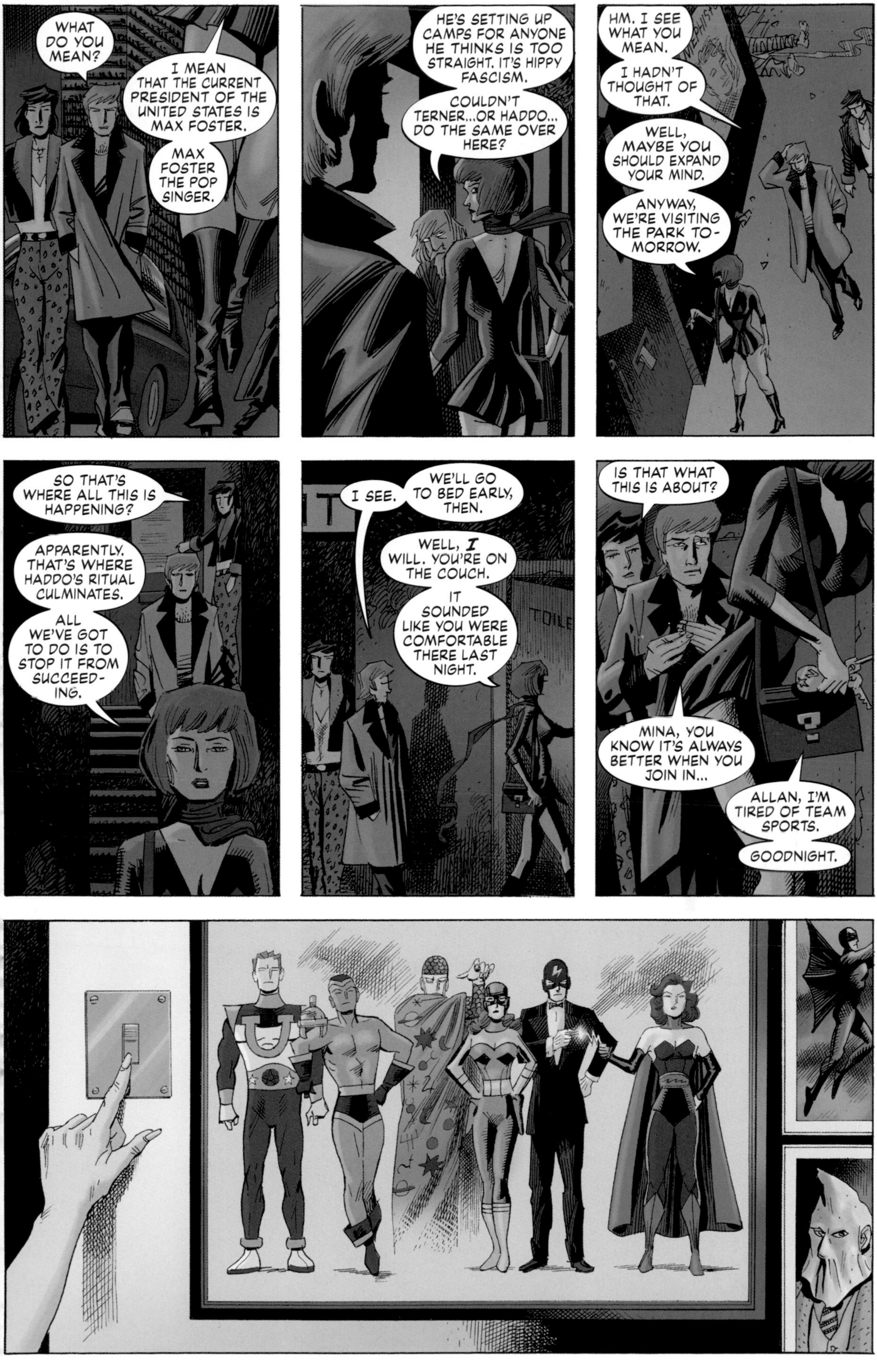
WHAT DO YOU MEAN?
I MEAN THAT THE CURRENT PRESIDENT OF THE UNITED STATES IS MAX FOSTER.
MAX FOSTER THE POP SINGER.
HE'S SETTING UP CAMPS FOR ANYONE HE THINKS IS TOO STRAIGHT. IT'S HIPPY FASCISM.
COULDN'T TERNER...OR HADDO... DO THE SAME OVER HERE?
HM. I SEE WHAT YOU MEAN.
I HADN'T THOUGHT OF THAT.
WELL, MAYBE YOU SHOULD EXPAND YOUR MIND.
ANYWAY, WE'RE VISITING THE PARK TO-MORROW.
SO THAT'S WHERE ALL THIS IS HAPPENING?
APPARENTLY. THAT'S WHERE HADDO'S RITUAL CULMINATES.
ALL WE'VE GOT TO DO IS TO STOP IT FROM SUCCEED-ING.
I SEE.
WE'LL GO TO BED EARLY, THEN.
WELL, *I* WILL. YOU'RE ON THE COUCH.
IT SOUNDED LIKE YOU WERE COMFORTABLE THERE LAST NIGHT.
IS THAT WHAT THIS IS ABOUT?
MINA, YOU KNOW IT'S ALWAYS BETTER WHEN YOU JOIN IN...
ALLAN, I'M TIRED OF TEAM SPORTS.
GOODNIGHT.

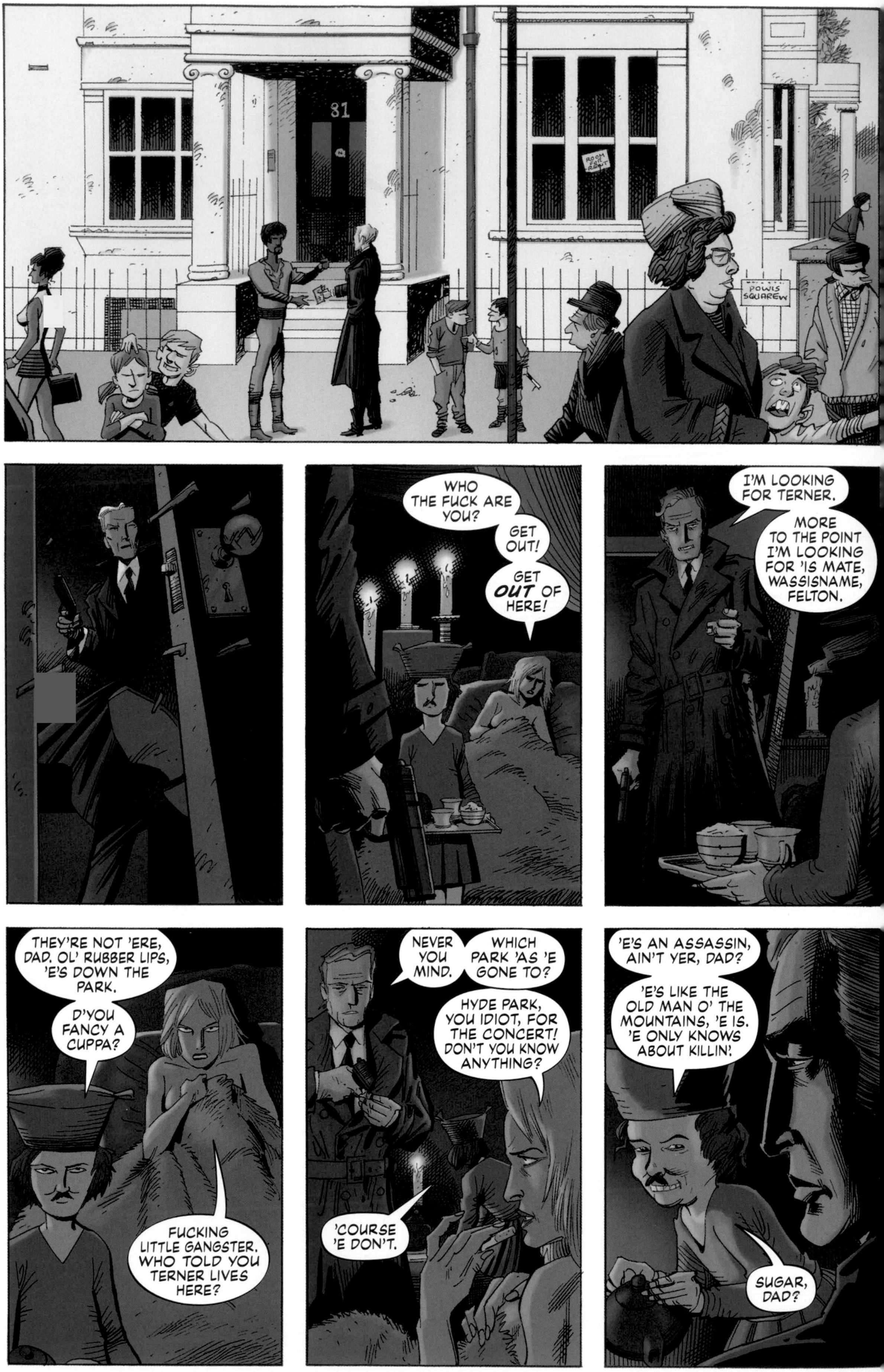
81
ROOM FOR RENT
POWIS SQUAREW
WHO THE FUCK ARE YOU?
GET OUT!
GET *OUT* OF HERE!
I'M LOOKING FOR TERNER.
MORE TO THE POINT I'M LOOKING FOR 'IS MATE, WASSISNAME, FELTON.
THEY'RE NOT 'ERE, DAD. OL' RUBBER LIPS, 'E'S DOWN THE PARK.
D'YOU FANCY A CUPPA?
FUCKING LITTLE GANGSTER. WHO TOLD YOU TERNER LIVES HERE?
NEVER YOU MIND.
WHICH PARK 'AS 'E GONE TO?
HYDE PARK, YOU IDIOT, FOR THE CONCERT! DON'T YOU KNOW ANYTHING?
'COURSE 'E DON'T.
'E'S AN ASSASSIN, AIN'T YER, DAD?
'E'S LIKE THE OLD MAN O' THE MOUNTAINS, 'E IS. 'E ONLY KNOWS ABOUT KILLIN'.
SUGAR, DAD?

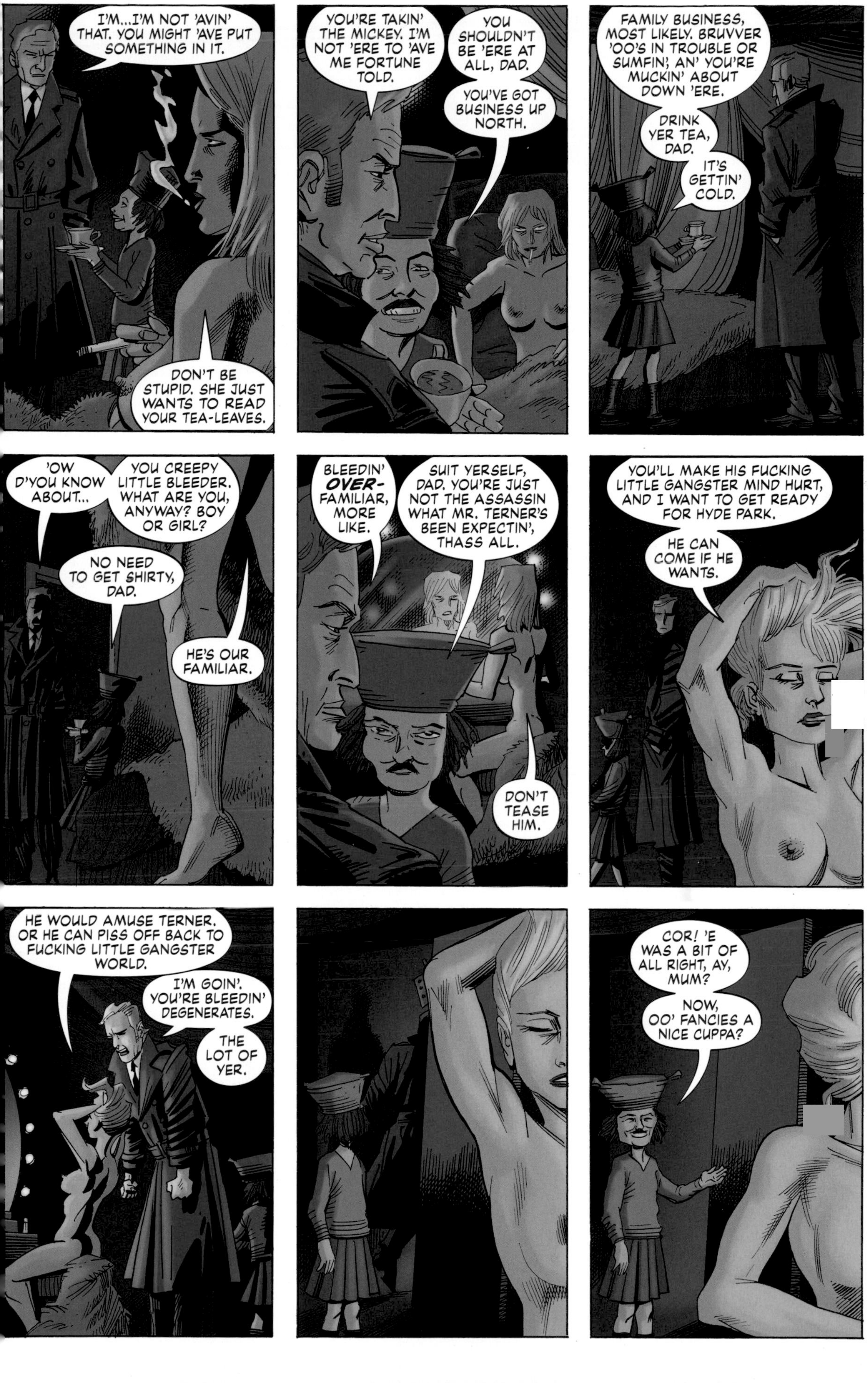
I'M...I'M NOT 'AVIN' THAT. YOU MIGHT 'AVE PUT SOMETHING IN IT.
DON'T BE STUPID. SHE JUST WANTS TO READ YOUR TEA-LEAVES.
YOU'RE TAKIN' THE MICKEY. I'M NOT 'ERE TO 'AVE ME FORTUNE TOLD.
YOU SHOULDN'T BE 'ERE AT ALL, DAD.
YOU'VE GOT BUSINESS UP NORTH.
FAMILY BUSINESS, MOST LIKELY. BRUVVER 'OO'S IN TROUBLE OR SUMFIN'; AN' YOU'RE MUCKIN' ABOUT DOWN 'ERE.
DRINK YER TEA, DAD.
IT'S GETTIN' COLD.
'OW D'YOU KNOW ABOUT...
YOU CREEPY LITTLE BLEEDER. WHAT ARE YOU, ANYWAY? BOY OR GIRL?
NO NEED TO GET SHIRTY, DAD.
HE'S OUR FAMILIAR.
BLEEDIN' OVER-FAMILIAR, MORE LIKE.
SUIT YERSELF, DAD. YOU'RE JUST NOT THE ASSASSIN WHAT MR. TERNER'S BEEN EXPECTIN', THASS ALL.
DON'T TEASE HIM.
YOU'LL MAKE HIS FUCKING LITTLE GANGSTER MIND HURT, AND I WANT TO GET READY FOR HYDE PARK.
HE CAN COME IF HE WANTS.
HE WOULD AMUSE TERNER. OR HE CAN PISS OFF BACK TO FUCKING LITTLE GANGSTER WORLD.
I'M GOIN'. YOU'RE BLEEDIN' DEGENERATES.
THE LOT OF YER.
COR! 'E WAS A BIT OF ALL RIGHT, AY, MUM?
NOW, OO' FANCIES A NICE CUPPA?

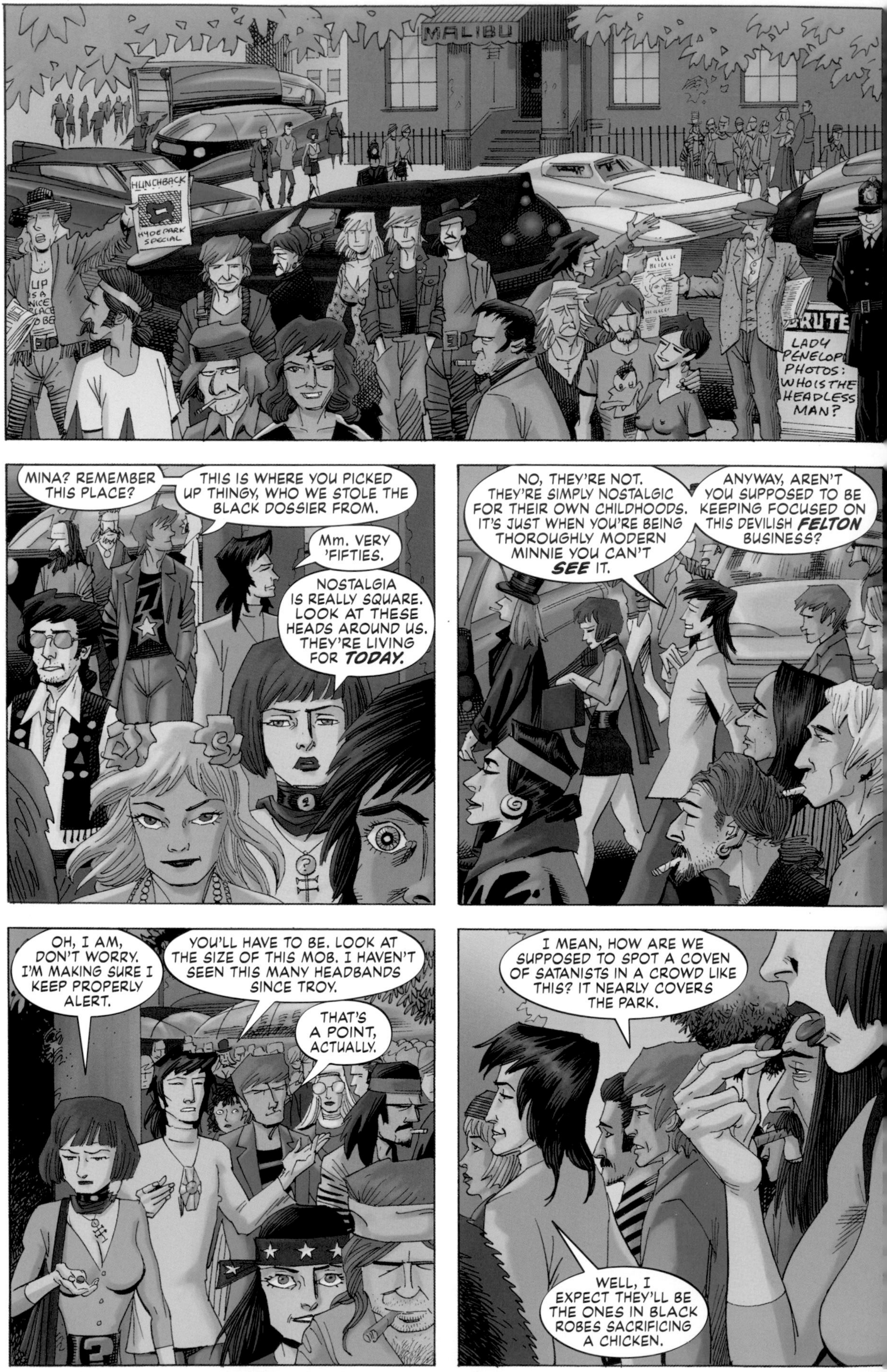
MALIBU
HUNCHBACK
HYDE PARK SPECIAL
LADY PENELOP PHOTOS: WHO IS THE HEADLESS MAN?
MINA? REMEMBER THIS PLACE?
THIS IS WHERE YOU PICKED UP THINGY, WHO WE STOLE THE BLACK DOSSIER FROM.
Mm. VERY 'FIFTIES.
NOSTALGIA IS REALLY SQUARE. LOOK AT THESE HEADS AROUND US. THEY'RE LIVING FOR **TODAY.**
NO, THEY'RE NOT. THEY'RE SIMPLY NOSTALGIC FOR THEIR OWN CHILDHOODS. IT'S JUST WHEN YOU'RE BEING THOROUGHLY MODERN MINNIE YOU CAN'T **SEE** IT.
ANYWAY, AREN'T YOU SUPPOSED TO BE KEEPING FOCUSED ON THIS DEVILISH **FELTON** BUSINESS?
OH, I AM, DON'T WORRY. I'M MAKING SURE I KEEP PROPERLY ALERT.
YOU'LL HAVE TO BE. LOOK AT THE SIZE OF THIS MOB. I HAVEN'T SEEN THIS MANY HEADBANDS SINCE TROY.
THAT'S A POINT, ACTUALLY.
I MEAN, HOW ARE WE SUPPOSED TO SPOT A COVEN OF SATANISTS IN A CROWD LIKE THIS? IT NEARLY COVERS THE PARK.
WELL, I EXPECT THEY'LL BE THE ONES IN BLACK ROBES SACRIFICING A CHICKEN.

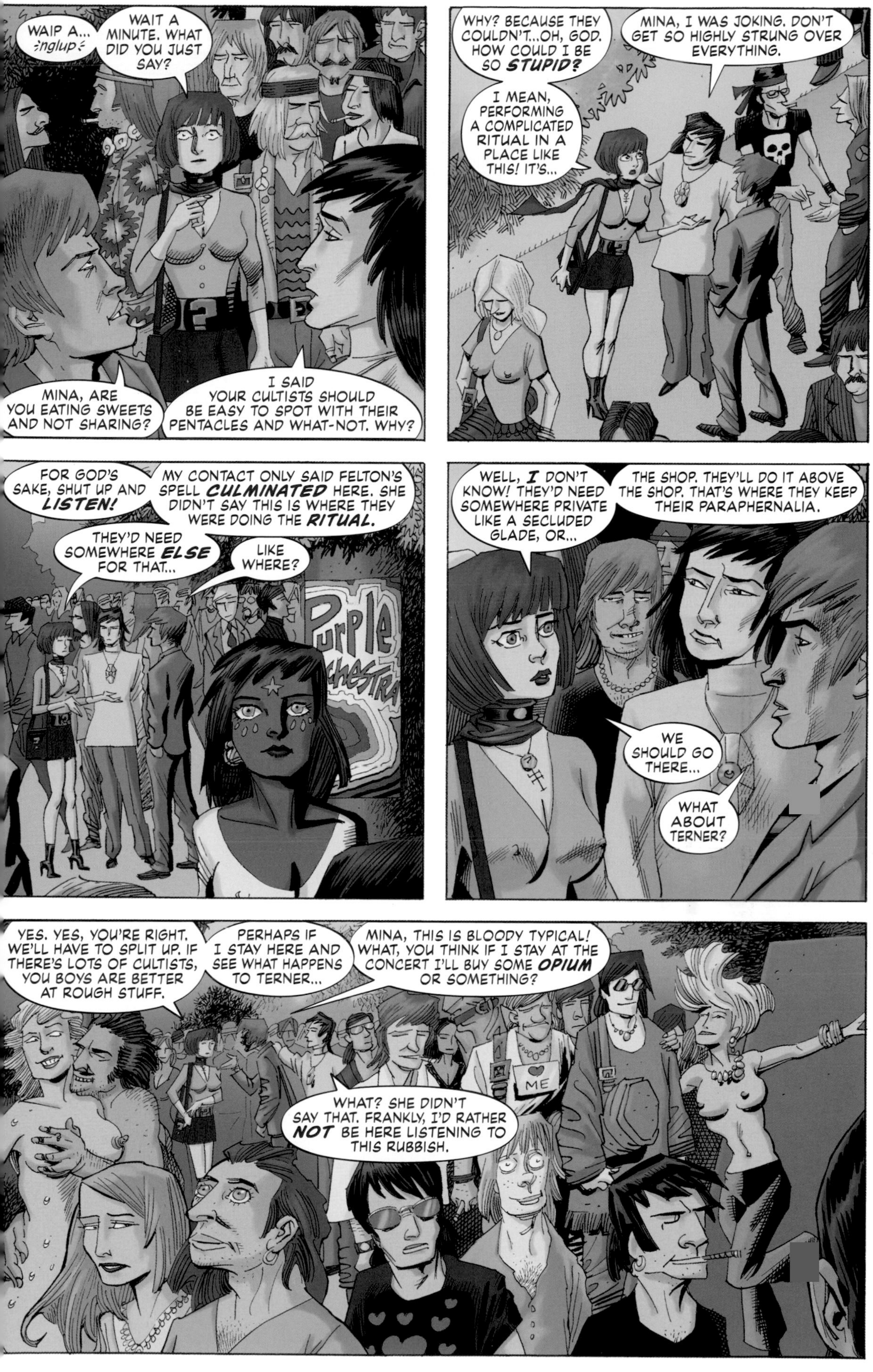
WAIP A... nglup
WAIT A MINUTE. WHAT DID YOU JUST SAY?
MINA, ARE YOU EATING SWEETS AND NOT SHARING?
I SAID YOUR CULTISTS SHOULD BE EASY TO SPOT WITH THEIR PENTACLES AND WHAT-NOT. WHY?
WHY? BECAUSE THEY COULDN'T...OH, GOD. HOW COULD I BE SO STUPID?
I MEAN, PERFORMING A COMPLICATED RITUAL IN A PLACE LIKE THIS! IT'S...
MINA, I WAS JOKING. DON'T GET SO HIGHLY STRUNG OVER EVERYTHING.
FOR GOD'S SAKE, SHUT UP AND LISTEN!
MY CONTACT ONLY SAID FELTON'S SPELL CULMINATED HERE. SHE DIDN'T SAY THIS IS WHERE THEY WERE DOING THE RITUAL.
THEY'D NEED SOMEWHERE ELSE FOR THAT...
LIKE WHERE?
Purple Orchestra
WELL, I DON'T KNOW! THEY'D NEED SOMEWHERE PRIVATE LIKE A SECLUDED GLADE, OR...
THE SHOP. THEY'LL DO IT ABOVE THE SHOP. THAT'S WHERE THEY KEEP THEIR PARAPHERNALIA.
WE SHOULD GO THERE...
WHAT ABOUT TERNER?
YES. YES, YOU'RE RIGHT. WE'LL HAVE TO SPLIT UP. IF THERE'S LOTS OF CULTISTS, YOU BOYS ARE BETTER AT ROUGH STUFF.
PERHAPS IF I STAY HERE AND SEE WHAT HAPPENS TO TERNER...
MINA, THIS IS BLOODY TYPICAL! WHAT, YOU THINK IF I STAY AT THE CONCERT I'LL BUY SOME OPIUM OR SOMETHING?
WHAT? SHE DIDN'T SAY THAT. FRANKLY, I'D RATHER NOT BE HERE LISTENING TO THIS RUBBISH.
ME

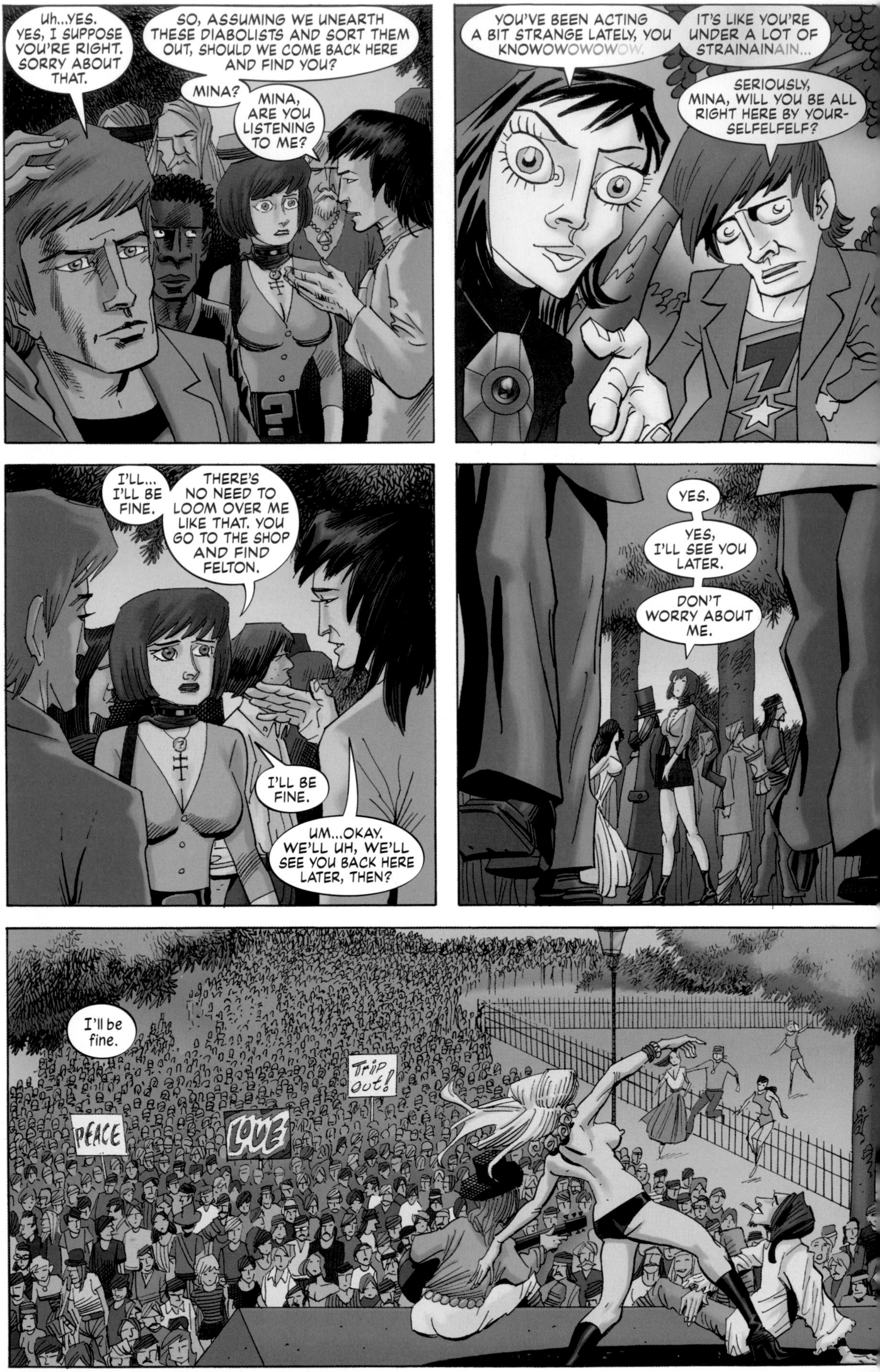
UH...YES. YES, I SUPPOSE YOU'RE RIGHT. SORRY ABOUT THAT.
SO, ASSUMING WE UNEARTH THESE DIABOLISTS AND SORT THEM OUT, SHOULD WE COME BACK HERE AND FIND YOU?
MINA?
MINA, ARE YOU LISTENING TO ME?
YOU'VE BEEN ACTING A BIT STRANGE LATELY, YOU KNOWOWOWOWOWOW.
IT'S LIKE YOU'RE UNDER A LOT OF STRAINAINAIN...
SERIOUSLY, MINA, WILL YOU BE ALL RIGHT HERE BY YOUR-SELFELFELF?
I'LL... I'LL BE FINE.
THERE'S NO NEED TO LOOM OVER ME LIKE THAT. YOU GO TO THE SHOP AND FIND FELTON.
I'LL BE FINE.
UM...OKAY. WE'LL UH, WE'LL SEE YOU BACK HERE LATER, THEN?
YES.
YES, I'LL SEE YOU LATER.
DON'T WORRY ABOUT ME.
I'll be fine.
PEACE
LOVE
Trip out!

HENRY EDWARD
JEKYLL

EDWARD HYDE

1851 - 1898

*Monstrous, he died
for Mankind.*

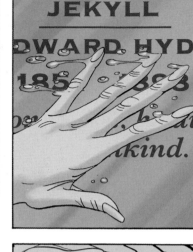

HEY, EASY, MAN...

I'M SORRY. SORRY.

HAS EVERYONE GOT THESE... THINGS...?

WHOOPS...

ARE YOU OKAY, LUVUVUVUV?

SHE'S COOL. SHE'S JUST TRIPPINGINGING.

LEAVE HER TO ENJOY HERSELFELFELFELF.

PEACE, SISTERISTER-ISTERISTER...

YEAH.

YEAH, I'M COOL. I'M JUST TRICK...TRICKING... I'M JUST TRIPPING.

YEAH? WELL, DON'T LOOK 'ROUND OR THAT BIG MONSTER WILL FREAK YOU OUT.

DON'T TELL HER THAT.

YOU JUST COME ON AND SEE THE PURPLE ORCHESTRA. THERE'S NO MONSTER.

WHAT? HA HA. WHAT ARE YOU TALKING...

...ABOUT...

HEY, LOOK COME ONONONON...

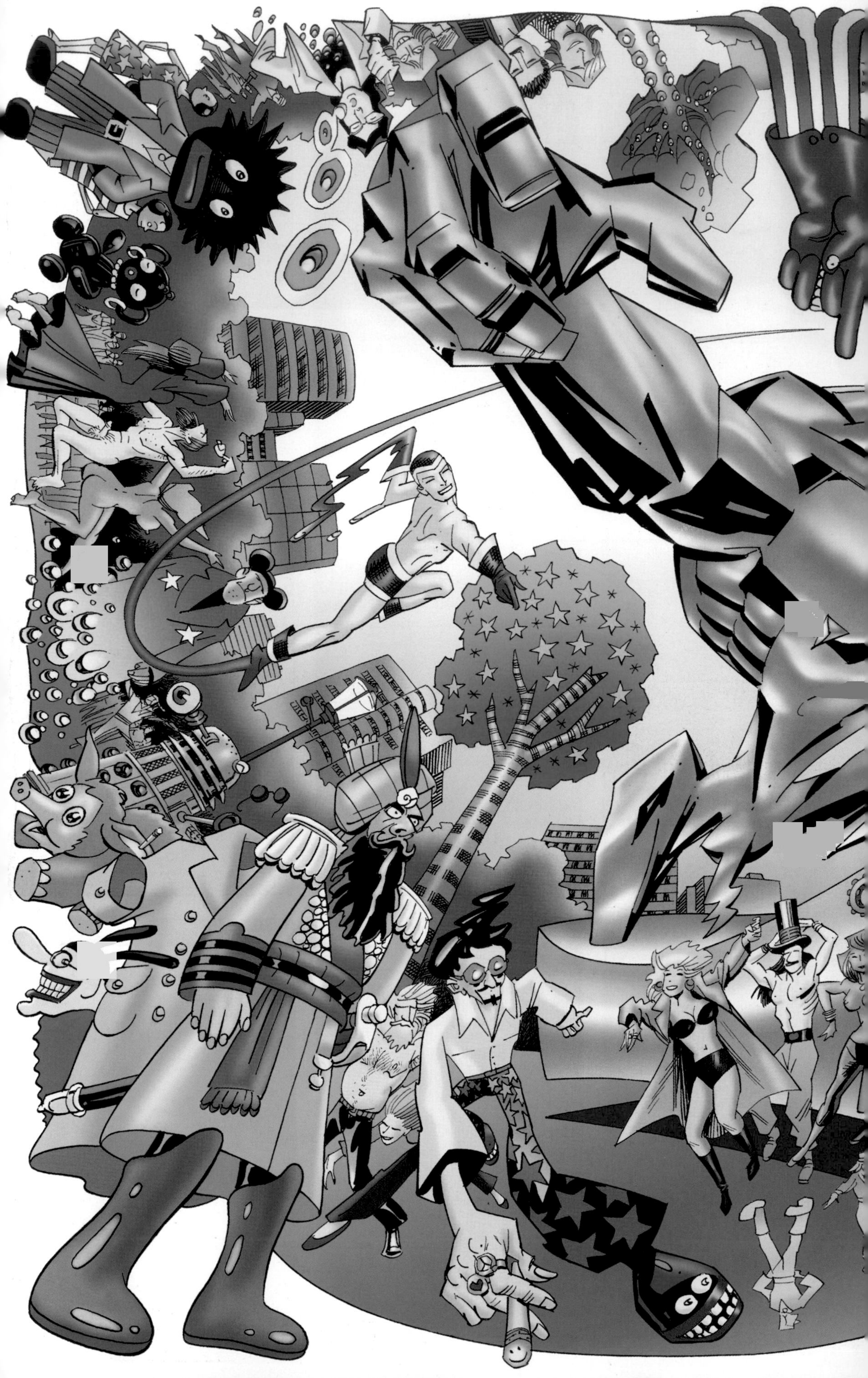

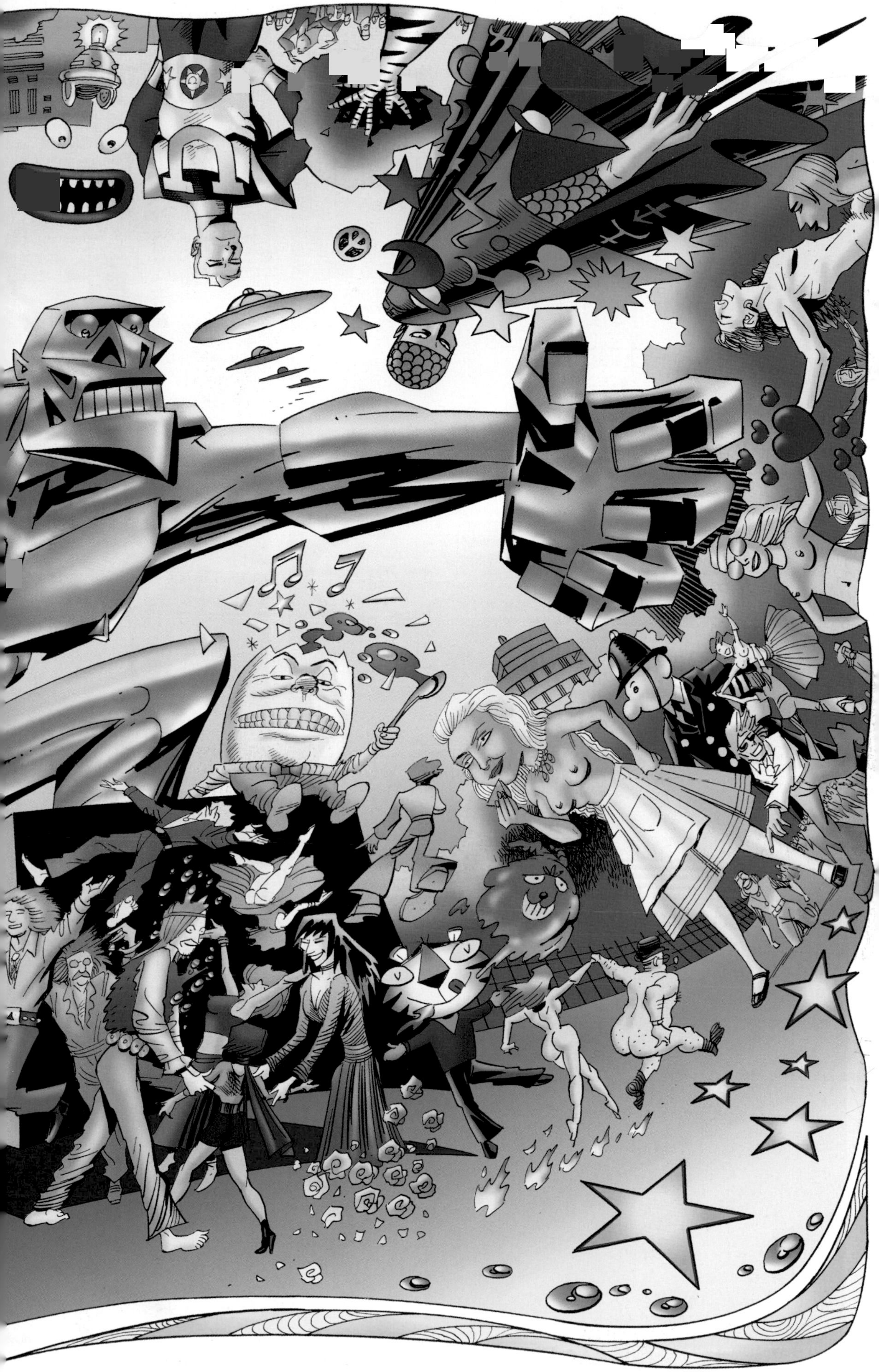

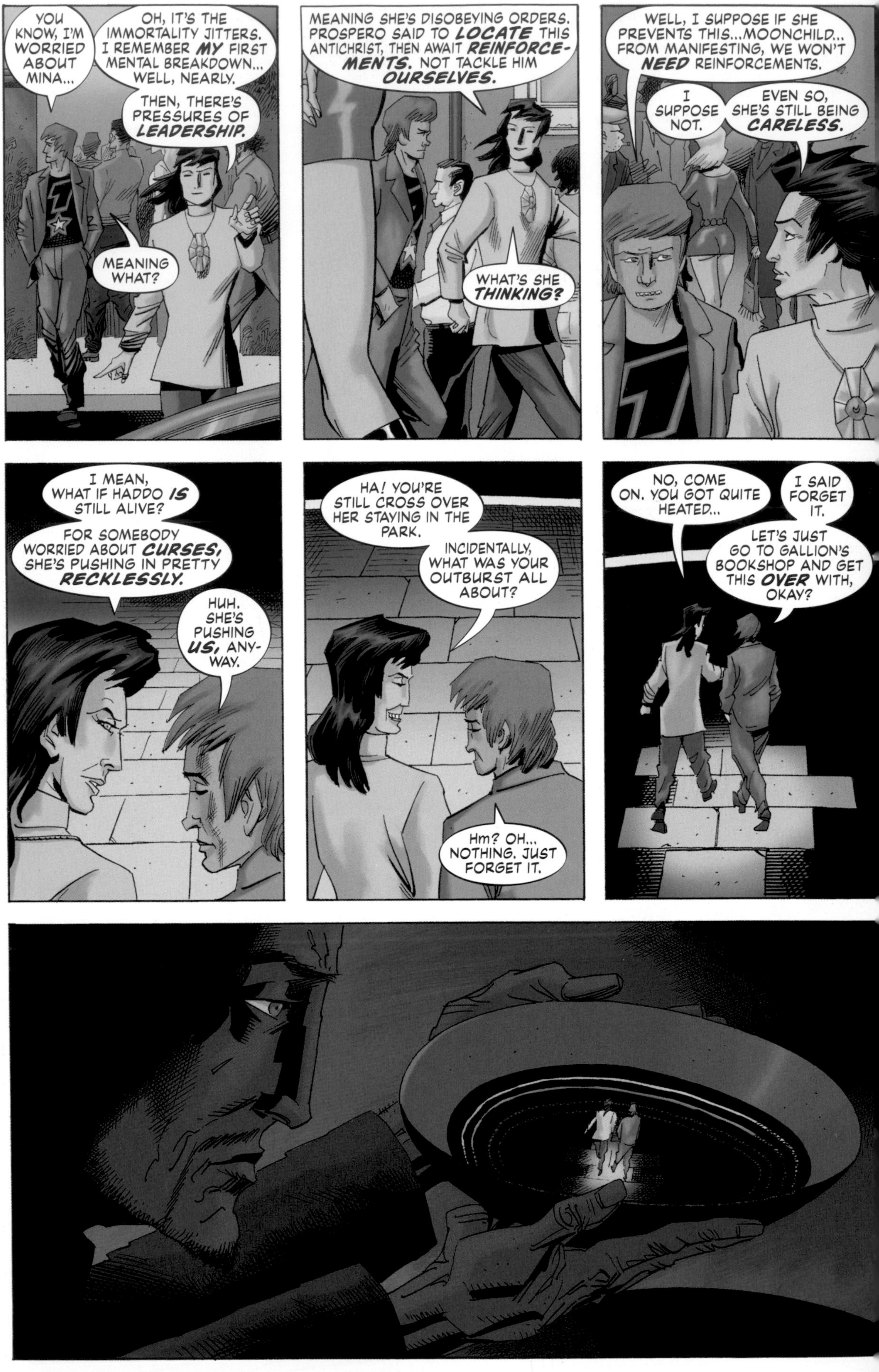
YOU KNOW, I'M WORRIED ABOUT MINA...
OH, IT'S THE IMMORTALITY JITTERS. I REMEMBER MY FIRST MENTAL BREAKDOWN... WELL, NEARLY.
THEN, THERE'S PRESSURES OF LEADERSHIP.
MEANING WHAT?
MEANING SHE'S DISOBEYING ORDERS. PROSPERO SAID TO LOCATE THIS ANTICHRIST, THEN AWAIT REINFORCE-MENTS. NOT TACKLE HIM OURSELVES.
WHAT'S SHE THINKING?
WELL, I SUPPOSE IF SHE PREVENTS THIS...MOONCHILD... FROM MANIFESTING, WE WON'T NEED REINFORCEMENTS.
I SUPPOSE NOT.
EVEN SO, SHE'S STILL BEING CARELESS.
I MEAN, WHAT IF HADDO IS STILL ALIVE?
FOR SOMEBODY WORRIED ABOUT CURSES, SHE'S PUSHING IN PRETTY RECKLESSLY.
HUH. SHE'S PUSHING US, ANY-WAY.
HA! YOU'RE STILL CROSS OVER HER STAYING IN THE PARK.
INCIDENTALLY, WHAT WAS YOUR OUTBURST ALL ABOUT?
Hm? OH... NOTHING. JUST FORGET IT.
NO, COME ON. YOU GOT QUITE HEATED...
I SAID FORGET IT.
LET'S JUST GO TO GALLION'S BOOKSHOP AND GET THIS OVER WITH, OKAY?

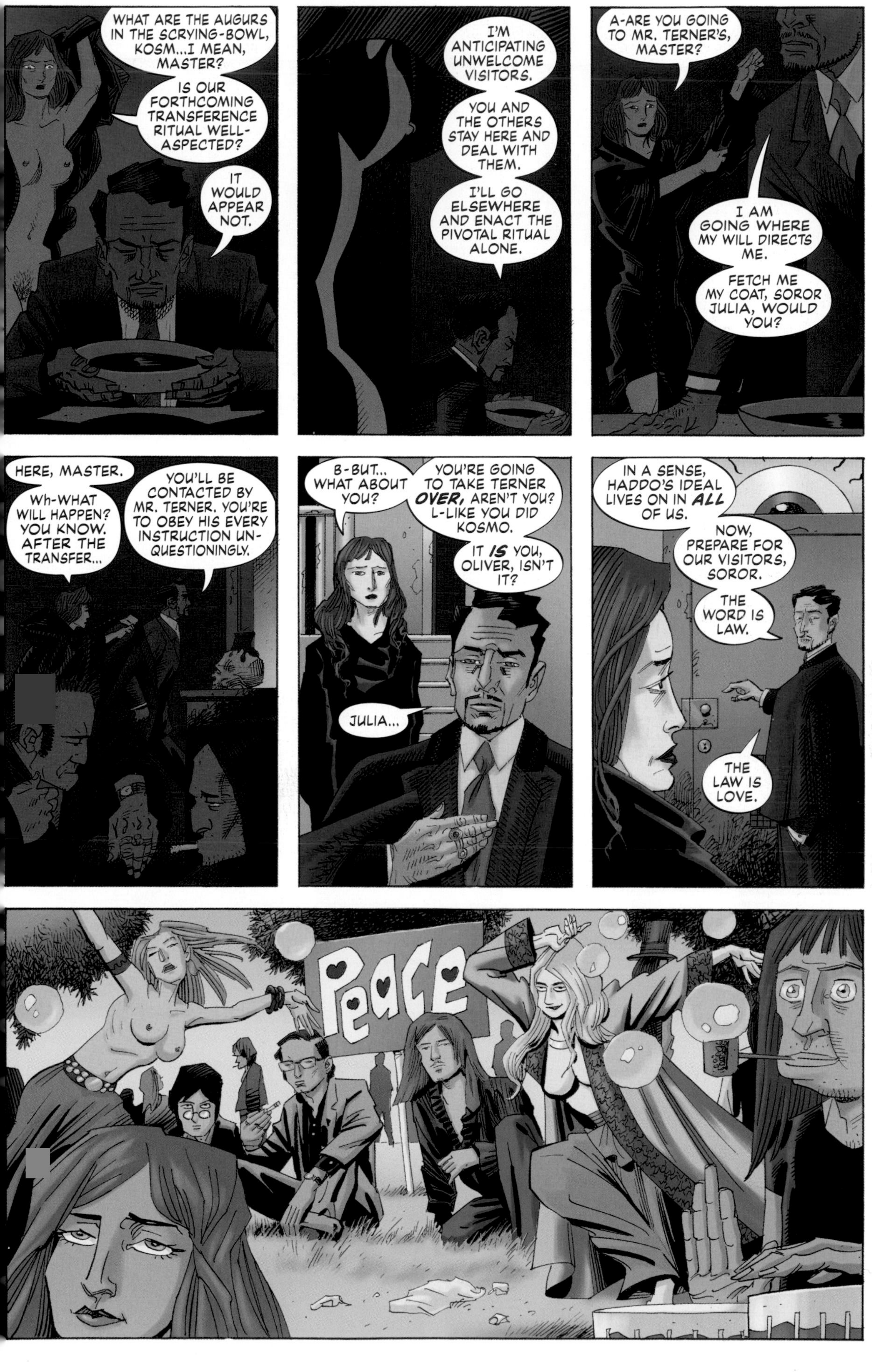
WHAT ARE THE AUGURS IN THE SCRYING-BOWL, KOSM...I MEAN, MASTER?
IS OUR FORTHCOMING TRANSFERENCE RITUAL WELL-ASPECTED?
IT WOULD APPEAR NOT.
I'M ANTICIPATING UNWELCOME VISITORS.
YOU AND THE OTHERS STAY HERE AND DEAL WITH THEM.
I'LL GO ELSEWHERE AND ENACT THE PIVOTAL RITUAL ALONE.
A-ARE YOU GOING TO MR. TERNER'S, MASTER?
I AM GOING WHERE MY WILL DIRECTS ME.
FETCH ME MY COAT, SOROR JULIA, WOULD YOU?
HERE, MASTER.
Wh-WHAT WILL HAPPEN? YOU KNOW. AFTER THE TRANSFER...
YOU'LL BE CONTACTED BY MR. TERNER. YOU'RE TO OBEY HIS EVERY INSTRUCTION UN-QUESTIONINGLY.
B-BUT... WHAT ABOUT YOU?
YOU'RE GOING TO TAKE TERNER **OVER,** AREN'T YOU? L-LIKE YOU DID KOSMO.
IT **IS** YOU, OLIVER, ISN'T IT?
JULIA...
IN A SENSE, HADDO'S IDEAL LIVES ON IN **ALL** OF US.
NOW, PREPARE FOR OUR VISITORS, SOROR.
THE WORD IS LAW.
THE LAW IS LOVE.
PEACE

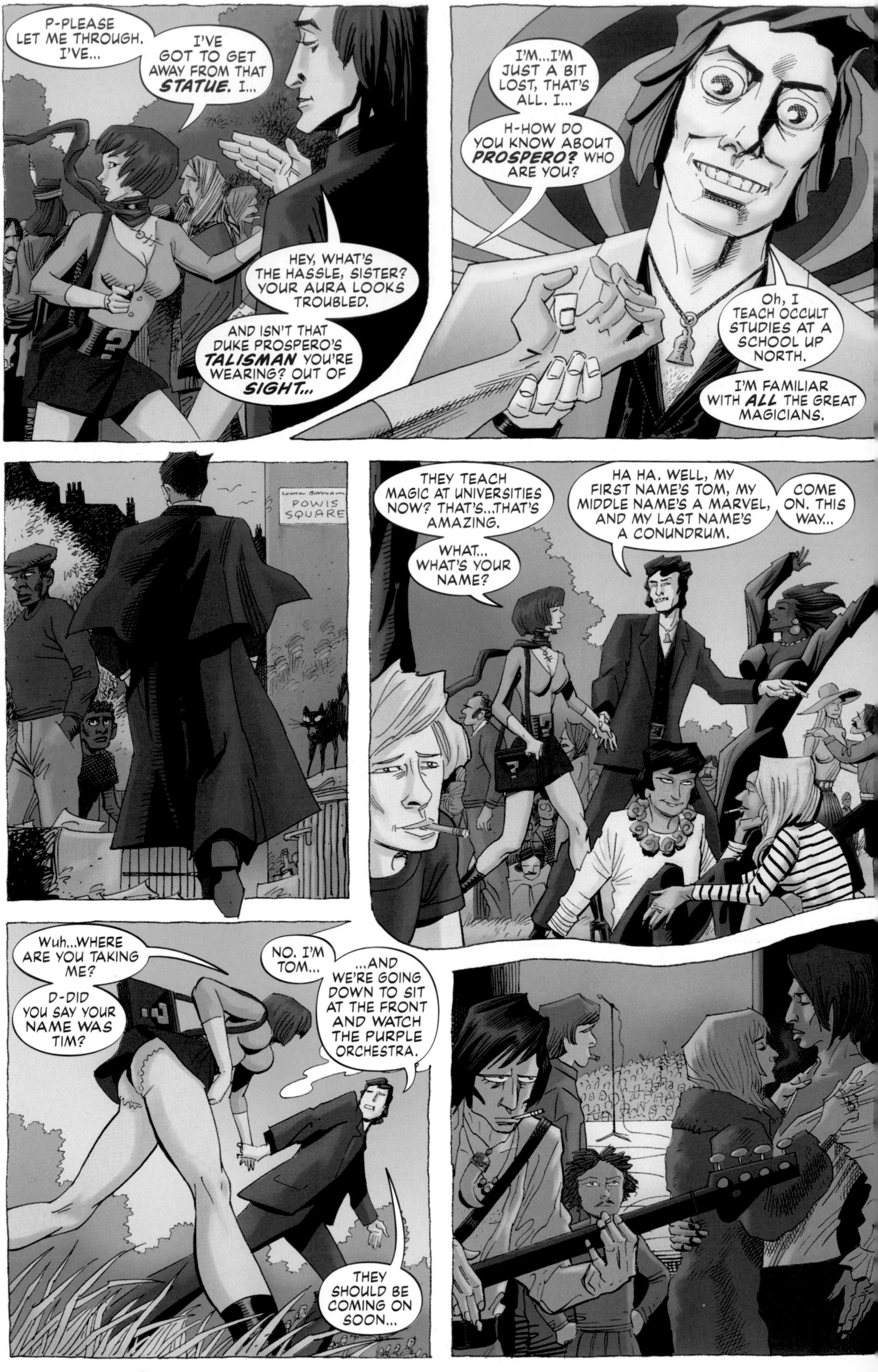
P-PLEASE LET ME THROUGH. I'VE...
I'VE GOT TO GET AWAY FROM THAT STATUE. I...
HEY, WHAT'S THE HASSLE, SISTER? YOUR AURA LOOKS TROUBLED.
AND ISN'T THAT DUKE PROSPERO'S TALISMAN YOU'RE WEARING? OUT OF SIGHT...
I'M...I'M JUST A BIT LOST, THAT'S ALL. I...
H-HOW DO YOU KNOW ABOUT PROSPERO? WHO ARE YOU?
Oh, I TEACH OCCULT STUDIES AT A SCHOOL UP NORTH.
I'M FAMILIAR WITH ALL THE GREAT MAGICIANS.
POWIS SQUARE
THEY TEACH MAGIC AT UNIVERSITIES NOW? THAT'S...THAT'S AMAZING.
WHAT... WHAT'S YOUR NAME?
HA HA. WELL, MY FIRST NAME'S TOM, MY MIDDLE NAME'S A MARVEL, AND MY LAST NAME'S A CONUNDRUM.
COME ON. THIS WAY...
Wuh...WHERE ARE YOU TAKING ME?
D-DID YOU SAY YOUR NAME WAS TIM?
NO. I'M TOM...
...AND WE'RE GOING DOWN TO SIT AT THE FRONT AND WATCH THE PURPLE ORCHESTRA.
THEY SHOULD BE COMING ON SOON...

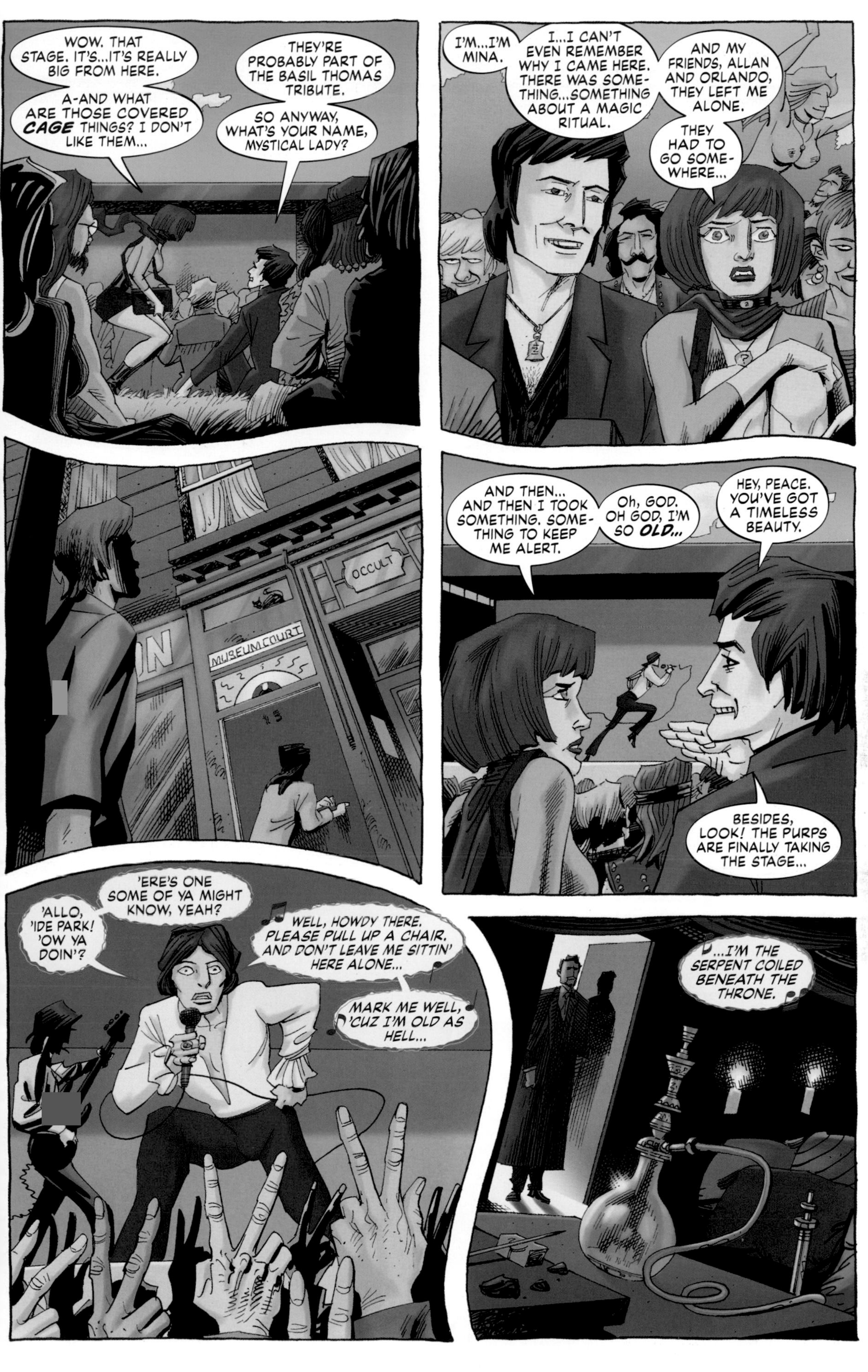
WOW. THAT STAGE. IT'S...IT'S REALLY BIG FROM HERE.
A-AND WHAT ARE THOSE COVERED **CAGE** THINGS? I DON'T LIKE THEM...
THEY'RE PROBABLY PART OF THE BASIL THOMAS TRIBUTE.
SO ANYWAY, WHAT'S YOUR NAME, MYSTICAL LADY?
I'M...I'M MINA.
I...I CAN'T EVEN REMEMBER WHY I CAME HERE. THERE WAS SOMETHING...SOMETHING ABOUT A MAGIC RITUAL.
AND MY FRIENDS, ALLAN AND ORLANDO, THEY LEFT ME ALONE.
THEY HAD TO GO SOMEWHERE...
OCCULT
MUSEUM COURT
AND THEN... AND THEN I TOOK SOMETHING. SOMETHING TO KEEP ME ALERT.
Oh, GOD. OH GOD, I'M SO ***OLD...***
HEY, PEACE. YOU'VE GOT A TIMELESS BEAUTY.
BESIDES, LOOK! THE PURPS ARE FINALLY TAKING THE STAGE...
'ALLO, 'IDE PARK! 'OW YA DOIN'?
'ERE'S ONE SOME OF YA MIGHT KNOW, YEAH?
WELL, HOWDY THERE. PLEASE PULL UP A CHAIR. AND DON'T LEAVE ME SITTIN' HERE ALONE...
MARK ME WELL, 'CUZ I'M OLD AS HELL...
...I'M THE SERPENT COILED BENEATH THE THRONE.

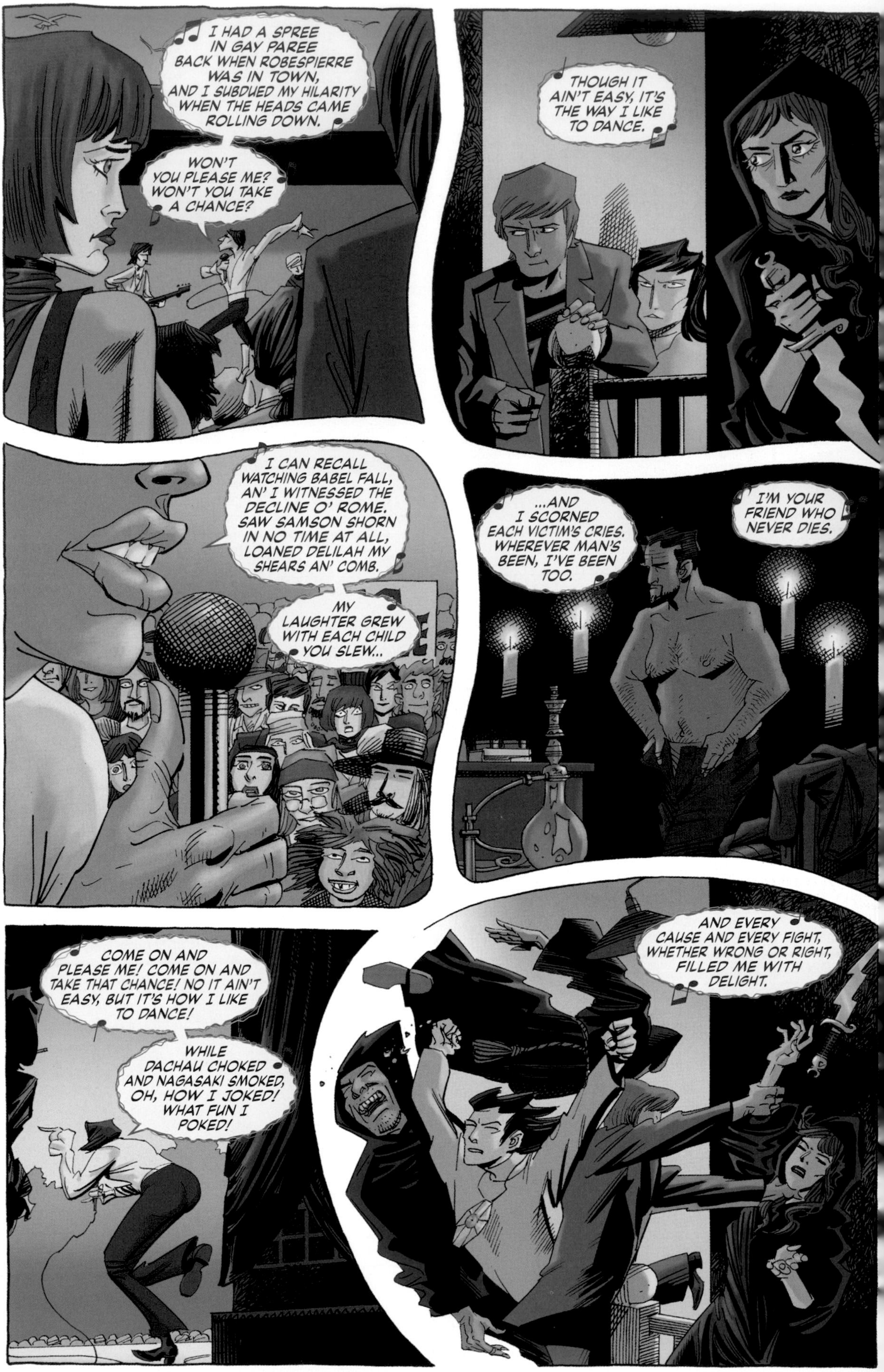
I HAD A SPREE IN GAY PAREE BACK WHEN ROBESPIERRE WAS IN TOWN, AND I SUBDUED MY HILARITY WHEN THE HEADS CAME ROLLING DOWN.
WON'T YOU PLEASE ME? WON'T YOU TAKE A CHANCE?
THOUGH IT AIN'T EASY, IT'S THE WAY I LIKE TO DANCE.
I CAN RECALL WATCHING BABEL FALL, AN' I WITNESSED THE DECLINE O' ROME. SAW SAMSON SHORN IN NO TIME AT ALL, LOANED DELILAH MY SHEARS AN' COMB.
MY LAUGHTER GREW WITH EACH CHILD YOU SLEW...
...AND I SCORNED EACH VICTIM'S CRIES. WHEREVER MAN'S BEEN, I'VE BEEN TOO.
I'M YOUR FRIEND WHO NEVER DIES.
COME ON AND PLEASE ME! COME ON AND TAKE THAT CHANCE! NO IT AIN'T EASY, BUT IT'S HOW I LIKE TO DANCE!
WHILE DACHAU CHOKED AND NAGASAKI SMOKED, OH, HOW I JOKED! WHAT FUN I POKED!
AND EVERY CAUSE AND EVERY FIGHT, WHETHER WRONG OR RIGHT, FILLED ME WITH DELIGHT.

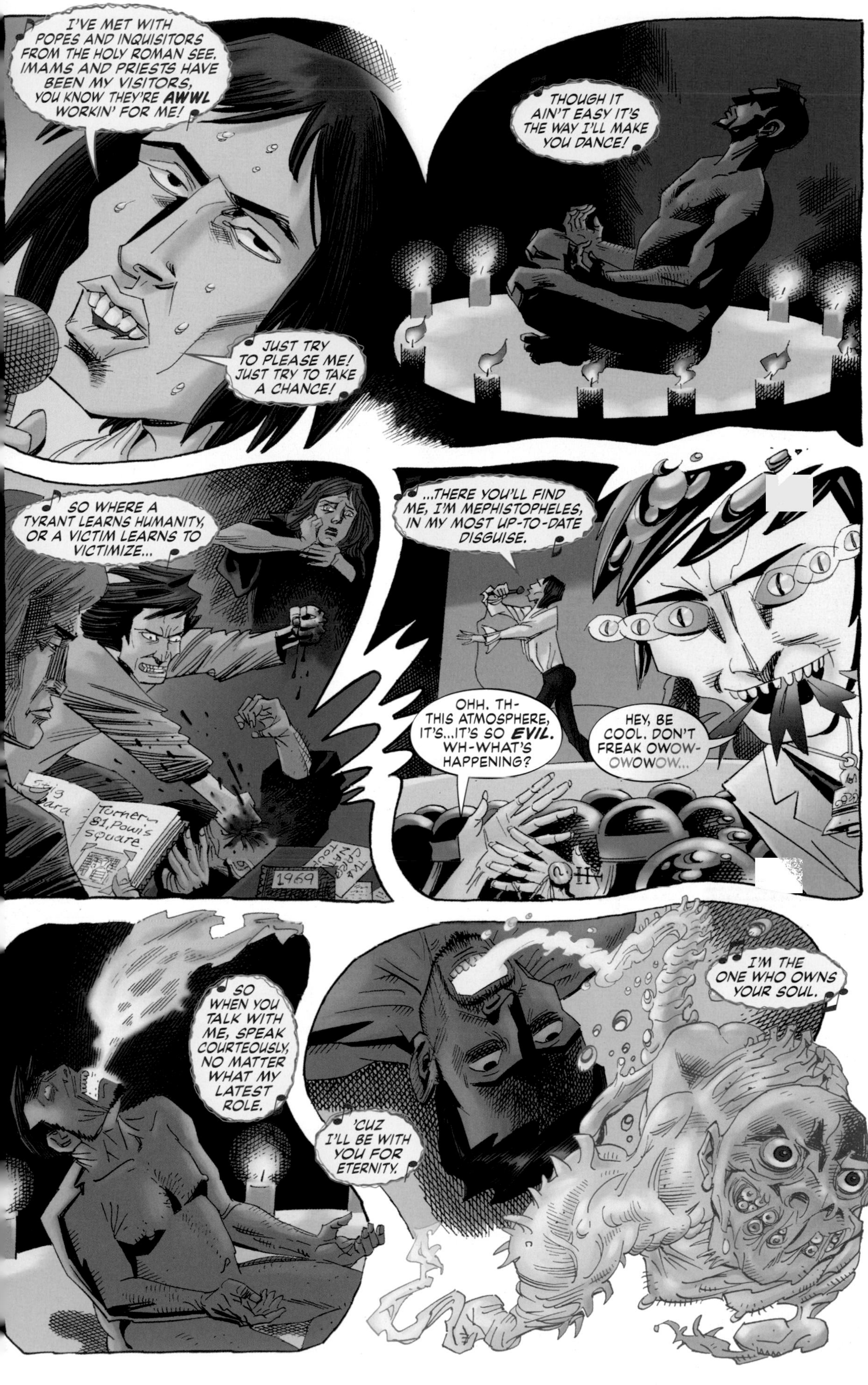
I'VE MET WITH POPES AND INQUISITORS FROM THE HOLY ROMAN SEE. IMAMS AND PRIESTS HAVE BEEN MY VISITORS, YOU KNOW THEY'RE **AWWL** WORKIN' FOR ME!
JUST TRY TO PLEASE ME! JUST TRY TO TAKE A CHANCE!
THOUGH IT AIN'T EASY IT'S THE WAY I'LL MAKE YOU DANCE!
SO WHERE A TYRANT LEARNS HUMANITY, OR A VICTIM LEARNS TO VICTIMIZE...
Turner 81, Powis square.
1969
...THERE YOU'LL FIND ME, I'M MEPHISTOPHELES, IN MY MOST UP-TO-DATE DISGUISE.
OHH. TH- THIS ATMOSPHERE, IT'S...IT'S SO **EVIL**. WH-WHAT'S HAPPENING?
HEY, BE COOL. DON'T FREAK OWOW-OWOWOW...
SO WHEN YOU TALK WITH ME, SPEAK COURTEOUSLY, NO MATTER WHAT MY LATEST ROLE.
'CUZ I'LL BE WITH YOU FOR ETERNITY.
I'M THE ONE WHO OWNS YOUR SOUL.

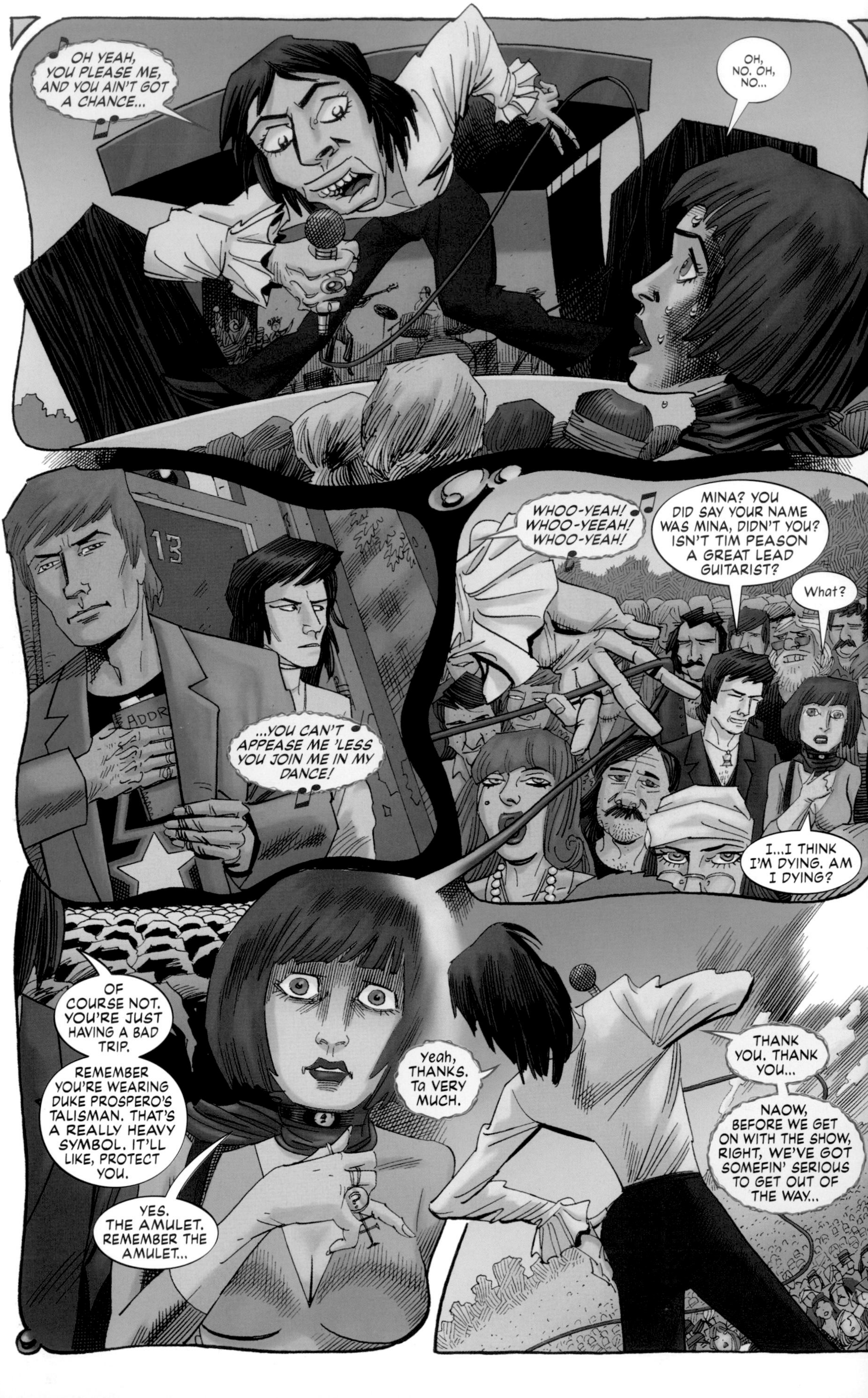
OH YEAH, YOU PLEASE ME, AND YOU AIN'T GOT A CHANCE...
OH, NO. OH, NO...
13
ADDR
...YOU CAN'T APPEASE ME 'LESS YOU JOIN ME IN MY DANCE!
WHOO-YEAH! WHOO-YEEAH! WHOO-YEAH!
MINA? YOU DID SAY YOUR NAME WAS MINA, DIDN'T YOU? ISN'T TIM PEASON A GREAT LEAD GUITARIST?
What?
I...I THINK I'M DYING. AM I DYING?
OF COURSE NOT. YOU'RE JUST HAVING A BAD TRIP.
REMEMBER YOU'RE WEARING DUKE PROSPERO'S TALISMAN. THAT'S A REALLY HEAVY SYMBOL. IT'LL LIKE, PROTECT YOU.
YES. THE AMULET. REMEMBER THE AMULET...
Yeah, THANKS. Ta VERY MUCH.
THANK YOU. THANK YOU...
NAOW, BEFORE WE GET ON WITH THE SHOW, RIGHT, WE'VE GOT SOMEFIN' SERIOUS TO GET OUT OF THE WAY...

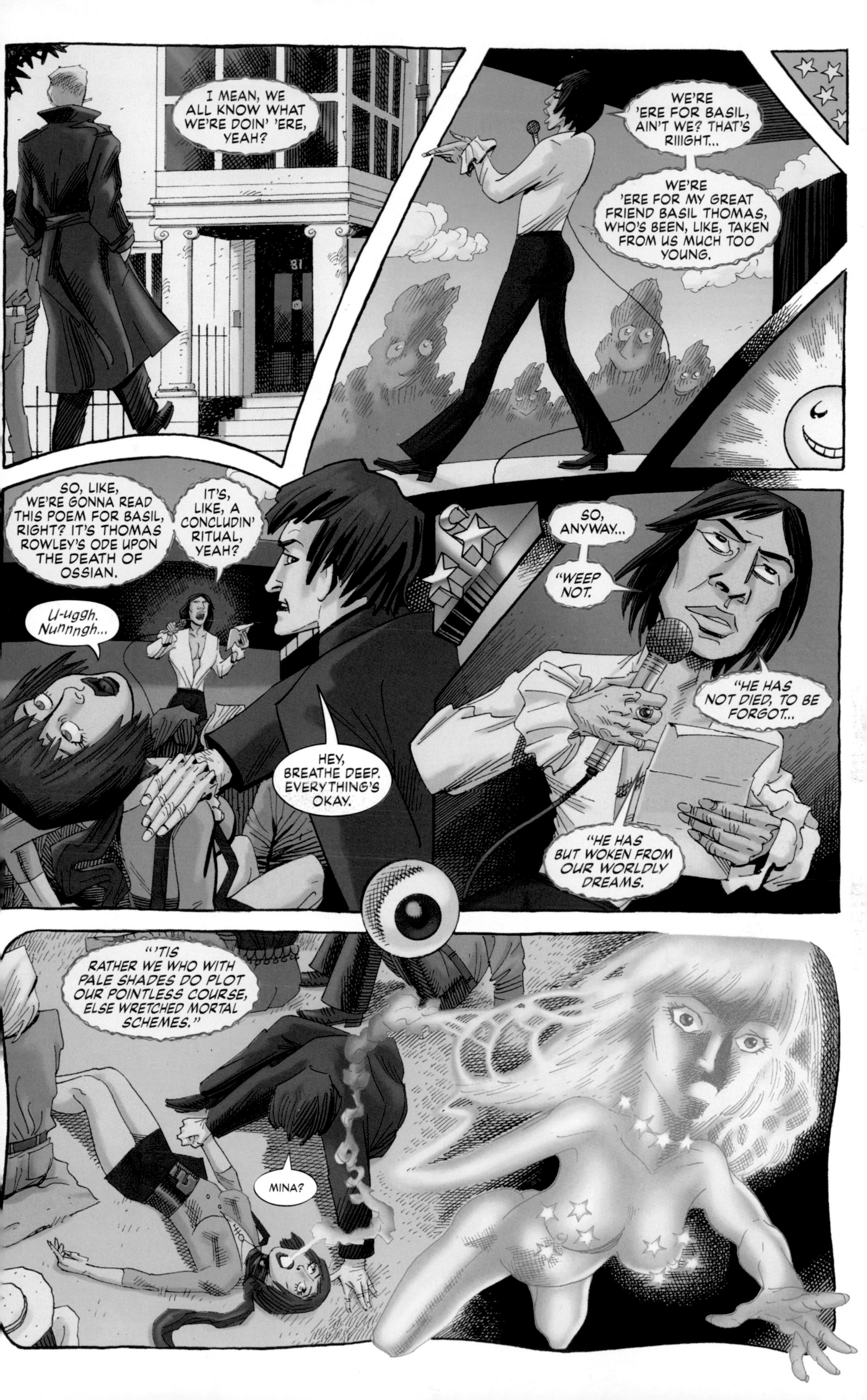
I MEAN, WE ALL KNOW WHAT WE'RE DOIN' 'ERE, YEAH?
WE'RE 'ERE FOR BASIL, AIN'T WE? THAT'S RIIIGHT...
WE'RE 'ERE FOR MY GREAT FRIEND BASIL THOMAS, WHO'S BEEN, LIKE, TAKEN FROM US MUCH TOO YOUNG.
SO, LIKE, WE'RE GONNA READ THIS POEM FOR BASIL, RIGHT? IT'S THOMAS ROWLEY'S ODE UPON THE DEATH OF OSSIAN.
IT'S, LIKE, A CONCLUDIN' RITUAL, YEAH?
U-uggh. Nunnngh...
HEY, BREATHE DEEP. EVERYTHING'S OKAY.
SO, ANYWAY...
"WEEP NOT.
"HE HAS NOT DIED, TO BE FORGOT...
"HE HAS BUT WOKEN FROM OUR WORLDLY DREAMS.
"'TIS RATHER WE WHO WITH PALE SHADES DO PLOT OUR POINTLESS COURSE, ELSE WRETCHED MORTAL SCHEMES."
MINA?

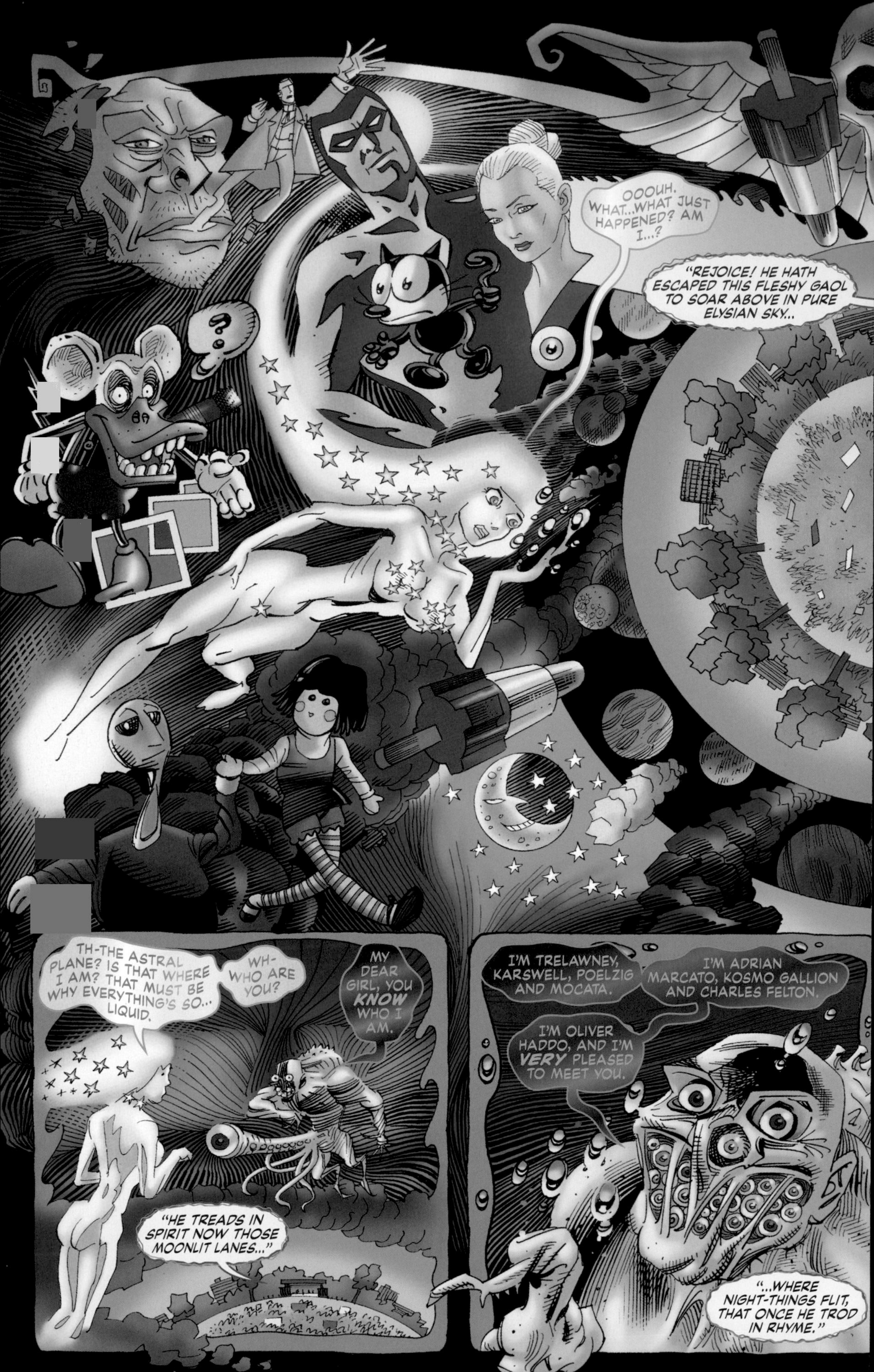
OOOUH. WHAT...WHAT JUST HAPPENED? AM I...?
"REJOICE! HE HATH ESCAPED THIS FLESHY GAOL TO SOAR ABOVE IN PURE ELYSIAN SKY...
TH-THE ASTRAL PLANE? IS THAT WHERE I AM? THAT MUST BE WHY EVERYTHING'S SO... LIQUID.
WH- WHO ARE YOU?
MY DEAR GIRL, YOU KNOW WHO I AM.
"HE TREADS IN SPIRIT NOW THOSE MOONLIT LANES..."
I'M TRELAWNEY, KARSWELL, POELZIG AND MOCATA.
I'M ADRIAN MARCATO, KOSMO GALLION AND CHARLES FELTON.
I'M OLIVER HADDO, AND I'M VERY PLEASED TO MEET YOU.
"...WHERE NIGHT-THINGS FLIT, THAT ONCE HE TROD IN RHYME."

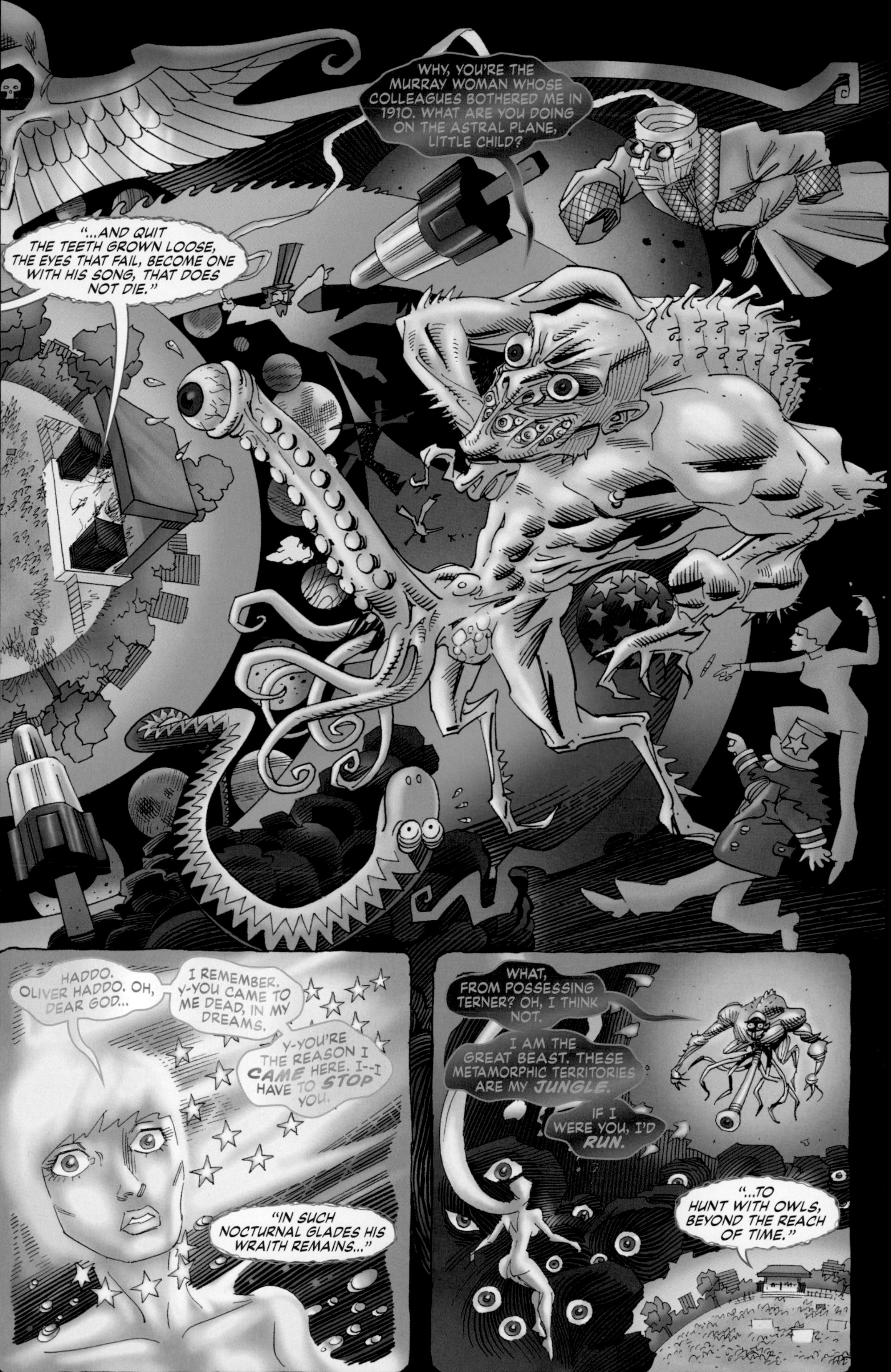
WHY, YOU'RE THE MURRAY WOMAN WHOSE COLLEAGUES BOTHERED ME IN 1910. WHAT ARE YOU DOING ON THE ASTRAL PLANE, LITTLE CHILD?
"...AND QUIT THE TEETH GROWN LOOSE, THE EYES THAT FAIL, BECOME ONE WITH HIS SONG, THAT DOES NOT DIE."
HADDO. OLIVER HADDO. OH, DEAR GOD...
I REMEMBER. Y-YOU CAME TO ME DEAD, IN MY DREAMS.
Y-YOU'RE THE REASON I CAME HERE. I--I HAVE TO STOP YOU.
"IN SUCH NOCTURNAL GLADES HIS WRAITH REMAINS..."
WHAT, FROM POSSESSING TERNER? OH, I THINK NOT.
I AM THE GREAT BEAST. THESE METAMORPHIC TERRITORIES ARE MY JUNGLE.
IF I WERE YOU, I'D RUN.
"...TO HUNT WITH OWLS, BEYOND THE REACH OF TIME."

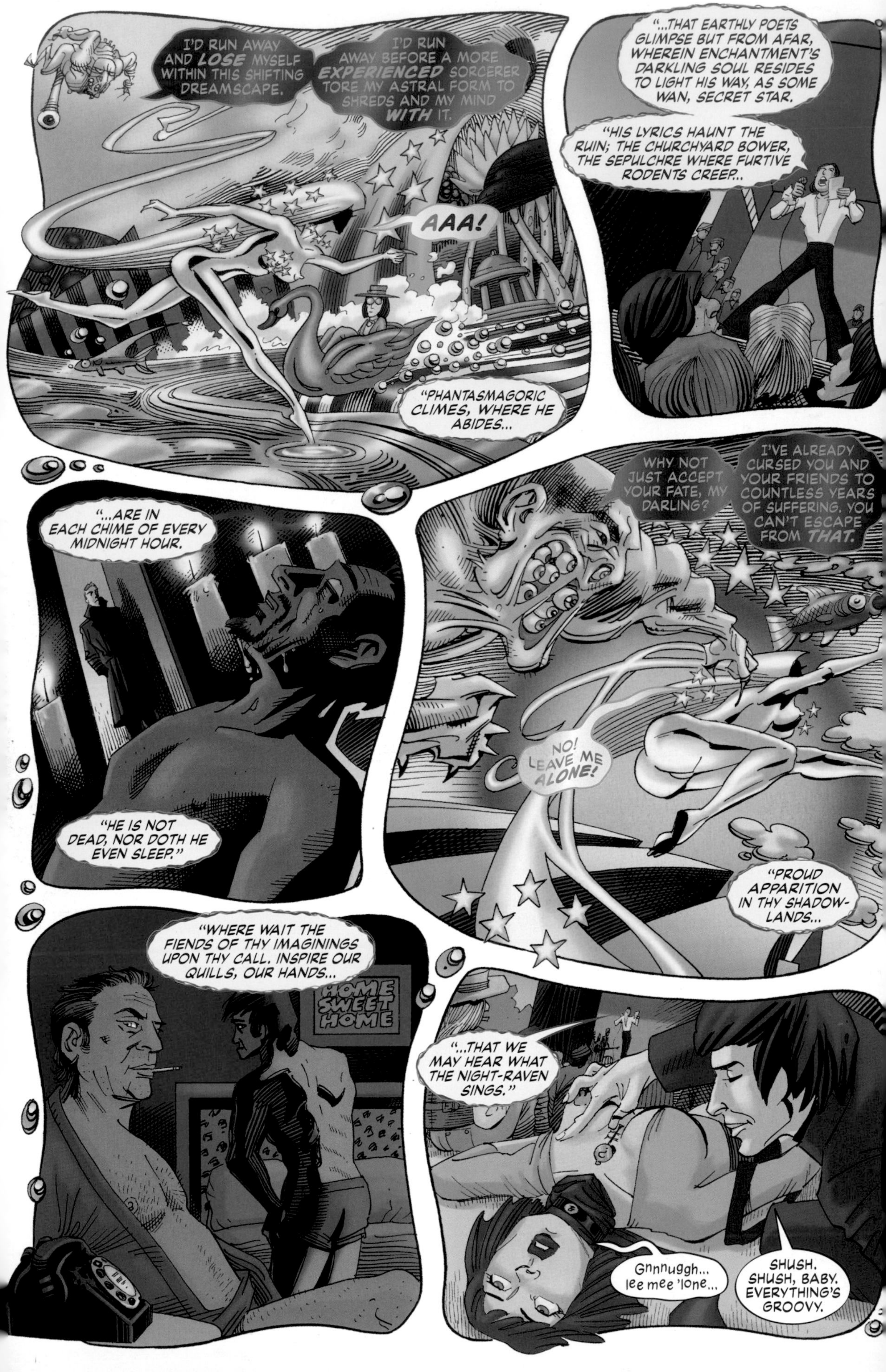
I'D RUN AWAY AND LOSE MYSELF WITHIN THIS SHIFTING DREAMSCAPE.
I'D RUN AWAY BEFORE A MORE EXPERIENCED SORCERER TORE MY ASTRAL FORM TO SHREDS AND MY MIND WITH IT.
AAA!
"PHANTASMAGORIC CLIMES, WHERE HE ABIDES...
"...THAT EARTHLY POETS GLIMPSE BUT FROM AFAR, WHEREIN ENCHANTMENT'S DARKLING SOUL RESIDES TO LIGHT HIS WAY, AS SOME WAN, SECRET STAR.
"HIS LYRICS HAUNT THE RUIN; THE CHURCHYARD BOWER, THE SEPULCHRE WHERE FURTIVE RODENTS CREEP...
"...ARE IN EACH CHIME OF EVERY MIDNIGHT HOUR.
"HE IS NOT DEAD, NOR DOTH HE EVEN SLEEP."
WHY NOT JUST ACCEPT YOUR FATE, MY DARLING?
I'VE ALREADY CURSED YOU AND YOUR FRIENDS TO COUNTLESS YEARS OF SUFFERING. YOU CAN'T ESCAPE FROM THAT.
NO! LEAVE ME ALONE!
"PROUD APPARITION IN THY SHADOW-LANDS...
"WHERE WAIT THE FIENDS OF THY IMAGININGS UPON THY CALL. INSPIRE OUR QUILLS, OUR HANDS...
HOME SWEET HOME
"...THAT WE MAY HEAR WHAT THE NIGHT-RAVEN SINGS."
Gnnnuggh... lee mee 'lone...
SHUSH. SHUSH, BABY. EVERYTHING'S GROOVY.

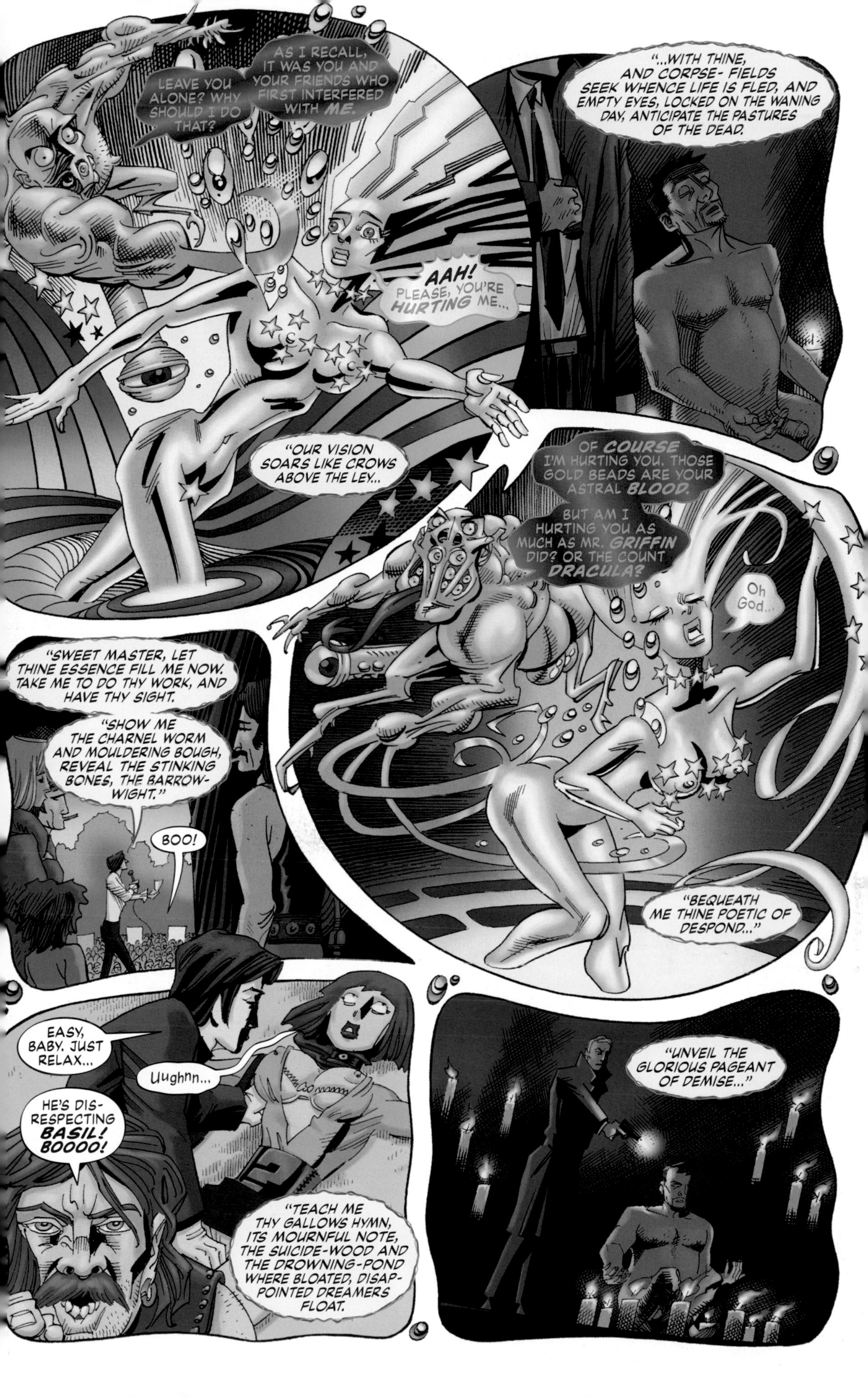

LEAVE YOU ALONE? WHY SHOULD I DO THAT?
AS I RECALL, IT WAS YOU AND YOUR FRIENDS WHO FIRST INTERFERED WITH ME.
AAH! PLEASE, YOU'RE HURTING ME...
"OUR VISION SOARS LIKE CROWS ABOVE THE LEY...
"...WITH THINE, AND CORPSE- FIELDS SEEK WHENCE LIFE IS FLED, AND EMPTY EYES, LOCKED ON THE WANING DAY, ANTICIPATE THE PASTURES OF THE DEAD.
OF COURSE I'M HURTING YOU. THOSE GOLD BEADS ARE YOUR ASTRAL BLOOD.
BUT AM I HURTING YOU AS MUCH AS MR. GRIFFIN DID? OR THE COUNT DRACULA?
Oh God...
"SWEET MASTER, LET THINE ESSENCE FILL ME NOW. TAKE ME TO DO THY WORK, AND HAVE THY SIGHT.
"SHOW ME THE CHARNEL WORM AND MOULDERING BOUGH, REVEAL THE STINKING BONES, THE BARROW-WIGHT."
BOO!
"BEQUEATH ME THINE POETIC OF DESPOND..."
EASY, BABY. JUST RELAX...
Ughhn...
HE'S DIS-RESPECTING BASIL! BOOOO!
"TEACH ME THY GALLOWS HYMN, ITS MOURNFUL NOTE, THE SUICIDE-WOOD AND THE DROWNING-POND WHERE BLOATED, DISAP-POINTED DREAMERS FLOAT.
"UNVEIL THE GLORIOUS PAGEANT OF DEMISE..."

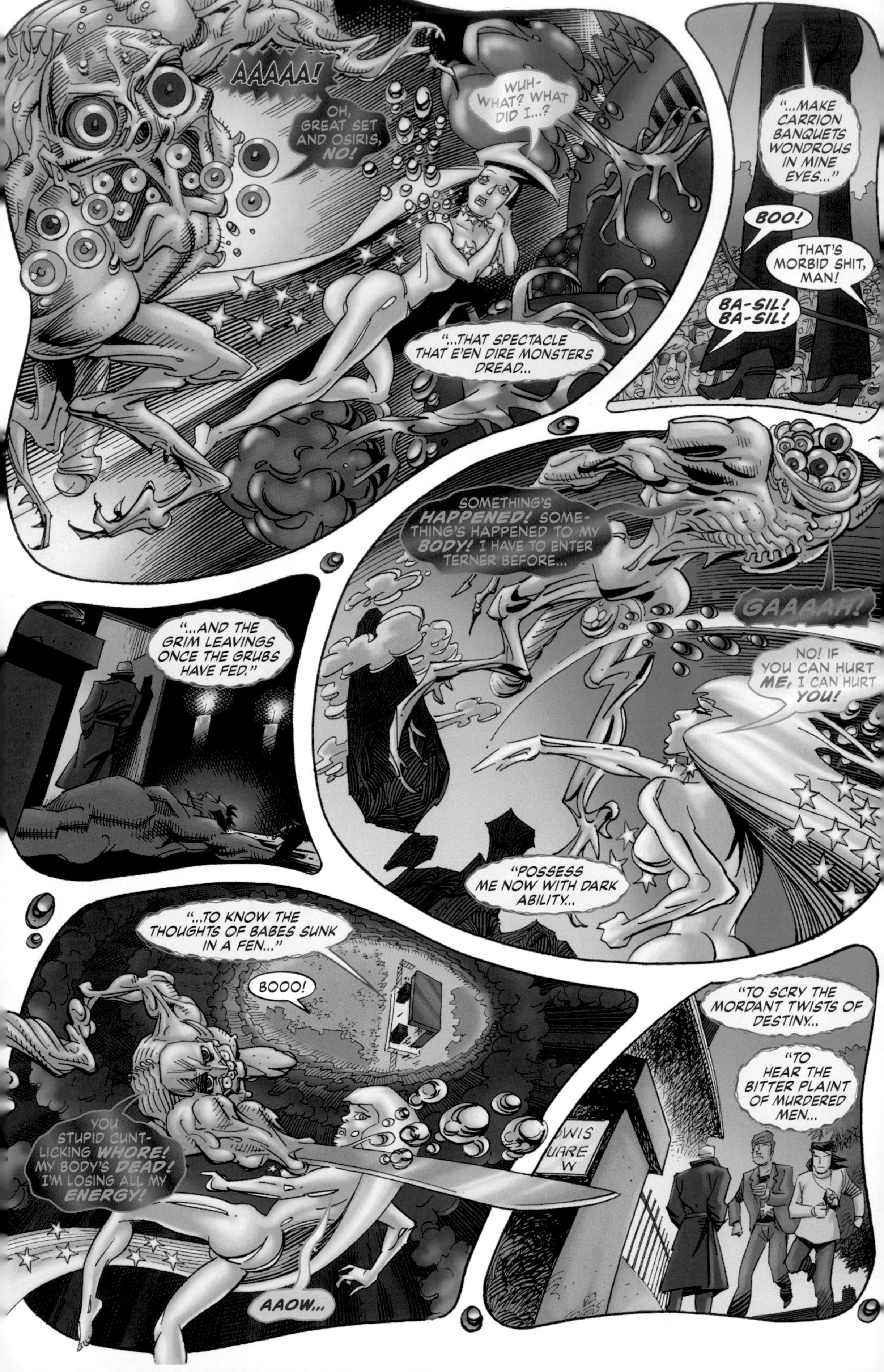
AAAAA!
OH, GREAT SET AND OSIRIS, NO!
WUH-WHAT? WHAT DID I...?
"...THAT SPECTACLE THAT E'EN DIRE MONSTERS DREAD...
"...MAKE CARRION BANQUETS WONDROUS IN MINE EYES..."
BOO!
THAT'S MORBID SHIT, MAN!
BA-SIL! BA-SIL!
"...AND THE GRIM LEAVINGS ONCE THE GRUBS HAVE FED."
SOMETHING'S HAPPENED! SOMETHING'S HAPPENED TO MY BODY! I HAVE TO ENTER TERNER BEFORE...
GAAAAH!
NO! IF YOU CAN HURT ME, I CAN HURT YOU!
"POSSESS ME NOW WITH DARK ABILITY...
"...TO KNOW THE THOUGHTS OF BABES SUNK IN A FEN..."
BOOO!
YOU STUPID CUNT-LICKING WHORE! MY BODY'S DEAD! I'M LOSING ALL MY ENERGY!
AAOW...
"TO SCRY THE MORDANT TWISTS OF DESTINY...
"TO HEAR THE BITTER PLAINT OF MURDERED MEN...

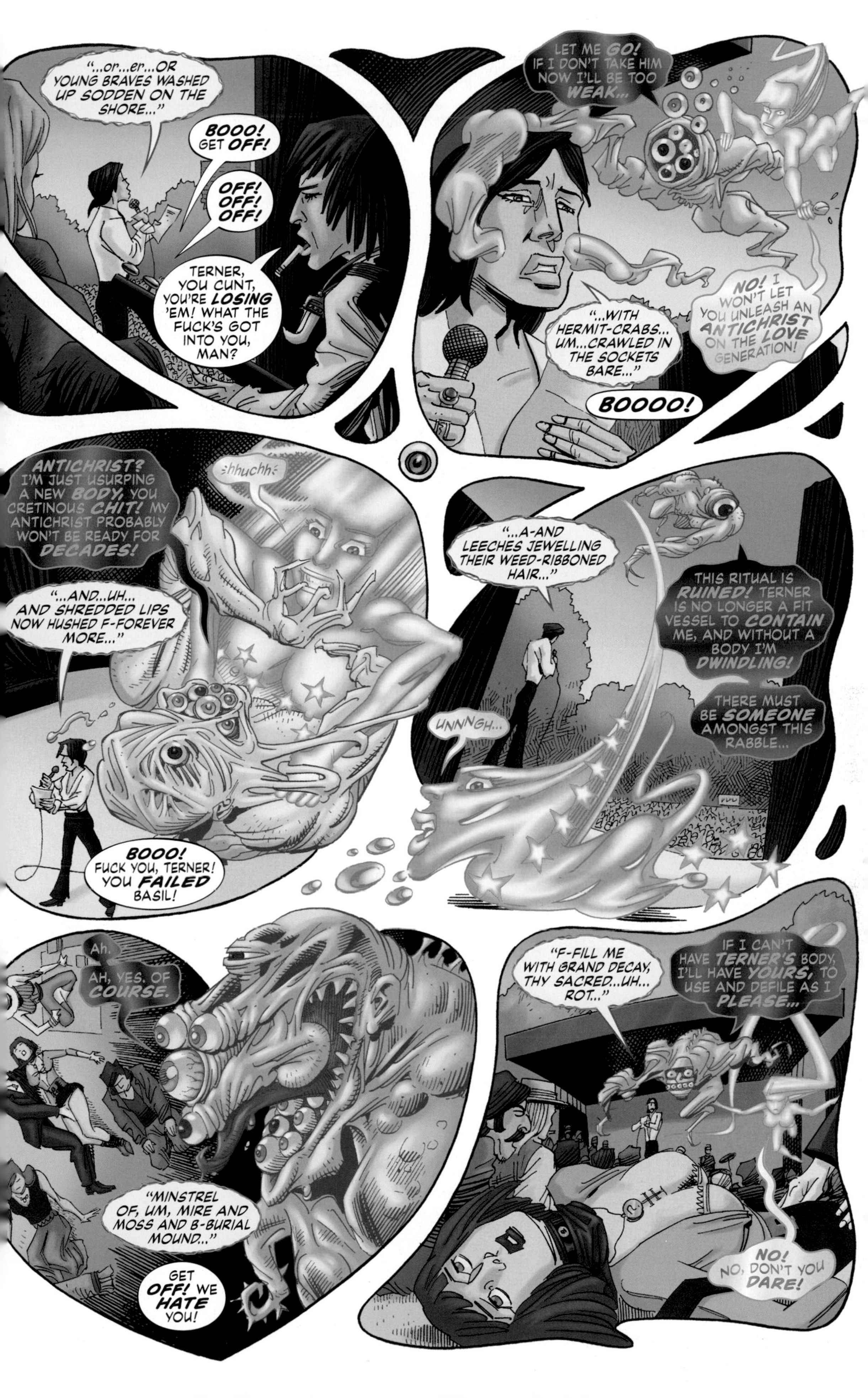
"...or...er...OR YOUNG BRAVES WASHED UP SODDEN ON THE SHORE..."
BOOO! GET OFF!
OFF! OFF! OFF!
TERNER, YOU CUNT, YOU'RE LOSING 'EM! WHAT THE FUCK'S GOT INTO YOU, MAN?
LET ME GO! IF I DON'T TAKE HIM NOW I'LL BE TOO WEAK...
"...WITH HERMIT-CRABS... UM...CRAWLED IN THE SOCKETS BARE..."
NO! I WON'T LET YOU UNLEASH AN ANTICHRIST ON THE LOVE GENERATION!
BOOOO!
ANTICHRIST? I'M JUST USURPING A NEW BODY, YOU CRETINOUS CHIT! MY ANTICHRIST PROBABLY WON'T BE READY FOR DECADES!
hhuchh
"...AND...UH... AND SHREDDED LIPS NOW HUSHED F-FOREVER MORE..."
BOOO! FUCK YOU, TERNER! YOU FAILED BASIL!
"...A-AND LEECHES JEWELLING THEIR WEED-RIBBONED HAIR..."
THIS RITUAL IS RUINED! TERNER IS NO LONGER A FIT VESSEL TO CONTAIN ME, AND WITHOUT A BODY I'M DWINDLING!
THERE MUST BE SOMEONE AMONGST THIS RABBLE...
UNNNGH...
Ah.
AH, YES. OF COURSE.
"MINSTREL OF, UM, MIRE AND MOSS AND B-BURIAL MOUND..."
GET OFF! WE HATE YOU!
"F-FILL ME WITH GRAND DECAY, THY SACRED...UH... ROT..."
IF I CAN'T HAVE TERNER'S BODY, I'LL HAVE YOURS, TO USE AND DEFILE AS I PLEASE...
NO! NO, DON'T YOU DARE!

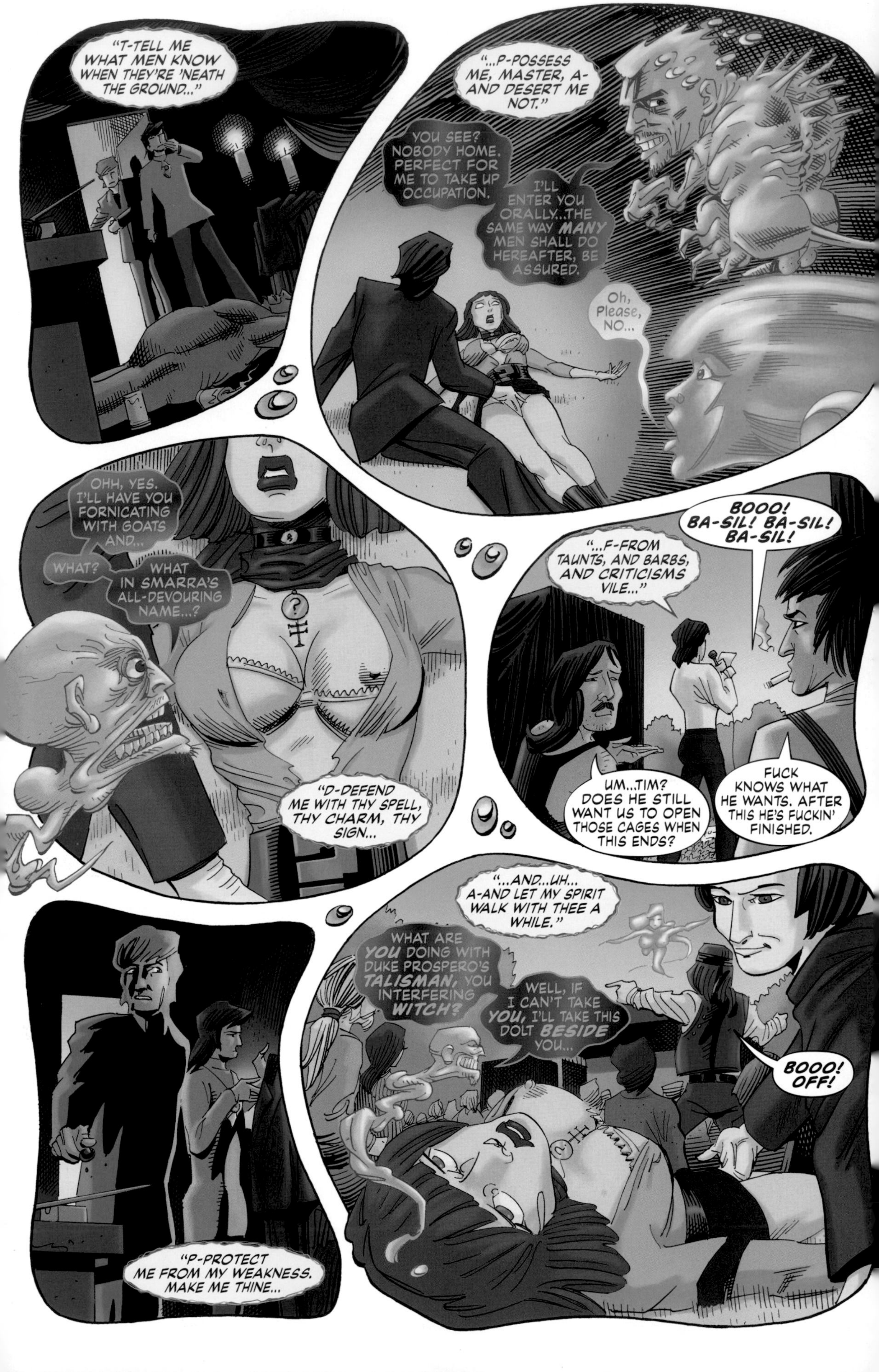
"T-TELL ME WHAT MEN KNOW WHEN THEY'RE 'NEATH THE GROUND..."
"...P-POSSESS ME, MASTER, A-AND DESERT ME NOT."
YOU SEE? NOBODY HOME. PERFECT FOR ME TO TAKE UP OCCUPATION.
I'LL ENTER YOU ORALLY...THE SAME WAY MANY MEN SHALL DO HEREAFTER, BE ASSURED.
Oh, Please, NO...
OHH, YES. I'LL HAVE YOU FORNICATING WITH GOATS AND...
WHAT?
WHAT IN SMARRA'S ALL-DEVOURING NAME...?
"D-DEFEND ME WITH THY SPELL, THY CHARM, THY SIGN...
"...F-FROM TAUNTS, AND BARBS, AND CRITICISMS VILE..."
BOOO! BA-SIL! BA-SIL! BA-SIL!
UM...TIM? DOES HE STILL WANT US TO OPEN THOSE CAGES WHEN THIS ENDS?
FUCK KNOWS WHAT HE WANTS. AFTER THIS HE'S FUCKIN' FINISHED.
"P-PROTECT ME FROM MY WEAKNESS. MAKE ME THINE...
"...AND...UH... A-AND LET MY SPIRIT WALK WITH THEE A WHILE."
WHAT ARE YOU DOING WITH DUKE PROSPERO'S TALISMAN, YOU INTERFERING WITCH?
WELL, IF I CAN'T TAKE YOU, I'LL TAKE THIS DOLT BESIDE YOU...
BOOO! OFF!

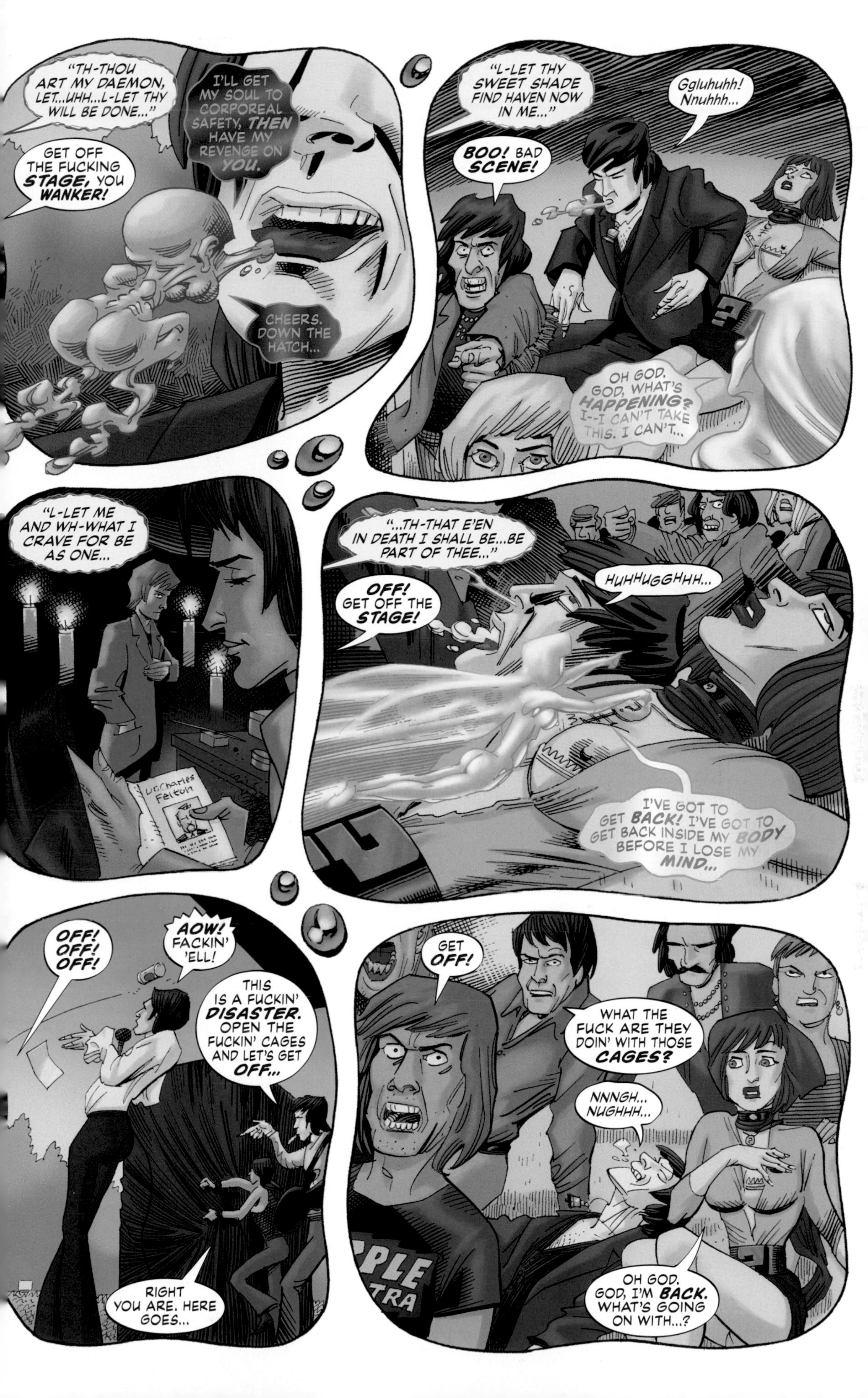
"TH-THOU ART MY DAEMON, LET...UHH...L-LET THY WILL BE DONE..."
I'LL GET MY SOUL TO CORPOREAL SAFETY, THEN HAVE MY REVENGE ON YOU.
GET OFF THE FUCKING STAGE, YOU WANKER!
CHEERS. DOWN THE HATCH...
"L-LET THY SWEET SHADE FIND HAVEN NOW IN ME..."
Ggluhuhh! Nnuhhh...
BOO! BAD SCENE!
OH GOD. GOD, WHAT'S HAPPENING? I--I CAN'T TAKE THIS. I CAN'T...
"L-LET ME AND WH-WHAT I CRAVE FOR BE AS ONE...
"...TH-THAT E'EN IN DEATH I SHALL BE...BE PART OF THEE..."
HUHHUGGHHH...
OFF! GET OFF THE STAGE!
I'VE GOT TO GET BACK! I'VE GOT TO GET BACK INSIDE MY BODY BEFORE I LOSE MY MIND...
OFF! OFF! OFF!
AOW! FACKIN' 'ELL!
THIS IS A FUCKIN' DISASTER. OPEN THE FUCKIN' CAGES AND LET'S GET OFF...
RIGHT YOU ARE. HERE GOES...
GET OFF!
WHAT THE FUCK ARE THEY DOIN' WITH THOSE CAGES?
NNNGH... NUGHHH...
OH GOD. GOD, I'M BACK. WHAT'S GOING ON WITH...?

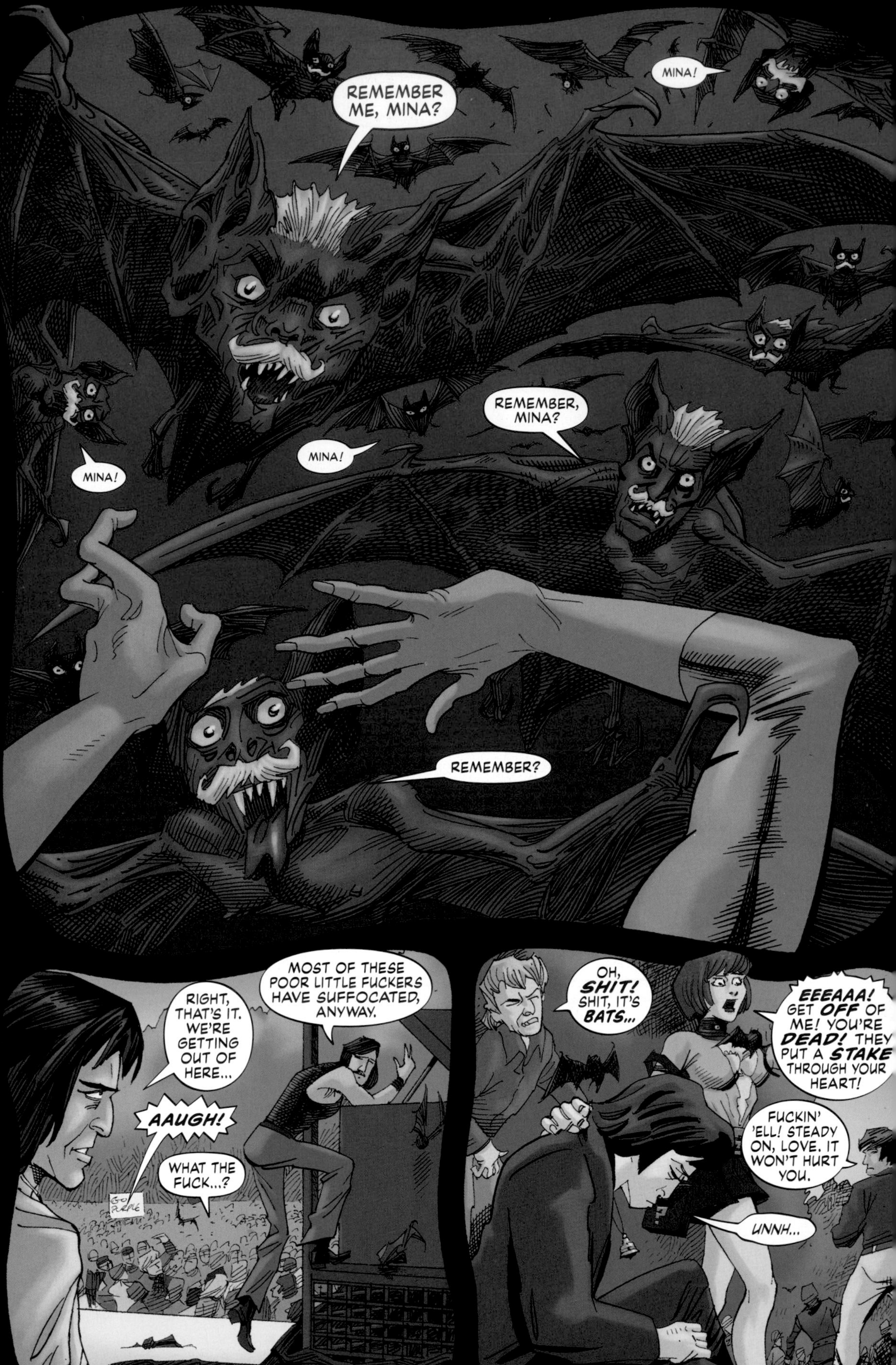
REMEMBER ME, MINA?
MINA!
MINA!
MINA!
REMEMBER, MINA?
REMEMBER?
RIGHT, THAT'S IT. WE'RE GETTING OUT OF HERE...
MOST OF THESE POOR LITTLE FUCKERS HAVE SUFFOCATED, ANYWAY.
AAUGH!
WHAT THE FUCK...?
OH, SHIT! SHIT, IT'S BATS...
EEEAAA! GET OFF OF ME! YOU'RE DEAD! THEY PUT A STAKE THROUGH YOUR HEART!
FUCKIN' 'ELL! STEADY ON, LOVE. IT WON'T HURT YOU.
UNNH...

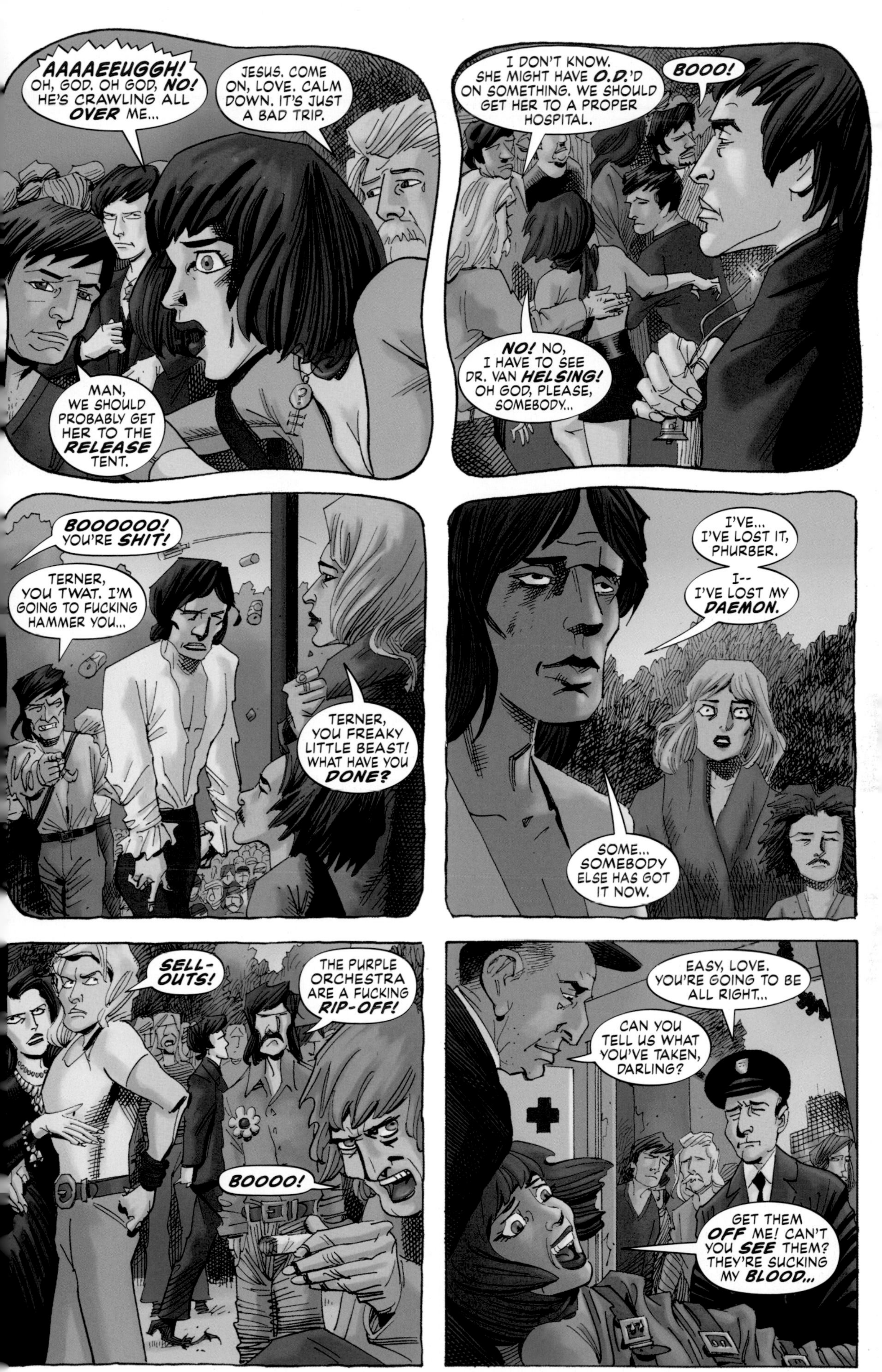
AAAAEEUGGH! OH, GOD. OH GOD, NO! HE'S CRAWLING ALL OVER ME...
JESUS. COME ON, LOVE. CALM DOWN. IT'S JUST A BAD TRIP.
MAN, WE SHOULD PROBABLY GET HER TO THE RELEASE TENT.
I DON'T KNOW. SHE MIGHT HAVE O.D.'D ON SOMETHING. WE SHOULD GET HER TO A PROPER HOSPITAL.
BOOO!
NO! NO, I HAVE TO SEE DR. VAN HELSING! OH GOD, PLEASE, SOMEBODY...
BOOOOOO! YOU'RE SHIT!
TERNER, YOU TWAT. I'M GOING TO FUCKING HAMMER YOU...
TERNER, YOU FREAKY LITTLE BEAST! WHAT HAVE YOU DONE?
I'VE... I'VE LOST IT, PHURBER.
I-- I'VE LOST MY DAEMON.
SOME... SOMEBODY ELSE HAS GOT IT NOW.
SELL-OUTS!
THE PURPLE ORCHESTRA ARE A FUCKING RIP-OFF!
BOOOO!
EASY, LOVE. YOU'RE GOING TO BE ALL RIGHT...
CAN YOU TELL US WHAT YOU'VE TAKEN, DARLING?
GET THEM OFF ME! CAN'T YOU SEE THEM? THEY'RE SUCKING MY BLOOD...

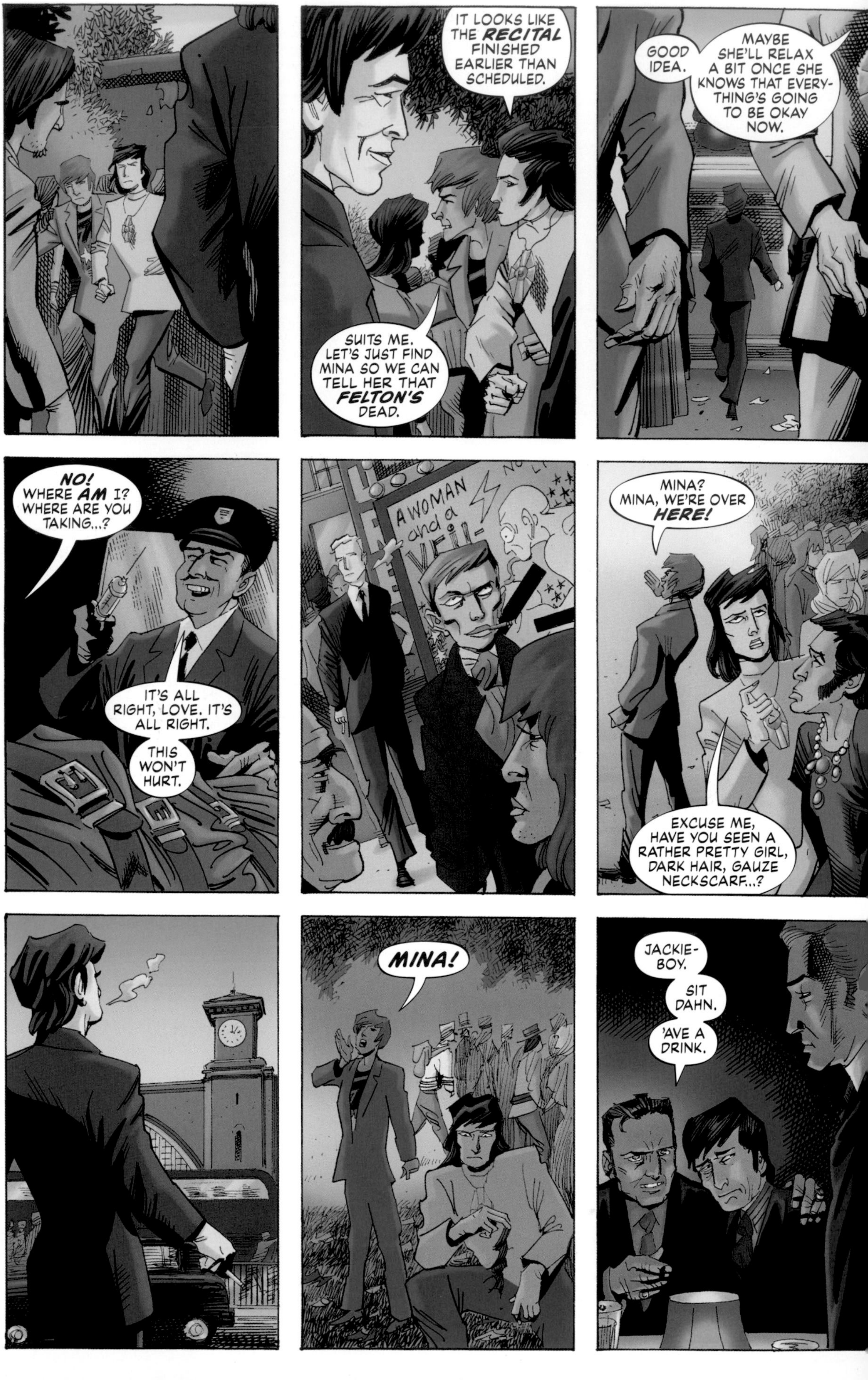
IT LOOKS LIKE THE RECITAL FINISHED EARLIER THAN SCHEDULED.
SUITS ME. LET'S JUST FIND MINA SO WE CAN TELL HER THAT FELTON'S DEAD.
GOOD IDEA.
MAYBE SHE'LL RELAX A BIT ONCE SHE KNOWS THAT EVERY-THING'S GOING TO BE OKAY NOW.
NO! WHERE AM I? WHERE ARE YOU TAKING...?
IT'S ALL RIGHT, LOVE. IT'S ALL RIGHT.
THIS WON'T HURT.
A WOMAN and a VEIL
MINA? MINA, WE'RE OVER HERE!
EXCUSE ME, HAVE YOU SEEN A RATHER PRETTY GIRL, DARK HAIR, GAUZE NECKSCARF...?
MINA!
JACKIE-BOY.
SIT DAHN.
'AVE A DRINK.

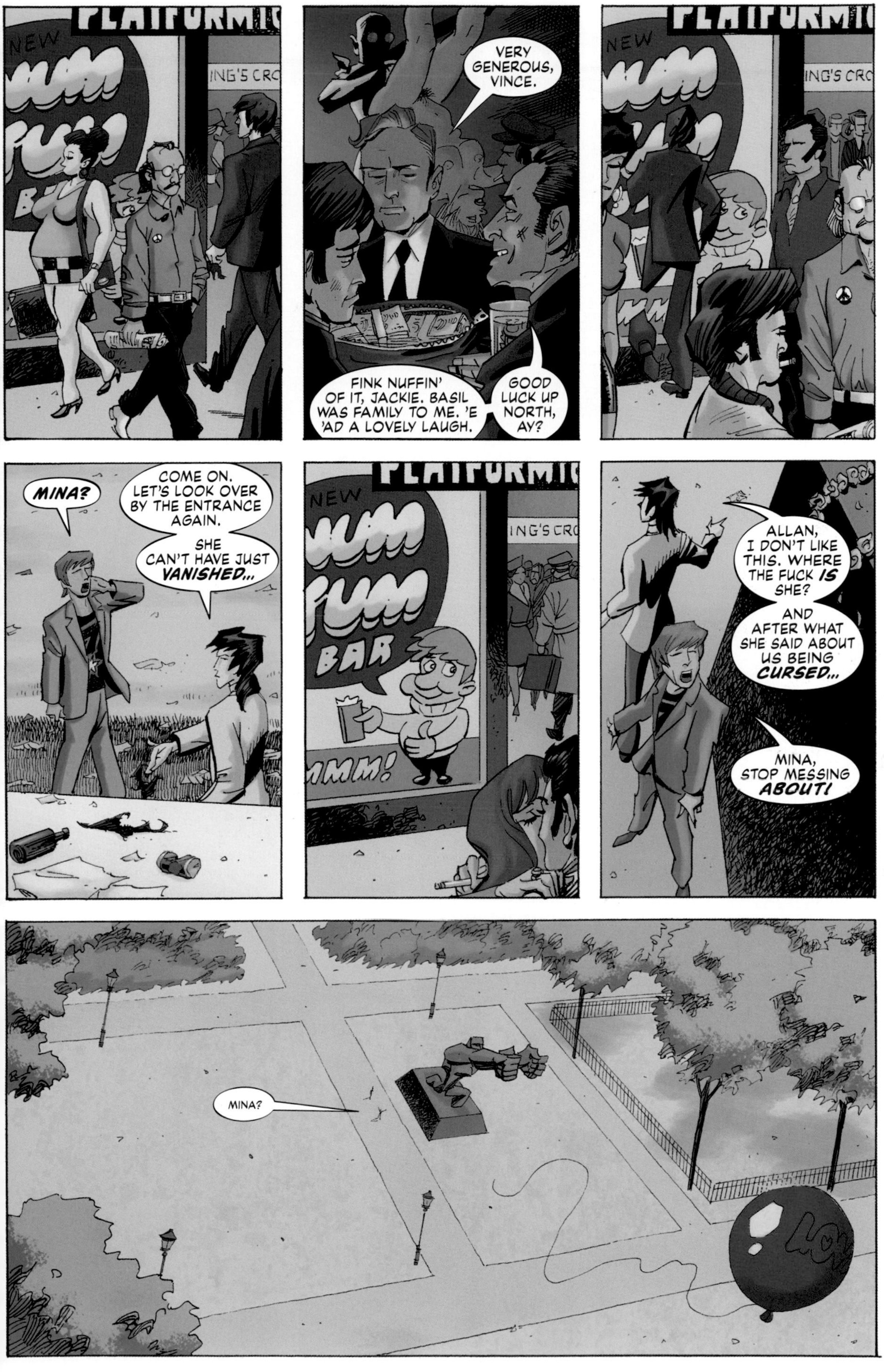

PLATFORMIC
NEW
ING'S CRO
VERY GENEROUS, VINCE.
FINK NUFFIN' OF IT, JACKIE. BASIL WAS FAMILY TO ME. 'E 'AD A LOVELY LAUGH.
GOOD LUCK UP NORTH, AY?
MINA?
COME ON. LET'S LOOK OVER BY THE ENTRANCE AGAIN.
SHE CAN'T HAVE JUST VANISHED...
BAR
MMM!
ALLAN, I DON'T LIKE THIS. WHERE THE FUCK IS SHE?
AND AFTER WHAT SHE SAID ABOUT US BEING CURSED...
MINA, STOP MESSING ABOUT!
MINA?

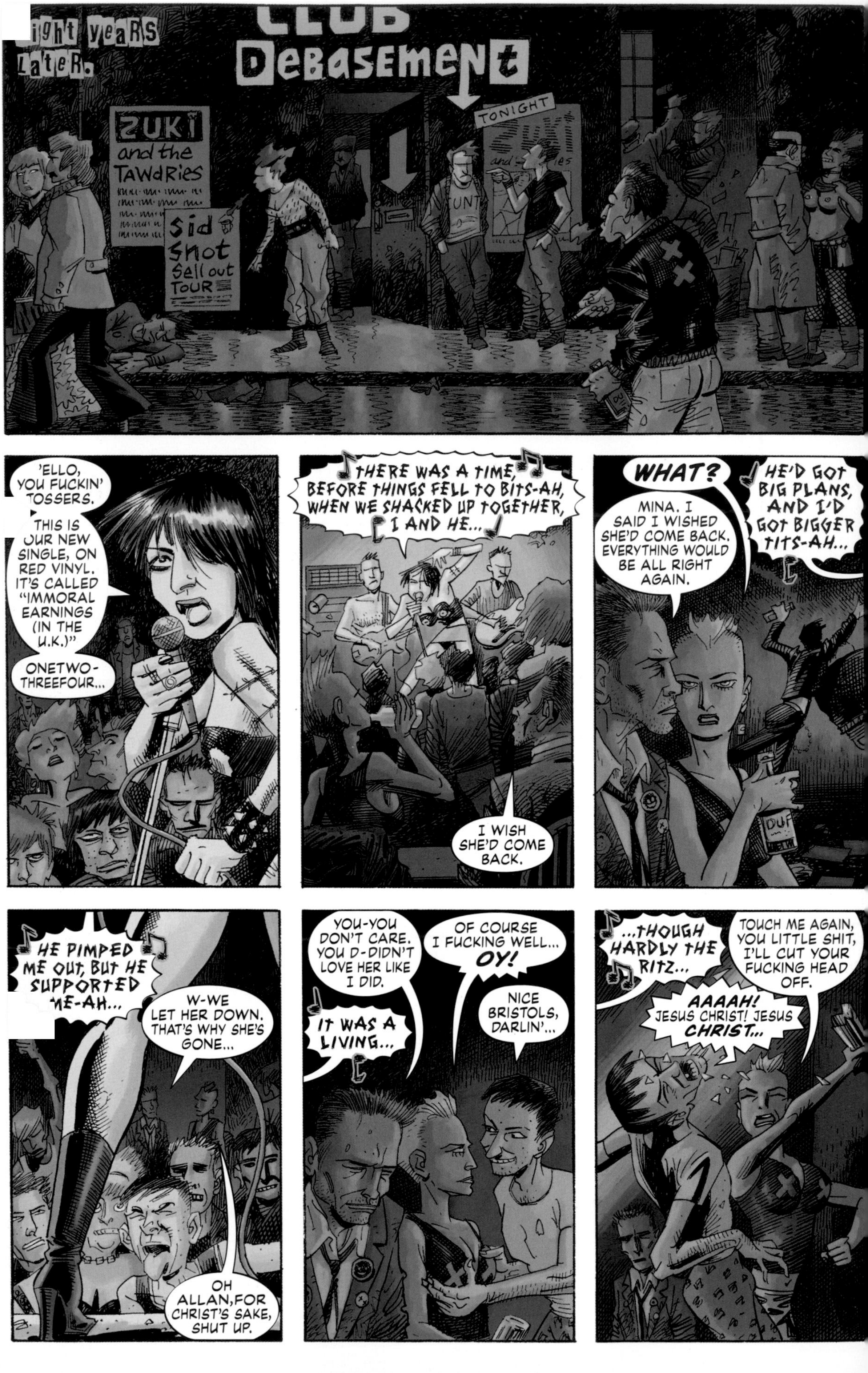

ight years Later.
CLUB Debasement
ZUKI and the TAWDRIES
Sid Snot Sell out TOUR
TONIGHT
'ELLO, YOU FUCKIN' TOSSERS.
THIS IS OUR NEW SINGLE, ON RED VINYL. IT'S CALLED "IMMORAL EARNINGS (IN THE U.K.)"
ONETWO-THREEFOUR...
THERE WAS A TIME, BEFORE THINGS FELL TO BITS-AH, WHEN WE SHACKED UP TOGETHER, I AND HE...
I WISH SHE'D COME BACK.
WHAT?
MINA. I SAID I WISHED SHE'D COME BACK. EVERYTHING WOULD BE ALL RIGHT AGAIN.
HE'D GOT BIG PLANS, AND I'D GOT BIGGER TITS-AH...
HE PIMPED ME OUT, BUT HE SUPPORTED ME-AH...
W-WE LET HER DOWN. THAT'S WHY SHE'S GONE...
OH ALLAN, FOR CHRIST'S SAKE, SHUT UP.
YOU-YOU DON'T CARE. YOU D-DIDN'T LOVE HER LIKE I DID.
OF COURSE I FUCKING WELL... OY!
IT WAS A LIVING...
NICE BRISTOLS, DARLIN'...
...THOUGH HARDLY THE RITZ...
TOUCH ME AGAIN, YOU LITTLE SHIT, I'LL CUT YOUR FUCKING HEAD OFF.
AAAAH! JESUS CHRIST! JESUS CHRIST...

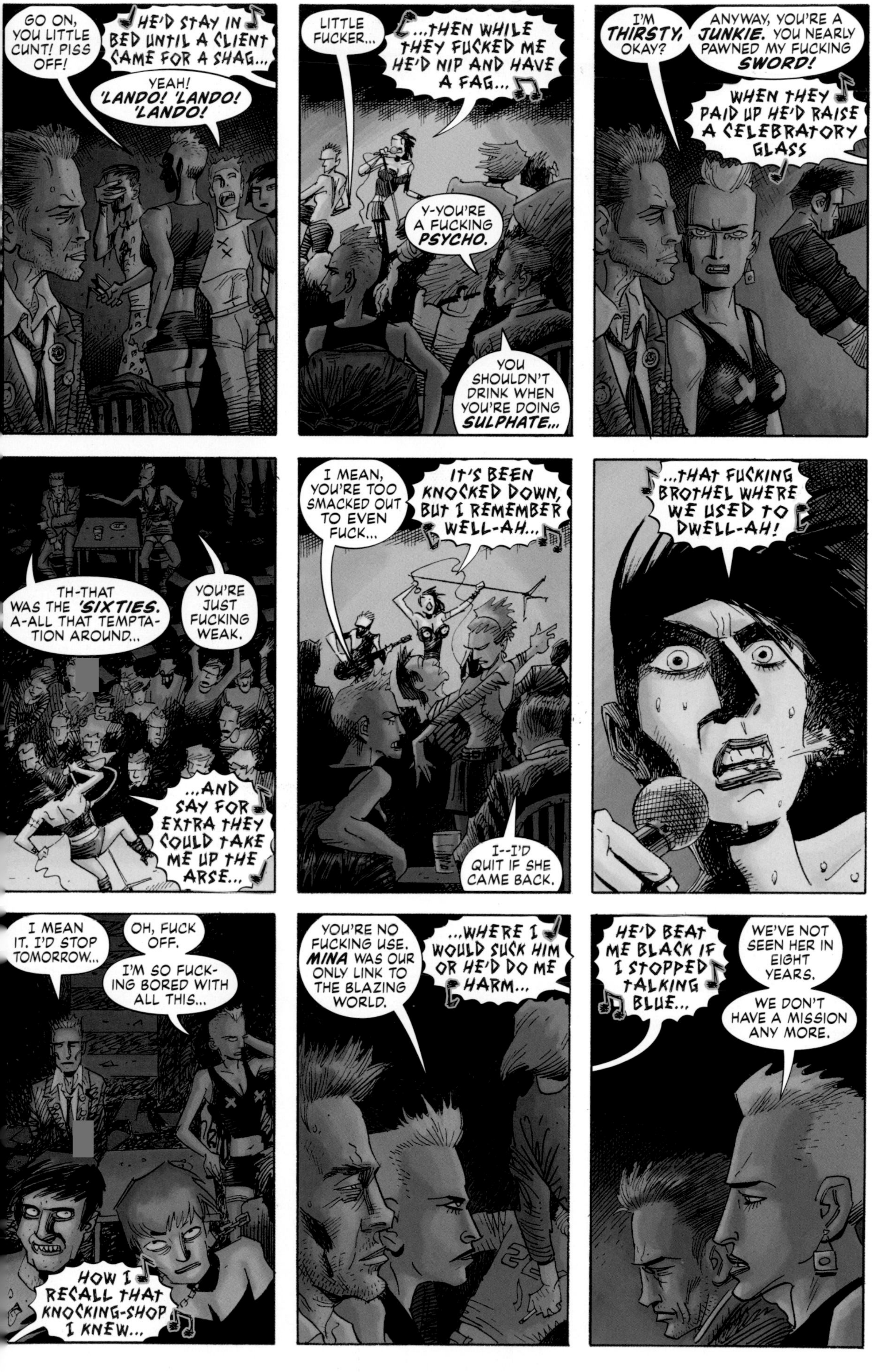
GO ON, YOU LITTLE CUNT! PISS OFF!
HE'D STAY IN BED UNTIL A CLIENT CAME FOR A SHAG...
YEAH! 'LANDO! 'LANDO! 'LANDO!
LITTLE FUCKER...
...THEN WHILE THEY FUCKED ME HE'D NIP AND HAVE A FAG...
Y-YOU'RE A FUCKING PSYCHO.
YOU SHOULDN'T DRINK WHEN YOU'RE DOING SULPHATE...
I'M THIRSTY, OKAY?
ANYWAY, YOU'RE A JUNKIE. YOU NEARLY PAWNED MY FUCKING SWORD!
WHEN THEY PAID UP HE'D RAISE A CELEBRATORY GLASS
TH-THAT WAS THE 'SIXTIES. A-ALL THAT TEMPTATION AROUND...
YOU'RE JUST FUCKING WEAK.
...AND SAY FOR EXTRA THEY COULD TAKE ME UP THE ARSE...
I MEAN, YOU'RE TOO SMACKED OUT TO EVEN FUCK...
IT'S BEEN KNOCKED DOWN, BUT I REMEMBER WELL-AH...
I--I'D QUIT IF SHE CAME BACK.
...THAT FUCKING BROTHEL WHERE WE USED TO DWELL-AH!
I MEAN IT. I'D STOP TOMORROW...
OH, FUCK OFF.
I'M SO FUCKING BORED WITH ALL THIS...
HOW I RECALL THAT KNOCKING-SHOP I KNEW...
YOU'RE NO FUCKING USE. MINA WAS OUR ONLY LINK TO THE BLAZING WORLD.
...WHERE I WOULD SUCK HIM OR HE'D DO ME HARM...
HE'D BEAT ME BLACK IF I STOPPED TALKING BLUE...
WE'VE NOT SEEN HER IN EIGHT YEARS.
WE DON'T HAVE A MISSION ANY MORE.

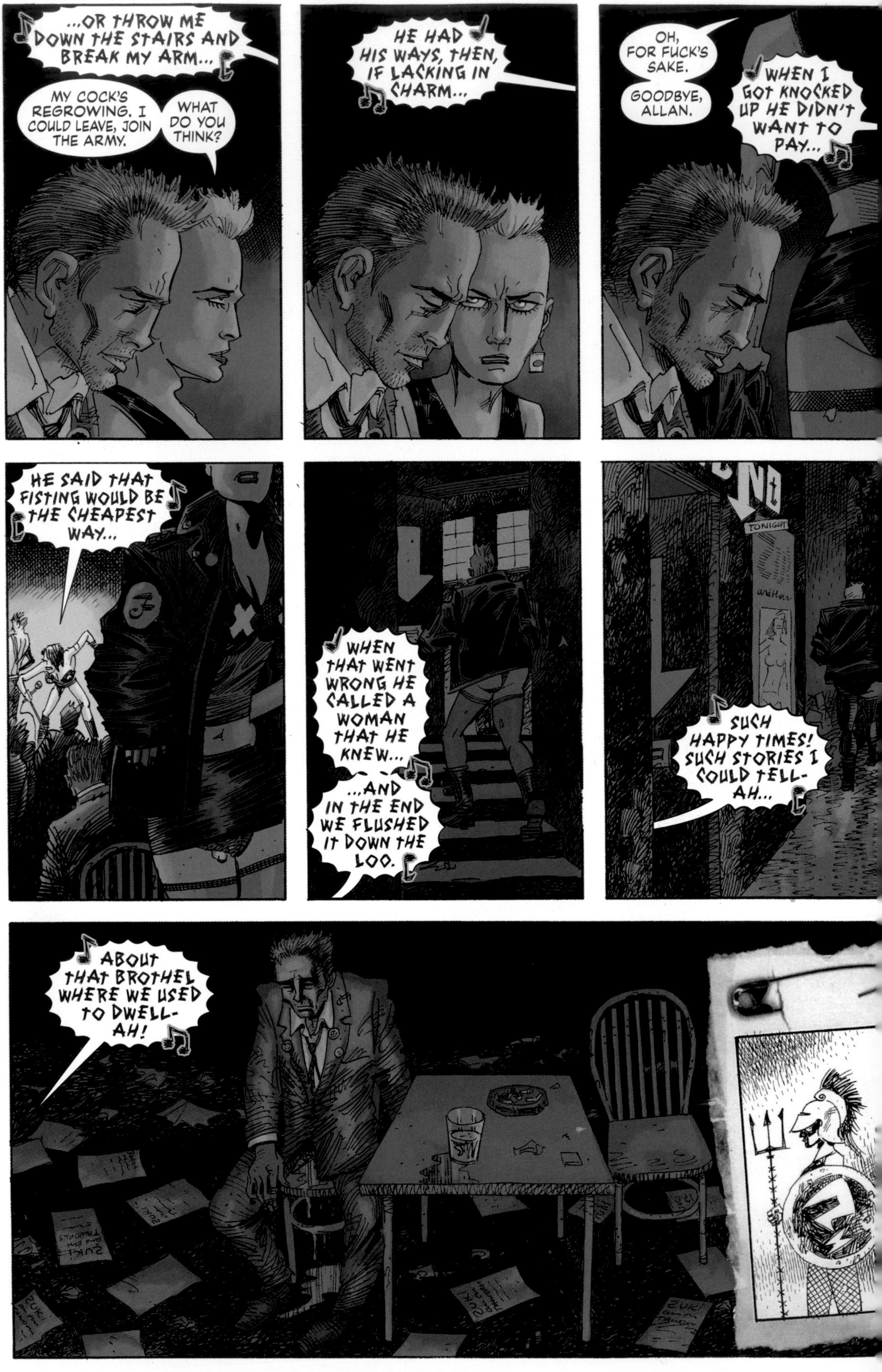
...OR THROW ME DOWN THE STAIRS AND BREAK MY ARM...
MY COCK'S REGROWING. I COULD LEAVE, JOIN THE ARMY.
WHAT DO YOU THINK?
HE HAD HIS WAYS, THEN, IF LACKING IN CHARM...
OH, FOR FUCK'S SAKE.
GOODBYE, ALLAN.
WHEN I GOT KNOCKED UP HE DIDN'T WANT TO PAY...
HE SAID THAT FISTING WOULD BE THE CHEAPEST WAY...
WHEN THAT WENT WRONG HE CALLED A WOMAN THAT HE KNEW...
...AND IN THE END WE FLUSHED IT DOWN THE LOO.
TONIGHT
SUCH HAPPY TIMES! SUCH STORIES I COULD TELL-AH...
ABOUT THAT BROTHEL WHERE WE USED TO DWELL-AH!

MINIONS OF THE MOON
by John Thomas

(Originally serialised in *Lewd Worlds Science Fiction*, Ed. James Colvin, 183-185, 1969.)

Chapter Two: The Distance From Tranquility

A tiny paper figure painstakingly cut from a jam-jar label and spread with adhesive paste is lodged unnoticed, stuck fast in the patient's straggly hair as they attempt to use the blunted plastic scissors despite fingers rendered numb and clumsy by repeated medication. Labouring obsessively on their collage, the patient has reduced all consciousness into a focused bead of present that refuses to acknowledge any past or future and therefore is spared even such basic existential questions as 'Where am I', much less 'How long have I been here?'

The clinic's proprietor, a woman doctor with what seem aggressively large breasts, stands at the patient's elbow and insists they take the first in that evening's procession of confounding medicines. The pill, dispersible in water, is served up in a small plastic cup. The patient gazes dully into this receptacle while the persistent doctor urges them to drink it down.

The small white tablet is disintegrating, fizzing into nothingness on its circumference and losing definition in the increasingly foggy liquid that surrounds it. It resembles the full moon in miniature, seen through obscuring cloud.

The Galley-wag, Black Matter Cosmos, circa 1896: Escape from Nowhere

As viewed by terrestrial eyes, the universe's fireball-dusted skin was all of it. The nine parts of its substance that were unaccounted for, its flesh and bones, remained concealed beneath this glittering epidermis. Thus invisible to human scrutiny, the core of the continuum existed as an unimaginably massive trans-galactic mountain range, a strangely-contoured topographic shape that hung unseen in stupefying folds millions of light-years deep. This was effectively the whole of spacetime, with the luminosities and nebulae known to mankind only cake-decorations on its surface.

Jackboy Sixty was, of course, not his true name… this was in actuality a finely modulated deep subsonic tone…but only a convenience bestowed on him by the pink masters, to distinguish him from all the other Jackboys that made up the blackboat's cargo. The pink masters had their origins in the star-pastures that were rumoured to exist upon those narrow margins of the cosmos said to somehow lie beyond the confines of this endless baryonic territory, this dark immensity that was the bulk of everything. In the phonetic language of

the masters…Jackboy Sixty had at first not recognised the bursts of separate, randomly pitched sounds as language but was learning rapidly in the characteristic manner of his kind…the vast atomic light that the pink humanoids originated from was known as 'Olodoria' or something similar, though some years later he would learn that in terrestrial astronomies it was referred to as 'Antares.' Here, then, was the home-world that had launched the blackboats into the dark guts of the continuum to trawl for sentient life as a commodity; as units to be sold upon the slave-blocks of the universe's flimsy, fiery surface.

The resourceful Jackboy, taken as an infant from his native planetoid in the night-system known as the Great Erebus Array, had realised some fifteen years into his captivity that the electro-shackle on his ankle had malfunctioned and could be removed during the sanctioned hours of sleep without alerting the pink masters. From that point on, whenever opportunity arose he'd quietly leave his fellow victims slumbering at their oars and make his way through the enormous galley's lightless innards to a disused storage hold that he'd discovered, empty and apparently unvisited due to the dangerously weak condition of the slave-ship's hull at this point, previously damaged by a hurtling blackball meteor and only partially repaired. For decades he had laboured in this secret chamber, navigating its dark contours by the bounce-back from his deep bass growl and handling work-tools by engulfing them in the soft substance of the pads with which his blunt arms terminated, until finally his magnificent folly was completed.

The escape craft nestled in a cradle of supporting struts, its all-important particle-sack hanging in limp folds across the vessel's upper surface. Jackboy Sixty knew that once he started the inflation process he'd have only moments before the tremendous loss of anti-particles leeched from the blackboat's drive was noticed, but knew also that he had no other option. Cranking round the wheel with a determined grunt he opened the gluino-valves and watched with satisfaction as the monstrous anti-matter bladder went into its primary then secondary expansion phases.

As he'd known it would, the bulkhead door of the abandoned cargo-hold abruptly hurtled inward on explosive bolts and two of the pink masters rushed into the chamber, jabbering in agitation. Jackboy Sixty recognised the taller of the pair as his own unit's whip-boss, a sadistic younger male named Kelger Vo, and knew that dozens of the compound-eyed and cerise-coloured slavers would be racing to assist their colleagues at that very moment. There would not be time for niceties.

The more diminutive of the two masters, a plump female that the naked and perspiring Jackboy thought was known as Vinvir Gu, had already pulled her control-wand from its holster and was levelling its tight beam of mind-scrambling micro-radiation at his over-sized and shaggy head. He whistled a shrill burst of hyper-sound, disintegrating the control-wand's crystal bulb, and then turned his attentions upon Kelger Vo. The wiry slaver, with his legs displayed unappetisingly by his short trousers, had realised the inefficacy of his comrade's control wand and was instead bringing out a much more daunting sonic weapon, this being the paralysing chime that would disrupt a nervous system's motor impulses and leave the target frozen in its tracks. Regretfully compressing his huge larynx, Jackboy Sixty first expressed a standing interference wave to cancel the vibrations of the gong-like apparatus and then went on to reduce both of the screaming galley-masters to flat puddles of undifferentiated protoplasm. By now, reinforcements were erupting through the chamber door with horror and surprise apparent in their wide, slack mouths and multi-faceted insectile eyes.

Stepping up to his makeshift vessel's steering wheel, he shouted down the cargo-hold's already weakened hull and was propelled out in a spore-burst of exploded debris and pink, twitching slaver bodies into the vast, unalleviated blackness of the baryonic cosmos. Navigating inexactly by the swelling thunder of approaching gravities or the dull roar of X-rays, Jackboy Sixty rode the howling dark out to its limits at velocities of such colossal magnitude that slowing down seemed an unlikelihood and stopping an impos-sibility. Bare-skinned and bellowing he clung tight to the rigging as his craft burst through into the rind of lights and galaxies, the shallow foam of spectacle that effervesced on the meniscus of the universe's giant midnight heart. Roaring at frequencies that stopped the dance of atoms and plunged temperatures towards a zero that was all but absolute, he fell into the blinding swirl of suns and worlds and magnetars. Nude and impossible in his fragmenting vehicle, he plummeted towards delirious adventure.

Mina, the Limbus of the Moon, 1964: Glass Shirts and Goose-Bones

Somewhere behind her she could hear the high-pitched chatter, all in Dutch, of the two giggling wooden automata as they assisted their intrepid captain with the mooring of The Rose of Nowhere there amongst the jagged molar rocks and grey dust-oceans of the moon. Picking her way carefully across the crunch and crumble of the powdery surface, Mina once again turned over in her tirelessly investigative mind the fact that she was breathing on the airless lunar satellite without respiratory apparatus; had in fact been breathing thus unaided on the deck of their improbable conveyance throughout the long trip from Earth. She was constructing a hypothesis based on the ancient anecdotal evidence of Baron Munchausen, apparently borne to the moon in a terrific waterspout. A waterspout, in Mina's understanding, was what hap-pened when tornados touched upon the sea, and she conjectured an immense tornado that might stretch its whirling tunnel of tormented air across the empty void of space between her planet and its silvery companion.

That would not, of course, explain how there could be a stable atmospheric bubble clinging to the lunar landscape (where she thought that there was insuffi-cient gravity for this to be achievable) nor yet how this precarious atmosphere might be replenished given the conspicuous lack of vegetation. She was still consider-ing this seemingly intractable conundrum some few moments later when the toe of her black leather boot connected with an object partly buried in the finely-ground precipitate surrounding her. Upon inspection this turned out to be a rusting crown of what looked to be Anglo-Saxon origins, while a short distance further on she came across a single Argyle sock, some ballpoint pens, a wooden doll that might have been Elizabethan and a damaged violin, perhaps a Stradi-varius. With mounting wonderment it dawned upon her that she must be situated in the fabled Limbus of the Moon, where all lost things were rumoured to accumulate. She thought her hypothetical tornado might at least provide a credible scientific means by which this curious displacement was accomplished, but as she traipsed further through the moon-sand with the squeals and answering growls of the Dutch dolls and their esteemed commander fading to inaudibility behind her, she discovered objects that did not appear to make an easy fit with any of her theories.

She found avian skeletons which she identified as those of geese, both wearing perished leather harness-es, and thought that they might be remainders from the fiercely-debated Godwin journey to the moon reputed to have happened long before Professor Cavor's mis-sion, sometime in the late seventeenth century. She had, however, no such likely explanation for what seemed to be two broken halves of a suspiciously large tunic made entirely out of solid glass; for what appeared to be the decomposing head and thorax of a hippopotamus-sized ant, or for the tightly-furled Titanium-white suede of moss that she found cover-ing one of the heftier lunar boulders. These seemed to be things that had originated on the moon rather than items snatched from a terrestrial source by some unproven interplanetary vortex. There were also faint impressions in the dust which she reluctantly conclud-ed were prints made by the bare feet of women.

Lifting up her head she scanned the pearly ribbon of what seemed a far-too-close horizon, noticing the bubbling froths of dome that marked both the Ameri-can and nearby British moon-bases, these settlements endangered by a war between two native lunar species which Mina had been instructed to prevent. Reasoning that the distant sealed environments suggested that the breathable pocket of atmosphere in which she was en-closed did not extend much further she elected to turn back, pulling her leather super-hero cloak about her in the icy climate as she trod through the ash-coloured dunes towards the tethered Rose of Nowhere and her waiting shipmates. It occurred to her that she was walking normally without the weightless, bouncing gait she'd heard described by other lunar voyagers. This tended to confirm her earlier observation that in lunar terms localised atmosphere implied localised gravity, although of course that didn't bring her any closer to an understanding of this baffling phenomenon or how it was supposed to work in scientific terms.

Later, over a frugal and yet filling meal of ra-tions from the hyper-galleon's lockers, Mina and her shipmates did their best to formulate a plan of action. It was finally agreed that while the Galley-wag and his enthusiastic wooden harem would attempt to find out more about the warring native races, Mina would employ breathing equipment and her borrowed helmet of invisibility to more closely investigate the vulner-able terrestrial moon-bases which were threatened by the conflict. This decided, the black-matter buccaneer elected to recite a raucous shanty that described a week spent in what sounded like an ultra-spatial bordello, with which Sarah Jane and Peg clapped happily along.

>   *'On my forst night a boxum humahedroid
> came ter me,
>   With her ninth hole so deep t'were more a
> stringularity...'*

Mina half listened to this listing of increasingly unfathomable and unlikely amorous encounters, usually involving topographically impossible erotic orifices or else sexual positions that could only be attained in higher mathematical dimensions. She mused briefly on a line that rhymed 'unnatural act' with 'tesseract', then turned her wandering attention to a starboard porthole where a clouded turquoise egg that she still found it difficult to think of as the Earth was at that moment slowly setting, all its tragedies and glories swallowed by the moon's bleakly vestigial skyline.

**The Galley-wag & the Frankenstein monster,
Arctic circle, 1896: Babes in Toyland**

He'd plunged through radiance incomprehensible to splinter his escape-craft on the icecaps of the first world that appeared to harbour any atmosphere conducive to survival. Waking in the ribcage wreckage of his crippled vessel, he had found himself sprawling amidst a silent swarm of airborne crystals that appeared to be composed of two parts hydrogen to one part oxygen, this mix existing in a hitherto undocumented frozen state. Shaking his head to clear the grogginess he found that he'd accumulated plump white ridges of the novel substance on the strangely-stiffened locks of his black mane. He also found himself surrounded by observers, stubby little bipeds with napped, yellowish-brown fur and glittering black eyes that at first glance seemed to be made from glass. The creatures, he observed, were clad in uniforms that had the bright extravagance of ceremonial costumes but which, viewed en masse, conveyed a strongly military impression. This impression was confirmed when, having realised that the former Jackboy was now conscious, all the fuzzy-textured beings simultaneously brought up hollow metal tubes which they directed at the new arrival, and which he deduced were some

archaic variety of weapon. He prepared to vent a low, disabling harmonic that he hoped would work on these bizarre bright-matter individuals, but was stayed from doing so by the appearance of a very different and much taller figure in his partly crystal-blinded field of vision.

This late entrant to the drama was a gangly and ectomorphic humanoid clad in what looked to be subdued formal attire surmounted by a grandiose cape of white fur held at the throat by an elaborate gold clasp. Where flesh was visible this was pale and translucent, so that an impression of the bones and musculature at work beneath the soapy skin was made disturbingly apparent. This sartorially splendid apparition gave a languid wave with one blanched hand at which the weapons of the short and furry regiment accompanying him were on the instant lowered. Stooping down so that his waxen and lugubrious countenance was brought into proximity with the escaped slave's own, he murmured a few indecipherable syllables which nonetheless seemed to be uttered in a questioning and sympathetic tone to which the prostrate baryonic mariner could only answer with a non-committal grunt and an ambiguous movement of his disproportionately large black cranium.

Though he discovered he was lapsing in and out of consciousness...presumably he'd greatly underestimated the enormous impact of his landing…in what seemed no time at all he and his incapacitated voidship had been loaded onto separate low, flat wagons raised on huge blades that were pulled by the diminutive militia-animals across the slippery white expanse in which he'd seemingly arrived. After an indeterminable while the towers of an impressive architectural structure became visible through the obscuring whirl of frozen crystals, a great rearing palace built from simple shapes…blocks, pillars, arches…that were painted in a motley of bright primary colours. Being borne across some sort of gate that lowered to become a bridge and passing underneath a lofty wooden arch that was a beautiful deep emerald green were his last conscious memories for several days.

He woke to find himself in a resplendent bedchamber, almost entirely healed, where he was waited on by the small fleecy beasts who'd rescued him, albeit now dressed in a style less martial and presumably more suited to domestic serving duties. He was also visited by the tall, mournful being who'd commanded the aforesaid rescue, and by an extraordinary feminine automaton that after some few days he realised was his saviour's mate or perhaps lover. Within two weeks of commencing his confinement, his innate abilities with language had enabled him to undertake a dialogue with his unusual hosts and thus to learn more of the circumstances into which his improvised escape-craft had delivered him. It turned out that he and his ship were currently located at the north pole of a world which had the humble, self-effacing name of 'Dirt', this being the third major orbit-mass from a gigantic, crackling source of energy known as a sun; itself one of perhaps a hundred billion such that had arranged themselves into a vast and flat irregular ellipse that was referred to as a galaxy.

He also came to realise that his benefactors were by no means representative of this world's general inhabitants. The artificial female, whom it transpired was the queen of this strange polar region, had been made more than a century earlier by one of the predominating primate population, an unusually intelligent example of the species called Doctor Copelius. After a series of misfortunes this ingenious inventor had removed himself and his creation to this frozen wasteland, where he had proceeded to construct a whole civilisation of automata, entrusting them with the instructions for their own self-manufacture so that they might propagate themselves even in the event of his inevitable death. Ruling this secret clockwork realm was the doctor's original creation, whom he'd named 'Olympia.' Magnificently engineered and yet also possessed of an unsettling and icy sensuality, Olympia had a perfect and immobile doll-like countenance, a bosom and a cleavage that resembled some variety of typographical contrivance and a voice that chimed and tinkled in the manner of a wind-up musical device. The erstwhile Jackboy, having enjoyed naught but male companionship for several decades, found himself responding physically to the robotic regent but thought that to pursue such idle fancies might be inadvisable in light of the queen's evident relationship with the grave giant who'd found him injured out among the icefields, the dapper grotesque with skin like gelatine.

This brooding personage was not one of Copelius's marvellous mechanical confections, being artificial in a wholly different and perhaps more ghastly fashion altogether. As he told the story, he had been assembled from the body parts of diverse male cadavers and then somehow brought to life electrically by his ambitious 'father,' a one-time associate of the more elderly Copelius named Doctor Viktor Frankenstein. A string of tragedies had finally delivered this reanimated composite of other men to these northerly territories where he had discovered Toyland, as Olympia's principality was called, and the alluring mechanism who would soon become his bride. Due possibly to a shared masculine affinity it was this shambling Royal consort who instructed his inventive subjects to repair and modify the black star-sailor's craft, and also he who influenced his wife in her decision to provide the stranded voyager with a quintet of highly personable and vivacious wooden female manikins that had been engineered and modelled with the arts of love primarily in mind.

All things considered, he was starting to enjoy the idea of a cosmos with the lights on.

Mina, the American moon-colony, 1964: A Long Way from Baltimore.

'No, see, this is very interesting. It's a documented fact that Kennedy Senior was running arms to Adenoid Hynkel during the war, but his son was an enthusiastic anti-fascist during the communist Thingmaker administration that followed. It just doesn't make sense that his assassin was a Red sympathiser. And then we hear these rumours about biological duplicates of Hynkel being reared in Brazil. Coincidence, my friend? I think not.'

Through the glass bubble of Pete Munch's helmet, his bespectacled and haggard face had the faintly superior and knowing look that made a growing number of his fellow moon-base operatives, Dave Rawls included, thoroughly dislike this wiry and persistent little man with his incessant idiot monologues concerning government conspiracy. The two men, Munch and Rawls, were working in the blue light of their thermite torches to repair one of the base's airlocks, damaged in the recent onslaught of gigantic moon-bugs that had so surprised the various lunar colonies. Even the Russian base had offered to share information in the hope of limiting the rampage of the monstrous insects before all of the terrestrial settlements were damaged or disrupted. Wearying of his companion's paranoid digressions, Rawls made an attempt to change the subject.

'Munch, if you don't mind, I'm getting sick of hearing all this shit. How 'bout you got a theory on where all these fucking giant ants are coming from? Now, that might be some fucking use.'

He instantly regretted asking his co-worker if he had a theory. Of course Pete Munch had a theory. There were rumours that the skinny self-styled intellectual liked to puff on the odd reefer with the niggers in the U.S. base's maintenance crew, and reefer-fiends have got a theory about everything.

'It's funny you should say that, Rawlsy, because it just so happens I do. You think about the moon, right? It was formed when a small planetoid crashed into the young Earth, billions of years ago. All of the debris from the impact gathered at the limits of Earth's field of gravity, where across the eons it coagulated into our moon, where we're standing now. But even back then, they've found fossils demonstrating that the Earth was home to primitive microbial life, surviving in conditions that are almost unimaginable. What if some of those tough micro-organisms got caught up in the exploding planetary wreckage that eventually congealed to form the moon? What if they'd evolved across the ages in the way that life evolved back home, but in a much different environment so that the most successful life-form is some kind of monster ant?'

Rawls wished he wasn't dressed up in his fishbowl helmet. Then he would have been at liberty to spit contemptuously. As it was, he had to settle for verbal disdain.

'Like I could give a shit. We've known about the moon-bugs since that limey Cavor's expedition came back from the moon without him in 1901. It's obvious they must have got here somehow. I don't care how. What I want to know is why they're suddenly attacking all Earth's lunar bases when we're not anywhere near their territory. I mean look at this! These fucking things got mandibles that cut through fucking steel! The fucking Baltimore Gun Club didn't plan for this.'

Munch nodded. All around, the pallid landscape stretched in silence to a black horizon.

'Well, I hear the Soviets believe the ants have got a rudimentary civilisation and even perhaps some kind of a religion. They say that the bugs' recent behaviour resembles violent uprisings on Earth…like Britain's Indian Mutiny…when people feel that their religious principles are somehow being violated. Boy, I wonder what an insect worships. Some kind of beetle Buddha, maybe?'

Pete Munch rambled on annoyingly, until his partner finally decided to just tune him out. As Rawls welded the airlock's sheared-through metal seal back into place his thoughts turned to the cute technician, Bayliss, who'd arrived here at the Pride of Baltimore moon colony with the last shuttle. Rawls had heard that Bayliss had a wife and son back home in Maryland, not that it necessarily meant anything: Dave Rawls was married with a kid as well, and he'd been blowing one of the administration guys from the main dome since he first got here. Men were lonely up here on the moon. Some of them even went insane and suffered from mirages of moon-pussy, naked women running through the brilliant lunar dust, slow-motion titties bouncing in the piss-weak gravity. Give pretty-boy Bayliss a few weeks of that and he'd be partying with Dave Rawls in the rover-hangars…

As lost in his erotic reverie as Munch was in his endlessly unreeling speculative discourse on insect theology, Rawls failed to notice the procession of small boot-prints that were forming magically in the soft pumice only a few feet away, heading off from the American dome-complex and into the empty lunar wastes. Through the receivers of her stolen helmet of invisibility, Mina had heard enough. She waded on towards her rendezvous with only rising plumes of dust to mark her passage.

The Galley-wag and company, above the moon, 1964: Skulls and Amazons

A thin film of translucent grey was slithering across the crater floor some several hundred feet below, cast by The Rose of Nowhere as she glided high above the lunar surface on her mission of reconnaissance. While Peg and Sarah Jane applied themselves to the great steering-wheel, their dark commander stood beside the rail and trained his huge light-drinking eyes upon the barren landscape crawling by beneath them. The remarkable black-matter privateer who'd once been known as Jackboy Sixty had already noted two or three intriguing incongruities in his appraisal of the reputedly lifeless satellite, and deep within his neuron-dense and disproportionately massive brain he was engaged in trying to connect these disparate impressions into a coherent narrative, attempting not to be distracted by the casually salacious chatter of his wooden women.

He had steered his marvellous balloon-boat past the nest of gentle swellings that were moon-hills and had seen the teeming city-hive of the clearly distressed and angry Selenites. Like unusually agitated armoured cars the giant insects milled in a belligerent confusion on the edges of a 'market square' arrangement at the centre of their colony, carefully avoiding a conspicuously empty spot right in the middle of this open area as if it were some kind of recently-denuded holy ground. Watching the urgent and incessant semaphore of the unsettled arthropods' antennae, the lost son of the Great Erebus Array had come to the conclusion that if the six-legged monsters had communicated by the means of sound rather than pheromones he would be hearing enraged bellows and wails of incredulous bereavement from the furiously churning mob. He'd idly wondered what could have upset them so.

Journeying on, occasionally squinting at the night sky through an astrolabe more to impress the Dutch dolls than for any practical considerations, he had reached a wide expanse that seemed to him to be possessed of an anomalously bumpy texture, so that he turned down The Rose of Nowhere's burners and descended to perhaps ten feet above the slumbering albino dunes for a closer inspection. At close range, he'd been bewildered to discover that the landscape's goose-bumped grain when viewed from overhead was at this lower altitude resolved into a field of what looked very much like human skulls. Locking the wheel into a pre-set automatic course, even the two womanikins ceased their squeaky flirtation long enough to join their baryonic lover at the rail and gaze in silent fascination at this ghastly spread of brittle eggshell relics, bleaching there in the reflected Earthlight.

Fearing at first that this morbid spectacle betrayed some massacre of Earthling colonists, it had been the

sheer number of the fleshless craniums which had convinced him that this could not be the case. There were at least two or three thousand of them, far too many to have vanished unremarked from the terrestrial moon-bases, and unless he was mistaken in his understanding of human anatomy all of the skulls were male. Did this imply that there was currently or had once been a human population on the moon that had not come here from Miss Murray's twentieth-century home planet? Reasoning that if this plane of death's-heads were a lunar cemetery or ossuary then that would suggest some form of major settlement nearby, he'd lifted up into the higher reaches of the star-sprayed firmament once more and glided on across those silver pastures, acne-scarred by meteorites.

Only when he had ventured some leagues further and had stumbled on the sprawling acreage of alabaster moss, the grazing alien livestock and, most trenchantly, the citadel of naked women did he feel it would be prudent to return The Rose of Nowhere to her moorings and consult with his human accomplice as to how they should proceed in these combustible, outrageous circumstances.

Mina, Mysta and Maza, the moon, 1964: Give Me the Moonlight, Give Me the Girls…

Only when the skull-fields first came into view over the starboard bow did she reluctantly believe the tale the Galley-wag had told her when he and the dolls had taken her aboard after their rendezvous in the moon's Limbus. The pale bulbs with staring, empty sockets called to mind a probably-apocryphal report she'd come across some decades previously of a so-called 'honeymoon in space,' where the adventuring young couple had described a field of skulls here on Earth's orbiting companion. This connection, although anecdotal, did at least suggest a precedent for the bone carpet above which The Rose of Nowhere drifted

onward through the dark. Mina had no such explanation, though, for the immense moss-garden when
they reached it, or for the odd fauna that were feeding
there. She rapidly identified the chalk-white growth as
being the same species that she'd previously noticed
near their landing-site, and thought that in these
quantities it might explain the intermittent presence of
an atmosphere...though not what kept that atmosphere
from drifting into space when the moon's gravity was
patently inadequate to do so. Then, of course, there
were the animals.

These were exotic almost to the point of being
comical. A herd of piglet-creatures that communicated
in low whistles and whose hides gave the impression they'd somehow been knitted were all clustering
around a wavering giant worm or salamander which
appeared to be secreting a clear, broth-like fluid that
the lunar swine found nourishing. Nearby a smaller
group of very different animals were nibbling con-
tentedly at the lush pelt of moss, these having skins
that were predominantly black albeit marked with a
distinctive pattern of white polka-dots. After observing
them for a few moments, Mina also noticed that these
black-and-white things seemed to possess an innate
ability to change their shape. There were at least three
or four other species present on the fleecy lunar veldt,
including a variety of plump yet brightly-patterned bird
whose stubby and vestigial-looking wings were nonetheless sufficient to propel it through the low-gravity
heavens.

Just beyond these fields of what were obviously
beasts reared as food they found the citadel that Mina
had until then thought to be either a bawdy joke or an
idyllic sexual fancy of her shaggy-haired companion.
Its towers and boulevards were thronged with stun-
ning amazons, all naked save for the occasional cape,
sword-belt or wrought silver helmet and all with eyes
fixed inquisitively on the Galley-wag's extraordinary
vessel as, at Mina's signal, it descended cautiously towards what seemed to be the city's central plaza where
a statuesque reception party waited.

Given the inherent strangeness of the situ-
ation, Mina barely blinked when it transpired that

the beguiling lunar nudes had an impressive grasp of
English and, apparently thanks to a radio transmitter
situated up in the high Andes, fluent Spanish. Mina
and her party were escorted to an opalescent chamber
where the Galley-wag sat with an ornate cushion in his
lap, as Mina later realised to conceal the generous tu-
mescence that their hostesses' nudity had instantly oc-
casioned, and there met with two astonishingly lovely
women whom it seemed were high-ranked representa-
tives of this remarkable all-female populace, a brunette
evidently known as Mysta and a blonde named Maza.
These conversed both amiably and willingly, although
the tale that they recounted was alarming.

Countless centuries ago, the women's native
race had been a great civilisation that existed near
the universe's rim, developing amongst those oldest
first-formed suns until an unavoidable catastrophe...a
deadly ray-emitting star known as a gamma-burster...
had threatened to sterilise their entire galaxy. Migrat-
ing to the inner cosmos, the ancestors of these women
and their erstwhile mates had settled on Earth's moon
in the terrestrial Neolithic period, discovering that
some zones had workable gravity caused by incred-
ibly dense obelisks of black material that had been
buried on the lunar satellite for unknown reasons by
a similarly unknown agency, sometime in the remote
primordial past. They'd introduced their oxygen-
producing moss and livestock, far from the native
ant-like creatures they'd discovered here, establishing
a thriving colony that had branched off at least twice
to investigate the possibilities for humanoid survival
on both Mars and Venus. Here upon the moon, their
enclave had been a utopia until just sixty-three years
earlier. Until the plague.

This plague, which Mina realised guiltily had co-
incided with Professor Cavor's 1901 lunar expedition,
had killed every last male in the colony, accounting
for the lawn of polished skulls. The bereaved females,
though of great longevity in human terms, had no
more than a century to find some means of making
themselves pregnant before even the youngest amongst
them would be past child-bearing age. Luckily, they
had recently found a solution in the form of a vacuum-
preserved and frozen human male cadaver which, it
was believed, might very well provide a source of still-
viable sperm. Ironically, the means of their salvation
was discovered in the midst of the indigenous moon-
insects, where it seemed to have no function save as
an object of veneration. It was most regrettable, Mysta
agreed, that their removal of the body had provoked
such a warlike reaction from the Selenites. And yet,
as Maza went on to enquire, given the women's dire
predicament, what else were they to do?

Even as the two lunar beauties led her and her
shipmates down to the refrigerated chamber where
the freeze-dried specimen of masculinity was held in
storage, Mina felt the fateful fragments of the puzzle
falling ominously into place somewhere within her
reeling mind. Before the bulkhead chamber doors
were opened in an icy cloud of crystallising vapour,
she knew just what she would see.

There in the bluish artificial light, rigid as the sar-
cophagus of an Egyptian king, stood a corpulent figure
that she had last met in better health almost seventy
years before. With cricket cap frost-welded to his head
and the fate of a species in his ice-encrusted loins, the
dead eyes of Professor Selwyn Cavor stared plaintively
through the rising billows of sub-zero condensation
into Mina's own.   *– To Be Continued –*